Making Sense of Organizational Change

This book offers a unique way to understand the processes of organizational change. Rather than being structured as a 'how to' book, *Making Sense of Organizational Change* provides the reader with practical insights and skills for managing (or resisting) organizational change.

Its strength lies in three key areas: first, and central to this book, is the discussion and explanation of a strategic sensemaking approach, for helping managers, management educators and students understand – and address – the process of organizational change. Second, through a longitudinal study of a major company which underwent several organizational changes, the book reveals some of the key problems and challenges that managers face when introducing, implementing and managing change. Finally, the book provides a detailed examination of the drive for organizational change among Western companies over the last twenty-five years. In particular, Jean Helms Mills asks pertinent questions about why companies feel the need to change, and discusses up-to-date research findings on the viability of culture change, re-engineering, ISO 9000 and TQM change programmes.

Applying an invaluable sensemaking framework to organizational change in both a practical and accessible way, and combining the theory and practice of implementing change, this book represents an instructive and informative view on the implications of change in the business world today.

Jean Helms Mills is Assistant Professor of Organizational Behaviour at Acadia University, Canada. She is the Associate Editor (for the Americas) of the journal *Culture and Organization*.

Making Sense of Organizational Change

Jean Helms Mills

Routledge
Taylor & Francis Group

LONDON AND NEW YORK

First published 2003 by Routledge
11 New Fetter Lane, London EC4P 4EE

Simultaneously published in the USA and Canada
by Routledge
29 West 35th Street, New York, NY 10001

Routledge is an imprint of the Taylor & Francis Group

Typeset in Garamond by
Florence Production Ltd, Stoodleigh, Devon
Printed and bound in Great Britain by
St Edmundsbury Press, Bury St Edmunds, Suffolk

British Library Cataloguing in Publication Data
A catalogue record for this book is available from the British Library

Library of Congress Cataloging in Publication Data
A catalog record for this book has been requested

ISBN 0–415–36938–X (hbk)
ISBN 0–415–36939–8 (pbk)

Contents

Illustrations

Figures

Tables

Foreword

Organization change is ubiquitous today, and for good reason. Organizations *must* keep changing in order to keep up with changing world, national, and local events and competitive conditions. If they don't change they will fall behind.

Of course, some types of change are better than others. This particular new type of change that I'm proposing is highly successful, as indicated by the very positive experiences of several organizations. It is a must for any company that is concerned about staying on the leading edge of innovation and competitiveness.

How many times have you heard this story line, or one very like it? How often has this story been told, with the only change in it being the particular change programme being advocated as effective? How much more cynical are you now than you used to be about claims like this, perhaps even while you are hoping that the story line about the change you're considering is at least plausible, if not fully accurate? Certainly you are convinced that on-going organizational change of some type is crucial; the only problem is to cull from the multiple offerings the type of change that will work best.

In this thoughtful and thought-provoking book, Jean Helms Mills explores the above story line in a fascinating way. She presents a detailed case study of multiple 'pre-packaged' organizational change initiatives that Nova Scotia Power (once Nova Scotia Power Commission) underwent between 1988 and 2002. These included a culture change programme, privatization, downsizing, business process re-engineering, leadership changes, strategic business units, and a balanced scorecard strategic plan. Based on careful interviews, observation, and archival data-gathering over a five-year period, she details the reasons that a particular change was adopted with great enthusiasm, how interest in it waned, how it was replaced by another enthusiastically adopted change initiative, how interpretations of prior change initiatives evolved over time, and how this process was repeated again and again, through multiple changes. Often one change initiative hadn't even been 'completed' before the next one, sometimes a type of change with values that seemed to contradict the prior one, began to be implemented.

This description of the multiple, overlapping changes is juxtaposed with a careful, detailed exposition and respectful summary and critique of Karl

Weick's work on sensemaking as this work has evolved over more than thirty years and as it may be applied to organization change (or, more properly, organizational changing). Helms Mills makes creative use of Weick's insights to explore multiple underlying dimensions of the change processes at Nova Scotia Power; without Weick's framework these underlying processes would not be evident either to participants in the change or to those of us who read about it. She also shows some of the limits of this framework for describing organizational change processes and supplements it with more macro approaches to change that add dimensions such as power, identity, structure, and context.

The description of Weick's work is absorbing for many reasons, not the least of which is how it contrasts with the depiction of Nova Scotia Power's (and many other organizations') 'flavours of the week' or 'fad surfing' approach to change. Think of it. Karl Weick has been developing and continually improving understandings of sensemaking in organizations at least since 1969. He hasn't totally switched approaches multiple times. He hasn't denigrated his prior work on a regular basis. Rather, he has, it would appear patiently, revised his understanding of cognitive processes in organizing over a long period of time in such a way that his later thoughts build on, expand, and clarify earlier ones and as a result make a very powerful contribution. What kind of model for change is that?

But Helms Mills does more than describe Nova Scotia Power's approach and use Weick's work as a lens for understanding its underlying processes. She also shows how the changes there reflect the more general story of organizational changing that has been prevalent in North America and other parts of the world as well, at least since the early 1980s. It is this story that I introduced at the beginning of the foreword. She critiques the general story in interesting ways, such as by providing socio-political contexts for multiple types of packaged change initiatives and showing how designers of change describe their change approaches (and who they blame when their change approach doesn't work).

At the heart of this book is the central question: What does organizational change really 'mean'? Does it mean almost unquestioning adoption of new, pre-packaged changes developed and promulgated by 'educators, prophets and missionaries' outside the organization? Does it mean awareness by organization members that the times change and that their organization must change with the times? Does it mean recognition that, as institutional theorists and others argue, organizations must at least give the impression of adopting the latest fashionable change in order to appear legitimate to their various publics?

And this central question evokes others for which there are no clear answers. Are organizations and their members able to reflect on and learn from their various change attempts? How easy is it for organizations to assess how successful a particular change attempt is and to learn from it? The latter is a particularly complicated issue, for at least two reasons. First, any particular change is likely to happen in conjunction with other organizational activity that might compete with it. Second, different organizational groups (e.g. top management and unions) may well have contradictory criteria for determining success. In fact, as a result of reading this book I gained much more appreciation of the difficulties managers and other organizational leaders face in trying to create successful change in their organizations. There are so many advocates of one change approach or another, so many changes in the types of change approaches deemed appropriate, and so many people at least questioning, if not outright challenging, any approach. The ability to discern between competing approaches to change and their likely value may be one of the most important skills for managers to learn.

In sum, this is a valuable book, carefully constructed. It offers new ways to think about organizational change at this time and place and evokes multiple important questions about the experience of change. I hope that it will provoke much interesting reflection and, perhaps, even some differences in how organizational change is managed and understood.

Jean M. Bartunek
Boston College

Acknowledgements

Since beginning this book, which started life as my Ph.D. thesis at Lancaster University, there have been so many people who have helped make it possible. First, I would like to thank my supervisor, Dr Colin Brown, not only for his help and support, but for believing in me. I would also like to thank the many employees of Nova Scotia Power for sharing their stories with me. Special thanks to Barry Anderson, and Osmundo Betancourt, who provided invaluable help and friendship, to Louis Comeau for giving me access to Nova Scotia Power, and to the late Jim Woods, without whose unwavering support, this study would never have taken place.

I would be remiss if I didn't mention my former colleagues at Mount Allison University, especially Gina Grandy, whose cheerfulness and sense of humour kept me going through the long Sackville winters. Also, thanks to my new colleagues at Acadia University, especially Jonathan Campbell and Hope Corkum for their technical assistance.

I am also grateful to David Wicks for his input on an earlier draft of this manuscript. Kathy and John Graney, you provided me with a home away from home. You will never know how much your friendship has meant to me. And to all my friends, old and new, thanks for putting up with me throughout this process.

I am forever indebted to my parents, Philip and Sue Helms for supporting me through all the ups and downs that such a process inevitably holds, and to my Aunt Polly, and my brother Stephen. I couldn't have done it without all of you.

Finally, none of this would have been possible without the encouragement, patience, support and love of my husband Albert, who has bestowed meaning on my life. Thank you.

1 Introduction

The little girl had the making of a poet in her who, being told to be sure of her meaning before she spoke, said: 'How can I know what I think till I see what I say?'

(Wallace, 1926 – quoted in Weick, 1995: 12)

Introduction

This book is about making sense of organizational change. To understand the change process and change management in action, the book focuses on a major North American utility company that underwent a series of changes between 1982–2002. Using a grounded theory approach (Glaser and Strauss, 1967), data was collected in Nova Scotia Power between 1991 and 1996, while it underwent two major processes of change. This longitudinal case study involved extensive content analysis of Nova Scotia Power's corporate documents, observations of numerous planning meetings and change practices in action, discussions and interviews with a number of senior managers, and a series of semi-structured interviews with employees in the organization. The events that led to the selection and implementation of a planned culture change and a re-engineering programme are made sense of through a strategic, retrospective use of Weick's (1995) sensemaking approach to organizational analysis.

Studying organizational change in action

Over the last two decades of the twentieth century, theories of organizational change have had a tremendous impact on business and not-for-profit companies. The extent of the influence of popular theories of change – including 'Culture Change', Total Quality Management (TQM), Business Process Re-engineering (BPR), Organizational Learning, and, more recently Six Sigma – is evidenced throughout the business world as application and outcomes are reported and debated in the business presses, consulting reports, management journals and 'best-selling' business trade books.[1] Thousands of companies, including many of the top corporations, have implemented one or other change programme over the last twenty years,[2] often at the cost of millions of dollars, and involving large-scale restructuring and extensive job losses. At the end of the day, while it is generally agreed that certain change programmes have become widely popular, there is considerable debate about the success or failure of the subsequent changes themselves. Business critics who support Culture Change, TQM or BPR blame suggested failure on incorrect implementation. Other business critics are less convinced, questioning the lack of evidence of a clear link between the implementation of selected change programme and subsequent business success (Grey and Mitev, 1995).

What has been missing from the debate so far is what actually happens when management adopts and applies a popular change programme, and what can be learned from this. Reminiscent of the pioneering work of Henry Mintzberg (1973) and the more recent study of Rick Delbridge (1998), we are reminded that Mintzberg's observations of managers in action cast a very different light from that of conventional ideal-typical constructions on the skills needed to be a successful manager.

Analysis of the data suggests that the implementation of organizational change, particularly selected change programmes such as Culture Change, TQM and BPR, does not follow the rational, orderly decision-making processes indicated by advocates (e.g., Hammer and Champy, 1993; Juran, 1988; Schein, 1985). Instead, processes of organizational change appear to be fraught with conflicting and constantly changing points of sensemaking in which various actors vie to make sense of a particular situation and its outcomes. These enactments owe more to the ability to develop a plausible account than to any notion of 'success' or 'failure'. Further, the data suggest that in the post-1980 era organizational change is experienced as a meta-discourse (Cooke, 1999; Foucault, 1980) that acts as an imperative to constant change. This, in part, may explain the faddish nature of change programmes (Abrahamson, 1996) which, in turn, indicates that the processes of organizational sensemaking occurs within broad contexts, which influence actors' choices of extracted cues.

Sensemaking as a theoretical framework for understanding change

Karl Weick (1995: xi) describes his organizational sensemaking approach as 'a developing set of ideas with explanatory possibilities'. This approach has gained in popularity since the mid-1990s because its focus on understanding organizational processes makes it flexible enough to be applied to a diverse range of organizational outcomes. In Weick's earlier work (1979), the notion of sensemaking took on theoretical properties as a 'recipe' for organizational analysis, and in subsequent studies of organizations sensemaking was used as a theoretical framework for analysis of organizational events and outcomes (1990a, 1990b, 1993a, 1993b, 1996). Yet later, in his book on sensemaking and organizations, Weick (1995: xi) presented his sensemaking approach as, 'a developing set of ideas with explanatory possibilities, rather than as a body of knowledge' or 'an ongoing conversation'. In the spirit of the latter comments I have taken up the conversation, seeking to make strategic use of the approach as the basis of a theoretical framework. Thus, my contribution to the conversation is twofold: one, to use some of the central ideas of sensemaking (viz. sensemaking properties) to analyse a case study of organizational change and, two, to explore the usefulness of the sensemaking approach itself as an heuristic for understanding organizational change.

In the course of this study, I have also discovered that while the sensemaking approach provides a valuable framework for analysis of key elements of organizational change (e.g., how implementation strategies and outcomes are influenced by sensemaking activities), it is limited in its ability to adequately account for structural influences on sensemaking activities (e.g., how certain decisions appear constrained by formative contexts and organizational rules), or their translation into social-psychological outcomes (e.g., the processes whereby, and through which, certain decisions become understood in meaningful ways). So, I have concluded that analysis of organizational change and change management needs also to take into account the sensemaking activities of the actors involved, in particular those factors that facilitate or mitigate against the ability of key actors to develop plausible accounts. To that end, the outline of a modified sensemaking approach will also be proposed.

The case study

Nova Scotia Power Corporation (NSP) provides a valuable case study because it has gone through a number of major organizational changes over the last two decades. In particular it provides valuable insights into the way that large corporations have been willing to adopt many, if not all, of the major change programmes that have been on offer since the advent of culture change in 1980.

NSP is a large electrical utility based in the maritime province of Nova Scotia, on Canada's Eastern Shore. Officially the company has been in continuous operation, in one form or another, for nearly eighty years and is headquartered in the provincial capital of Halifax. The company operated as a government-owned 'Crown Corporation' until 1992 when it was privatised. Today Nova Scotia Power operates as the largest subsidiary of Emera Inc., which describes itself as 'a diversified energy and services company' (Emera Annual Report 2001: 18), whose shares trade on the Toronto Stock Exchange (TSE). Since its acquisition of Bangor Hydro-Electric on 10 October 2001, Emera Inc., currently employs a total of 2,248 people in a number of offices, call centres, and generating plants throughout the province of Nova Scotia and the state of Maine. In 2002, the vision of Nova Scotia Power is to be 'the customer's choice in energy and services' (Ibid.: 19).

In recent history, the company has been through a series of major changes that include a company-wide attitude survey (1987), a culture change programme (1988–93), privatization (1992), downsizing (1993 and 1995), a business process re-engineering programme (1993–5), key leadership changes (1983 and 1996), 'strategic business units' (1996) and, most recently (1999–2000), the introduction of a 'balanced scorecard' strategic plan. Many of these changes were reported, often applauded, in the business presses (Bruce, 1991; Comeau, 1994; Conrad, 1995; *et al*., 1995; Kaplan and Norton, 2000; McShane, 1998; Myrden, 1993, 1994). Arguably, NSP is a classic serial change company that has much to tell us about how and why senior managers adopt change programme and what the outcomes are. The focus of this case study is on two of NSP's early change programmes, which significantly contributed to their penchant for adopting the latest in management fads and fashions.

In 1991 and again in 1993 I was fortunate to gain access to the company to study, respectively, the Culture Change and BPR programmes that the company was undergoing. In the first phase of the research (1991–3) I was given almost unlimited access to the company to study the 'success' of its 'Culture Change program'. With the full support of senior management, including the Chief Executive Officer (CEO) Louis Comeau, I was given full access to travel the province, making site visits, sitting in on company meetings, conducting interviews with managers and employees, and observing various processes at work. In the second phase of the research (1993–6) I was given more limited access to study aspects of the re-engineering process. Despite initial resistance from company BPR consultants, Ernst & Young, I was able to sit in on several re-engineering planning meetings, to observe a key re-engineering process – the call centre – at work, and to interview a number of associated managers and employees. Access to the Human Resources Director was maintained throughout both phases of the research and provided invaluable insights to the various processes underway and to 'the thinking of senior management'.

Through numerous observations, interviews and content analysis of company documents over a considerable period of time (1991–6), my unique access allowed me to construct a case study of a major company undergoing change. Instead of being limited to a study of isolated changes in a number of different organizations, I was fortunate to be allowed to observe the influence and impact of change and how it was understood. Although it is contentious to argue that a case study can be taken as representative of a class of phenomena or events, I contend that NSP is in many ways 'typical' of a number of organizations of the time. Certainly NSP shared with numerous organizations the experience of adopting and implementing change programmes, adopting culture change and re-engineering programmes at a time when each was in vogue and at a peak of popularity among business practitioners and educators. On a different front, NSP was typical of many state-owned organizations throughout Britain and North America that underwent privatization. While many of the practices of Nova Scotia Power are not generalizable to an understanding of other companies, the sense-making properties and processes, I contend, are.

Making sense of the change process at Nova Scotia Power

My analysis of events at Nova Scotia Power raised many issues pertaining to the management and enactment of organizational change, that eventually led me to adopt a sensemaking perspective. What are the factors that encourage senior managers to perceive a need for change and how do these perceptions influence the consequent change process? For example, Nova Scotia Power's culture change programme was introduced at a time when the company was operating as a Crown Corporation and certain senior managers perceived a need to unify the disparate elements of the publicly owned company. Whereas, re-engineering was introduced at a point when the company was facing privatization and senior managers were primarily concerned with efficiency and profitability.

The role of 'experts' in the social construction of change scenarios and of the epistemological nature of change, itself, I felt, was also worthy of exploration. Again, in both the culture change and the re-engineering situations, I was struck by the fact that change decisions were influenced by knowledge of 'successful examples' of other change programmes, and the activities of selected consultants. For instance, the company's 'Culture Change' programme was influenced by the success of another local company, MT&T, and they hired a Nova Scotia consultant who focused exclusively on building unity around four 'core values'. This, in turn, raised questions about whether or not specific choices influenced the outcomes of change and about the nature of change itself. What, I wondered, would the outcome have been if the company had chosen a consultant that had focused, not on values, but on a different set of characteristics, e.g., sub-cultures. This in turn led me to wonder about the implications of the socially constructed nature of change and of specific change programmes for the management of change. What problems might organizations face in attempting to implement a culture change programme that relies on a specific notion of culture and organizational reality?

Finally, some of the problems that I observed with the implementation of change programmes led me to question the relationship between pre-packaged change problems and local realities. I observed that the introduction of the 'Culture Change' programme had mixed results from the beginning, due, in part, to differences among employees, depending on their location. For example, Cape Breton employees, based in a militant region of the province, were far less likely to accept any management change that did not address their fears and anxieties about the outcomes of change. In this case NSP's universal approach to culture change exacerbated local difficulties.

Eventually, a focus on change as socially constructed led me to the notion of sensemaking, as I was interested in understanding how senior managers come to perceive a situation in a particular way, and how these disparate understandings of organizational change could be managed. For example, if there are competing notions of change and of the character of the organization, how can a specific situation of change be successfully managed? In attempting to answer this and other questions I was drawn to Weick's (1995) theory of organizational sensemaking and the way it draws attention to the development of 'knowledge' as 'socio-psychological frameworks'.

Beyond sensemaking: towards a theoretical framework of change management

While Weick's (1995) sensemaking framework is a valuable tool for analysis of change and change management processes, it is limited in so far as it does not fully capture the richness of the social, organizational and social-psychological contexts in which frameworks develop, are enacted and changed. Two key sets of questions in particular dogged my thinking as I pursued a sensemaking approach: one concerned the context in which sensemaking occurs and the second concerned the institutionalization of sensemaking decisions.

An example of the former type of question arose when I began to search for explanations of why NSP moved from a culture change programme to one of re-engineering. Here I was led, in part, to the view that while the 'Culture Change' programme – with its focus on humanistic values – meshed well with extant notions of the purpose of a Crown Corporation, re-engineering – with its focus on efficiency – meshed well with the needs of a privatized company. This comparison led me to wonder about the broad contexts in which sensemaking occurs.

An example of the latter type of question arose when I began to search for explanations for why employees in the Cape Breton region were less willing to accept the 'Culture Change'. Here, in part, I was led to the view that the proposed changes clashed with existing expectations and practices. This led me to wonder about the influence of established practices on on-going sensemaking processes.

As I grappled with these questions I was drawn, respectively, to the work of Blackler (1992a, 1992b, 1993) and Mills (1988a, 1988b; Mills and Murgatroyd, 1991). Blackler's work on activity systems, as I shall argue later, provides a more comprehensive explanation of the 'social' element in Weick's notion of sensemaking while providing a way of conceptualizing a link between socio-cultural factors, discourse and organizational rules. In particular Blackler's (1992a) use of Unger's notion of 'formative contexts' (i.e., institutional and imaginative frameworks that shape the way people view reality) contributes to an understanding of the contexts in which sensemaking occurs and which influence sensemaking outcomes. Of equal importance is Blackler's (1993) notion of 'activity systems' (i.e., a series of inter-relationships which form a social-psychological context that mediates people in action), which he develops from the work of Vygotsky and Engestrom. The notion of the activity system contributes not only to an understanding of the social-psychological context in which sensemaking occurs but, through reference to differences that people bring to a situation, reveals the potential for ambiguity and change in a given situation.

Embedded in both the notion of formative context and of activity systems is the idea of rule-bound activity, but this remains underdeveloped in Blackler's work. Here the work of Mills, centrally focused on organizational rules (i.e., broad sets of expectations and practices which serve to guide, direct and constrain people in action), contributes to an understanding of the organizational influences on sensemaking.

Summary

In summary, this book sets out to improve our understanding of the process and management of organizational change by (a) a strategic utilization of Weick's (1995) sensemaking approach as both a theoretical framework for making sense of the data and, through its application, an argument for a sensemaking approach to change management; (b) undertaking a longitudinal case study of a major North American company involved in the introduction and implementation of two popular change programmes; and (c) drawing conclusions from the data to evaluate the strengths and limitations of the sensemaking model, in order to develop new ways forward for sensemaking and the understanding of change management.

2 Identifying cues

A history of Nova Scotia Power

History is one of a series of discourses about the world ... [that] do not create the world ... but they do appropriate it and give it all the meanings it has.
(Jenkins, 1994: 5)

[Historiography is a] manifestation of the historian's perspective as a 'narrator'.
(Jenkins, 1994: 12)

Introduction

This chapter presents an overview of the case, laying out the central cues (Weick, 1995) that influenced my reading of it. The story presented is not a conventional history but rather a narrative shaped by a particular perspective (Jenkins, 1994). In telling the story I have tried to reflect those issues that were experienced by some of the key players and influenced the decisions that they made. To that extent, this chapter is a narrative about the cues that were used to make sense of key situations of change (such as the introduction of a Culture Change programme). Some of the cues were brought to my attention by various managers and employees of Nova Scotia Power, and some by the writers of company documents, annual reports, newspaper reports or histories. Ultimately, the selection of cues is my own, as my sensemaking led me to focus on some features in the situation to the neglect of others.

A question of history

To say that this is not a conventional history of Nova Scotia Power is not to suggest that the story is unreliable or that it should be read as a work of fiction. To begin with, I have departed from the empiricism, not the rigour, associated with conventional historiography (Carr, 1990). As has been argued elsewhere, 'an historiographic approach, as with all methodological approaches, is framed by the worldview or paradigm ... of the researcher, and that this has implications for the research project' (Mills and Hatfield,

1998: 3). In Dellheim's (1986) functionalist historiography, for example, organizational culture is treated as a social fact whose linear progress is traced over time. Dunkerley's (1988: 85) radical structuralist account, on the other hand, questions the very notion of organization, arguing that 'organization structure is a reflection and expression of particular modes of rationality'. My approach differs from Dellheim (1986) in two key regards. First, I view organizational realities as social constructs rather than social facts; and, second, history is viewed not as progressive or linear but as a series of sense-making events that are sometimes on-going and sometimes disjointed over time (Mills and Hatfield, 1998). In my case a sensemaking event needs to be understood in the context of the particular cues that presented themselves, the character of the on-going realities within which the cues were embedded, the actors involved and their network of relationships, and what factors were acceptable as plausible accounts (Weick, 1995).

Second, my earlier statement that organizational culture is a heuristic for making sense of organizational life does not mean that I reject the notion of organizational culture as somehow 'unreal'. I would argue that 'real' (i.e., embodied) persons, engage in 'real' organizational activities (i.e., the perception of action within a limited entity), shaped by 'real' (i.e., felt) experiences (Helms Mills and Mills, 2000).

Third, this work is informed by a managerial realist perspective (Reed, 1992: 133) to the extent that it sets out to formulate a 'systematic understanding and explanation of the political and ideological practices through which "organizations" are assembled and sustained as viable social collectives'. To that end, I have focused on observations, statements and content analysis that indicated the felt experiences of the actors involved and their contribution to sensemaking outcomes (e.g., declarations of success in regard to the completion of a re-engineering process).

Mergers and mindsets

In 1983 Nova Scotia Power appointed Louis Comeau as its new President. It was the beginning of a series of major changes that was to reshape the company over the next two decades (see Table 2.1).

When Comeau joined the company it had 'been in business, under one name or another, for about one hundred years and [had] grown through acquisition and amalgamation of other utilities' (Nova Scotia Power, 1990b). By the early 1920s, the company had become a government agency known as the Nova Scotia Power Commission. The primary mandate of the company was to supply electricity to all areas of the province that didn't have access to power through private companies. A major change took place in 1972 when the Commission incorporated small companies, including Eastern Light and Power in Cape Breton and Nova Scotia Light and Power in Halifax and Yarmouth. The new company was called Nova Scotia Power Corporation and merged the senior management from the various smaller utilities

Table 2.1 Key changes at Nova Scotia Power, 1983–99

1983		Appointment of Louis Comeau as company President
1987		Employee attitude survey
1988		Introduction of culture change
1991		Assessment of culture change
1992	(12 August)	Privatization
—		Employee development initiatives
1993	(March)	'Effectiveness' stage of culture change
		Downsizing: 400 jobs eliminated
—	(May)	Re-engineering introduced
1994	(July)	Re-engineering consultants leave
1995	(31 July)	Downsizing: 250 jobs eliminated
1996	(3 April)	Retirement of Louis Comeau
		Gerald Godsoe appointed new President
		Godsoe dies before taking office
1996	(17 April)	Tom Hall appointed interim President
	(22 July)	David Mann appointed new President
1996		Introduction of strategic planning
1999		Balanced scorecards

with the management of the Commission. The situation remained unchanged until 1992 when the company was privatized and became known as Nova Scotia Power Inc., or Nova Scotia Power (see Figure 2.1).

The merger history was to play a role in the thinking of Comeau in the first half of his presidency as he set out to 'unify' the company. On his appointment Comeau toured the company to meet with staff. In his discussions with different employees at different locations he came to the view that over time the mergers of companies, amalgamations of various departments and the blending of different management styles had created a fragmented organization that was operating as several different companies, often with conflicting organizational goals. A subsequent employee attitude survey confirmed Comeau's opinion that the company was fragmented. This strengthened his resolve to find a way to unify the organization. He was to find it in the notion of organizational culture. The problem was summed up in an internal company document on 'Culture Change at Nova Scotia Power'. Noting the role of acquisitions and mergers in the growth of the company, the document stated that, 'By the middle of the late 1980s it became apparent that the "culture" of the Corporation was unsuited to the times' (Nova Scotia Power, 1990b).

Maps and mapmakers[1]

Nova Scotia Power is a Canadian company based in the Atlantic province of Nova Scotia. Within Nova Scotia itself, the company is spread over a radius of 300 miles (see Figure 2.2). The province shares with its US neighbours

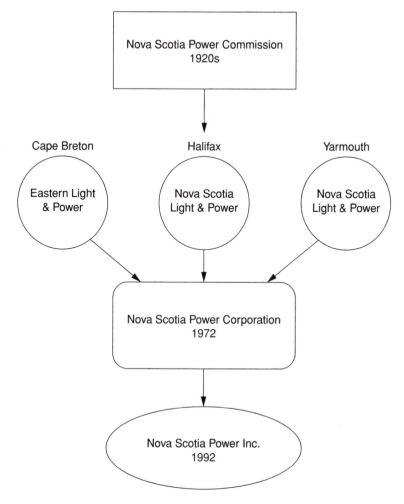

Figure 2.1 Merger and development of Nova Scotia Power, 1920–92

on the eastern seaboard a history of political patronage and Tammany Hall politics.[2] To understand something about public office in Nova Scotia, it is important to know that public appointments at all levels of government owe much to political favours or favouritism. To be appointed to a key position in a Crown Corporation in Nova Scotia it is important to be 'in' with the political party in office. At least this was the situation when Louis Comeau, a man with a track record in the Progressive Conservative Party, was appointed by the Conservative Government of John Buchanan to head up Nova Scotia Power in 1983. Patronage, until very recently, was an important formative context (Unger, 1987a, 1987b) in which corporate decision-making occurred.

Figure 2.2 Map of Nova Scotia

Political and structural changes

Nova Scotia Power has undergone several important changes since the 1920s.

Politically, the company developed from a series of small private companies operating in a competitive market situation, to a single province-owned Crown Corporation operating as a monopoly (1972–92), and then to a privatized, privately owned monopoly (since 1992). As I will argue later, the different ownership situations, particularly in the period 1988–92 and 1993–5 reflected broad periods of political discourse which, in addition to local politics, influenced sensemaking processes at NSP.

Structurally, the company has gone through numerous major changes, including a series of mergers (see Figure 2.1). More recent changes, as the company moved through a process of culture change to privatization and then to re-engineering, have led to a dramatic restructuring of the company.

The Thermal Division   In 1988 the Thermal Division of the organization consisted of a number of gas turbine, hydro and thermal plants throughout the province. Of the thermal plants three were located in the Cape Breton region at Lingan, Glace Bay, and Point Tupper, one at Trenton near Stellarton, and one at Tufts Cove close to Halifax.

By 1996 there were still five thermal plants,[3] but in some cases the plant manager was in charge of two plants instead of one. The Thermal Division was eventually renamed 'Power and Production' and operated a separate company within the division, selling electricity and knowledge to external buyers.

Transmissions and Distributions (T&D)   While the Thermal Division was responsible for the generation of electricity the Transmissions and Distributions Division was responsible for supplying electricity to the customer, servicing the equipment, and dealing directly with customer inquiries, collections, hook-ups and complaints.

In 1987 T&D constituted the largest segment of employees within the organization and comprised four zone offices – Eastern, Western, Central and Halifax. Zone offices were sub-divided into three areas of responsibility – administrative, customer and engineering service – and also had a number of district offices reporting to them. District offices acted as smaller versions of the zone offices and were located in the more isolated communities.

By 1996, T&D had been restructured and renamed the 'Customer Service and Marketing Division'. Instead of the previous four zones the new division was sub-divided into two very broad divisions, Metro and Provincial. The Metro division has two regions and the Provincial has five regions (replacing the district offices) reporting to them. The functions of the new division remained basically the same as before but some of the issues that had previously been handled by head office were now decentralized to the divisions. Hiring, for example, was moved from the head office personnel department and handled locally in each of the respective divisions by a human resources specialist. As part of the decentralization process several small call centres were re-opened and located within the division and regional offices throughout the province.

Head office   The head office of Nova Scotia Power is situated in an eighteen-storey office tower in Halifax. When Comeau took over as president he occupied, what was known as, 'the tower', along with his vice presidents, division directors, the finance department, the MIS department, human resources, and the administrative support staff. Following the introduction of a widespread culture change programme in 1988 (see Table 2.1) division directors were relocated on the same floors as the administrative staff to address some of the trappings of division between managers and staff (see 'attitude survey' below).

Privatization and the introduction of a programme of BPR in 1993 (see Table 2.1) led to new changes at head office to reflect the new situation. Two entire floors were given over to the newly centralized Customer Service Centre, which replaced all the regional call centres in the rest of the province.

Following the appointment of a new President (David Mann), and a move towards strategic business units, further changes have occurred at head office.

Although there is still a large call centre in head office, small call centres have been reinstated in the outlying areas, and there has been, once again, a decentralizing of some of the human resource and personnel functions to the divisional offices. As I shall argue later, an understanding of the process of change and its outcomes at Nova Scotia Power needs to take into account the various structural changes, as both responses to change and, more importantly, as sensemaking frameworks in which change decisions were made.[4]

Background to the Culture Change programme

In 1988 Nova Scotia Power embarked on a process of culture change. It was a process that was influenced by the political climate of the time (the company was becoming increasingly unpopular with Nova Scotians), a change in company leadership (with the appointment of a change-minded President), widespread expressions of low morale within the company (captured in an internal survey), and the growing popularity of culture change programmes throughout the industry in particular and a number of other companies throughout North America (see Appendix A and Table 4.3).

Leadership

If one factor was crucial in the decision to introduce a culture change, it was the 1983 appointment of Louis Comeau to head up Nova Scotia Power (see Table 2.1). It was Comeau who, sensing widespread morale problems, instigated an attitude survey and responded by identifying culture change as the method of dealing with the problem.

A former President of a small French university in the southwest of the province and Federal Member of Parliament for the Progressive Conservative Party, Comeau's appointment was seen by many to be a political one. Critics at the time complained that the company was being run in the best interests of the ruling Conservatives rather than the people of Nova Scotia: 'Under the Buchanan government, Nova Scotia Power had become, in the words of one Halifax economist, "a political toy"' (Dreyfuss, 1989).

Certainly the government of the day needed someone at the helm of Nova Scotia Power that they could trust to turn around the company's bad public image. As Comeau was later to note in an interview with the *Commercial News*:

> The utility, in 1983, was not in very good shape. From the basic point of government relations and public and community relations, it was a disaster. The utility had received two massive rate increases, one in 1978 and one in 1982. The public really didn't have a lot of sympathy for it when it came. The government had no confidence in Nova Scotia Power . . .
>
> (Bruce, 1991)

And he was soon to discover that internal employee–management relations were also 'a disaster'.

Government concerns meshed well with Comeau's political will and, combined with a natural inclination to reach out to employees and create a situation of trust, propelled him to seek a solution to the low morale he sensed throughout the company. From the outset Comeau was concerned to build strong inter-personal relations between himself and his employees. To that end, and in an effort to 'get to know' the company, he held a series of meetings through the organization at which he talked with employees to get a sense of their knowledge and concerns.[5] By the end of this process Comeau sensed a deep sense of apathy in a company that was seen as having little regard for the customer or the employee: 'There was little recognition of good performance. Management appeared aloof and uncaring' (Nova Scotia Power, 1990b).

It was not surprising that Comeau gained the distinct impression that morale was low. It was a feeling held by others throughout the company. As a senior draftsman[6] told me, 'the morale *is* poor . . . I've worked in different zones and we have to get rid of this ivory tower idea'. For a company lineman, 'The decision-making was done at the top. The person who does the job had no say. Things were running backward'. Reflecting on the period immediately prior to Comeau's appointment a line foreman expressed the view that, 'Attitudes had gone way done hill since the 1970s. A lot of people didn't enjoy working anymore. Nova Scotia Light and Power policies were being shoved down our throats.'

The wheels were turning. Comeau had taken the first step towards a solution that would result in the introduction of a Culture Change programme.

The attitude survey

Comeau eventually set out to deal with the issue of low morale by commissioning an external consulting firm to conduct an employee attitude survey. The results confirmed much of Comeau's initial impressions, indicating a highly dissatisfied workforce who perceived management as:

1   Lacking in empathy
2   Having an inability to communicate effectively
3   Unresponsive to media criticism
4   Portraying an aloof and uncaring image to the employees and the general public
5   Lacking in leadership skills
6   Offering no feedback
7   Placing more emphasis on the job than on the employee.[7]

It was clear to Comeau that he had inherited a task-oriented leadership generally lacking in employee consideration:[8] 'Paternalistic at best, task accomplishment was the objective. Inanimate resources were being given more consideration than human resources' (Nova Scotia Power, 1990b).

The consultants involved in the development and administration of the attitude survey informed the senior management team that the gap between employees and managers was, in large part, due to the large numbers of engineers who held management positions. Often managers had not had any formal leadership training and had been promoted based on technical rather than people skills. The managers' leadership style was seen as too rigid and autocratic, allowing employees little input or discretion in doing their jobs.

Problems between management and employees were not the only source of division. It was also noted that there was a considerable gap between the Thermal and T&D divisions to the extent that they had the feel of two different and separate companies. In the words of an administrative services supervisor, 'The divisions are almost like separate companies. We need to bring the walls down.'

The die was cast. Comeau was confronted with a serious problem that needed resolve. From his perspective the problem was rooted in inadequate communication between head office and the rest of the organization, and poor communication skill between managers and employees. What he needed was a way to overcome those problems, to deal with low morale and to unite the disparate Thermal and T&D divisions into a single company.

Comeau did not have to look far for a solution. Culture change was by now not only a popular method of dealing with a variety of organizational problems but was a growing part of the lexicon of managing within Nova Scotia Power. As Comeau and his senior managers looked for answers to their problem they could not have failed to notice that, throughout the industry, other utilities had implemented or were in the process of implementing culture change, as were a number of other large companies in Nova Scotia.

In the early part of 1988, only a few months after the completion of the attitude survey, the senior management of Nova Scotia Power took the first step towards enacting a new sense of organization throughout the company; they opted for culture change: 'The executive committee (President, Vice Presidents) made the initial decision to make an organized effort at changing our culture in March 1988 and chose a consulting firm specializing in culture change to provide their expertise' (Nova Scotia Power, 1990b).

The next step was in deciding what form the culture change would take. In that regard Comeau was influenced by the belief that his managers needed to be retrained in leadership skills and that employees needed some sense of involvement in the company. It was a view that later became enshrined in the company's 'vision for the year 2001', which envisioned: 'Participative management . . . with employees being fully involved as team members in problem solving and decision-making within an organizational structure that operates with few levels of management' (Nova Scotia Power, 1991c).

Looking back on the process, Comeau stated: 'I believe in people. In the sense that you achieve your goals through people and people only produce those results when they feel good about their work' (Nova Scotia Power, 1991a).

It was this approach that shaped the choice of consulting firm to develop a programme of culture change for Nova Scotia Power. That was the second stage of the enactment process. Nova Scotia Power sought a consulting firm that offered personal service and was able to devote the time necessary to 're-educate' managers to learn leadership skills, and employees to become more participatory and open to change. The aim was to find a consultant who specialized in culture change, could help the senior executive formulate a new mission statement, and would guide them through the implementation of a unifying culture. After receipt of competitive bids from a number of consulting firms, a local firm of consultants was chosen.

The consultant then convinced the executives of Nova Scotia Power to adopt an approach that she had used with a number of other government organizations, and the process began of 'training' managers and employees to build commitment around four key corporate values (see Table 6.1):

1   The *province*: 'being responsive to and respective of community needs'
2   The *employee*: recognizing 'employee contributions'
3   The *customer*: providing 'customer satisfaction'
4   The *environment*: 'responsibility for the quality of the environment.[9]

For a company leadership under pressure to make the organization appear more customer-oriented, responsible to the province, and concerned for its employees, the first three values made perfect sense. They also provided the basis of a plausible account of the new changes being enacted. In the late 1980s, at a time when environmentalism was a popular discourse throughout North America, the fourth value also made sense to a company that was otherwise in danger of being seen as a polluter. In short, the four corporate values were accepted as a highly plausible account of Nova Scotia Power's problems and what was needed to redress them. A major element in the construction of the company's account of events can be seen in the document, 'Culture Change at Nova Scotia Power' (Nova Scotia Power, 1990b). Commenting on the 'impetus for the change', the document identifies four major problems that needed redressing:

1   In many ways, customers were not being treated as the lifeblood of the business. Keeping the lights on was a priority, but little attention was being paid to the interrelationships between the Corporation and its customers.
2   As the largest employer of engineers in the province, the Corporation was often referred to as a construction company, rather than an electric utility. Certainly, there was a tremendous focus of resources on building things, as opposed to the provision of electricity and associated services.

3   Little attention was being paid to the human element; i.e. employees.
     Paternalistic, at best, task accomplishment was the objective. Inanimate
     resources were given much more consideration than human resources.
4   Although government-owned, management seemed to be trying to
     operate in isolation from the government, resenting direction being
     given to them based on political objectives, rather than good business
     practices. There was a failure to recognize the Corporation as an instru-
     ment of public purpose for the overall socio-economic benefit of the
     province.

This statement seems to capture the essence of what Weick (1995) calls retrospective sensemaking in that it provides a perfect justification for the
introduction of the first three of the four values. It was left to other corporate documents to deal with the fourth value, focused on the environment:

> Environmental protection and, indeed, enhancement of the environment
> go hand in hand. For this reason we support the goal of sustainable eco-
> nomic development, that is development which ensures that the utiliza-
> tion of resources and environment today does not damage the prospects
> for their use by future generations. As part of our support for the goal of
> sustainable economic development, we are committed to a progressive
> program of environmental protection which addressed preservation and,
> where possible, enhancement of the quality of the environment.
>
> (President's Report, Nova Scotia Power, 1990a)

Over the next four years the new image of the company was reinforced
through a series of practices, symbols, slogans and documentation. The
process of change began in the late spring of 1988 with a series of senior
management team meetings to discuss the types of culture changes that
the company wanted to achieve. In October 1988, all the members of the
senior management team attended a 'four-day awareness program' dubbed
'Values in Action'. This was accompanied by a 'pre-program Management
Practices Questionnaire' that was completed on each participant by 'himself/
herself, boss, peers and subordinates' with the results 'fed back to the participants during the program'. The next major step was a series of one-day
meetings for all the company's 120 middle managers. Next, in the late winter
and spring of 1989, came the 'Leadership and Values' phase, involving
'bosses' and 'subordinates' in a series of four-day training sessions. This was
followed with a series of four-day sessions for all the company's 330 supervisors. Between October 1990 and February 1991 a series of 'Values
Information and Endorsement' sessions were held for all remaining employees. Alongside these training sessions important symbolic changes were
made, including changes in the colours of hard hats: the use of white and
yellow hard hats to distinguish, respectively, managers from other employees
was replaced by the universal provision of yellow hard hats for managers and

employees alike. The four corporate values, constructed in symbolic form (see Table 6.1), were used in all major documents and it became common-place to include the words 'at Nova Scotia Power we value' in major documents and statements.[10]

As I shall show later, many of the processes of culture change were prob-lematic. Leaders differed in their understanding of 'organizational culture' and 'culture change':

> I think we are changing. So much of the change depends on individual members of management and their style of management. Therefore, we find varying degrees of change as we have different types of people.
> (Jim Woods, Director of Organizational and Employee
> Development, quoted in Nova Scotia Power, 1991a)

Some employees openly resisted the culture changes, viewing the process with suspicion:

> [M]anagers had major problems in communicating the change process to their people. They seemed to have difficulty in articulating what they had learned about change and about themselves while on the 'Leadership and Values Program' . . . The union leaders (table officers and safety committee members) were eager to participate but very leery, at the beginning at least, of the management propaganda or even brainwashing that they were going to be subjected to.
> (Nova Scotia Power, 1990b)

The division of the initial training programme into four-day sessions for senior managers and one-day sessions for middle managers and other employees led to misunderstandings and resentment, with those in the one-day sessions charging that the system was unfair: 'The message came through loud and clear. Unless the first and second line supervisors had the same four-day program our change efforts would not be successful' (Nova Scotia Power, 1990b).

Even the development of new symbolism, particularly the move to a universal yellow hard hat, led to some confusion and anger among managers. They felt they had earned the right to a symbol of status, while the employees felt nervous at their inability to distinguish between the approach of a colleague or a manager.

Nonetheless, in the early 1990s senior managers felt able to construct a plausible account of the 'successful' outcome of the Culture Change programme and I was hired at this point to report on the progress to date. Although I did not realize it at the time, there was never any real question about whether the Culture Change programme was a success but rather how much of a success, and where could improvements be made. Introducing me to Nova Scotia Power employees, Louis Comeau commented that,

> Now that we are three years into the culture change program, it is time
> to take a look at where we are in this 'never-ending journey'.... Are
> we making progress? Is change happening in the workplace? Are we
> living our values? Is Nova Scotia Power becoming a better place to work?
> To help us answer these questions, Mrs Jean Hatfield has joined us for
> the summer.
>
> (President's Bulletin)[11]

Background to privatization and re-engineering

As a Crown Corporation, it is not surprising that Nova Scotia Power's four
key values emphasized political more than economic concerns. In his 1989/90
President's annual report, for example, Louis Comeau stressed the political,
rather than the economic, benefits of the culture changes:

> I am pleased to report that we made significant progress during the
> past year in three key areas that are of importance to our customers:
> environmental protection, customer assistance in the area of energy
> utilization, and strengthening of Nova Scotia Power's financial self-
> sufficiency.

In the context of a Crown-owned company, the term 'customer' is rooted in
notions of political expediency. For Nova Scotia Power the customer was
seen, in large part, as an elector whose vote was influenced by the company's
service provision, pricing policy and spending habits. Thus, Comeau's reference to 'financial self-sufficiency' is not primarily to an organizational goal
of profitability but as an 'area of importance to our customers', i.e., a political
expedient that addresses voter concerns about the use of government money.
Comeau's report ends with the statement that:

> I am particularly grateful for, and proud of, the efforts made by our
> employees in maintaining our corporate values – our customers, our envir-
> onment, our employees, and our province. This annual report highlights
> just some of the examples of the contributions made by Nova Scotia
> Power employees to the overall benefit of Nova Scotia.

Downplayed to some extent, the goal of efficiency, nonetheless, formed a part
of the company's broad strategy of culture change. Senior managers saw a
change in values as the 'education phase of the change process'. The next
major phase was an emphasis on effectiveness.

When I embarked on a 'check-up on cultural change' at Nova Scotia
Power[12] in 1991 the company was just beginning its effectiveness phase of
the culture change. At that point in time the notion of effectiveness was very
much wedded to the culture change and the four key values:

We feel it may take five, seven, or even ten years to completely change our culture. After all, it has taken 100 years to create the old. We are also still in the education phase of the change process. To be sure, change is taking place on an individual basis throughout the Corporation, but our Corporate resources have been fully occupied with education. During the next phase of the culture change process, which we have dubbed 'Effectiveness – In Pursuit of Values', our efforts will be directed towards employee involvement, team building, and skills training, with the primary objective of making Nova Scotia Power a more effective organization.

(Nova Scotia Power, 1990b)

Indeed, a closer look at the company's vision of effectiveness in action reveals just how much its conceptualization owed to the culture change and the four key values:

We want to achieve certain features of an effective organization, for example:

- Perform only meaningful and necessary tasks.
- Empower our employees, delegating to the lowest possible level.
- Flatten the organization pyramid: reduce the number of management levels.
- Tap into the brain power of employees; involve employees in problem solving and decision-making; encourage their creativity; work smarter, not harder.[13]

Anyone studying Nova Scotia Power in 1991 may have expected the ongoing Culture Change programme to frame the company's focus on effectiveness, but it was not to be. Several key developments were beginning to impact decision-making within the company and causing a major change in thinking.

When Louis Comeau took over as head of Nova Scotia Power in 1983 Margaret Thatcher in the UK and Ronald Reagan in the US were marking the end of their first terms in office. The radical twins of late capitalism, Thatcherism and Reaganism, were entering a mature stage as large vestiges of the welfare state were dismantled and numerous government agencies were privatized. By the time Nova Scotia Power had completed the 'education phase' of its culture change the Berlin Wall had fallen and Soviet communism was in ruins. Entrepreneurship replaced socialism as the organizational buzzword of the former Eastern Bloc countries. The term 'revolutionary' was coming to be associated with new radical management techniques rather than left-wing activism as the term 're-engineering' entered the language of managing.[14]

In Canada in the early 1990s, the country had entered into a North American Free Trade Agreement (NAFTA) with the United States that promised (or threatened) to open up a number of areas new to competition, including telecommunications and electricity supply. As I will argue in more depth later, all these changes were shaping new discourses of management and of organizational change, providing new formative contexts in which Nova Scotia Power's management came to make sense of the company and the direction it was going in.

Privatization

By the middle of 1991 plans were underway to privatize Nova Scotia Power. On 9 January 1992 the privatization of the company was officially announced and three months later, on 16 April the government introduced Bill No. 204 to effect the sell-off. Following 'the longest debate in the history of the Committee of the Whole House' the Bill passed Third Reading on 19 June and shares were offered for sale between 7 July and 12 August 1992 (Nova Scotia Power, 1993a). It was to be the largest share offering in Canadian history, yielding $851 million. Nova Scotia Power's first official day of operation as an investor-owned utility was 13 August.

Top management welcomed the changes but it was clear that they were facing new and very different challenges. In a classic statement of sense-making, Louis Comeau welcomed privatization as 'a logical step' in the company's history:

> Privatization made eminent good sense at this stage in our history. Despite the company's extensive asset holdings in plant, equipment and expertise, prior to privatization equity represented only 5% of our capital structure. The remaining 95% was debt guaranteed by the Government of Nova Scotia. Electrical generation and distribution is a capital-intensive business often requiring substantial borrowing to finance major projects. As a Crown Corporation, Nova Scotia Power's borrowing power and flexibility to determine its own future would always be limited.
>
> (President's Report, 1992 Annual Report,
> Nova Scotia Power, 1993a)

Despite the fact that Nova Scotia Power was now free of (party) political pressures the change was, in Weick's (1995) terms, a shock to the on-going discourse of culture change. As we scan subsequent events it is clear that privatization acted as a catalyst that forced senior management at Nova Scotia Power to re-evaluate the Culture Change programme as it developed ways to deal with issues of competition, deregulation, high electrical rates and the need to make a profit. The company also had a new, powerful group of stakeholders to deal with – shareholders. In a nod to the existing cultural change a commitment to 'Our Shareholders' became a part of the company's key values. But other pressures were pulling decision-makers in new directions.

It was becoming 'obvious' that something would have to be done to reduce operating costs and 'unnecessary spending'. The government was no longer responsible for paying Nova Scotia Power's debts, and although the company provided a necessary service as a utility company, the possibility of deregulation and co-generation was making competition fiercer. Louis Comeau, in his President's Report for 1992, was to warn employees:

> We cannot . . . be complacent. The future brings with it many challenges. First of all, electricity in Nova Scotia is not as competitive as it can be. We must continue the progress made in productivity so that electricity becomes a more cost-effective choice for our customers. We must also become more aggressive in the way we run our business. Nova Scotia Power experienced a 4% average annual growth in electrical demand during the last 10 years but, based on projected provincial activity, our forecasts indicate that 1.6–1.7% appears to be a realistic rate for the future. As electricity currently occupied only 19% of the total energy market in Nova Scotia, as opposed to 24% nationally, there appears to be plenty of room for us to grow in the next 10–15 years. As a public company we can now strengthen our financial status by investigating new opportunities in a competitive marketplace. By increasing research and development we can open new doors to ourselves and our customers.

If we look closely at Comeau's statement it provides very different cues from those found in earlier statements. The new statement is the language of competition, cost-effectiveness, financial status and an 'aggressive' approach to business. In this context the idea of the 'customer' takes on new meanings, as people and businesses who provide Nova Scotia Power with the potential for financial growth and development. In marked contrast to his report two years earlier, Louis Comeau's President's Report for 1992, from the opening paragraph, focuses exclusively on effectiveness and profitability:

> It is no exaggeration to say that the past 12-month period has been the most significant in Nova Scotia Power's history. To evolve from a Crown Corporation to a fully functional, free-standing public company with 30,000 shareholders, in less than a year was a singular achievement. Particularly gratifying in a year of such challenge was the company's operational and financial performance. I am happy to report that we achieved our financial goals for the year. Our 1992 combined net income for the nine months since the last year-end was $38.0 million, an improvement of $0.4 million over the forecast in the prospectus. For the period from privatization to year-end, the company's net income was $29.0 million, or $0.34 per share. We also declared our first quarterly dividend, $0.1875 per share, which was paid on November 16, 1992.

Clearly, unlike in previous years, this was a statement addressed to shareholders.

Re-engineering

Towards the end of 1992 a small but significant event occurred in the life of Nova Scotia Power – they changed auditors. Prior to privatization the company had employed the firm of Peat Marwick Thorne (PMT) to audit their financial statements. It was PMT who audited the company's last accounts as a Crown Corporation in May 1991. Following privatization the company turned to chartered accountants Ernst & Young for auditing, and it was that company that signed off the financial statements on 2 February 1993.

By now senior management's interest in efficiency had taken on a new sense of urgency and they turned to their accountants, Ernst & Young for advice. Ernst & Young referred Nova Scotia Power to their consulting wing. The consultants had little difficulty in convincing Nova Scotia Power's senior management that re-engineering was the key to creating an effective organization, and that Ernst & Young was the company who could help them do so. In many ways it was a good match.

On the one hand, senior managers at Nova Scotia Power had, for some time, planned for an 'effectiveness phase' of the culture change. Privatization had not only speeded up an interest in effectiveness but was also changing the way managers viewed effectiveness. Increasingly, effectiveness was being expressed in terms of profitability. As in the past, Nova Scotia Power's senior management team was open to popular management ideas and the employment of consulting 'experts' to help them introduce and apply those ideas.

On the other hand, Ernst & Young offered a 'revolutionary' new management change technique that promised untold efficiencies. Here was a company that, with some justification, presented itself as on the cutting-edge of management development. Two years prior to the publication of Hammer and Champy's (1993) pioneering *Re-engineering the Corporation*, H. James Harrington, the International Quality Adviser for Ernst & Young, published *Business Process Improvement (1991)*. Ernst & Young came to Nova Scotia Power with an established reputation in the 'successful' re-engineering of a number of major companies, including Calgary Power and Ontario Hydro,[15] and their own publications on quality (Ernst & Young, 1992a, 1992b).

The re-engineering plan that Ernst & Young put before Nova Scotia Power promised to streamline the organization, make it more productive, increase profits and still maintain the integrity of the corporate culture. To this end Ernst & Young helped Nova Scotia Power formulate a new strategic plan which, in order to be effective, would have to involve participation by the entire organization. Almost immediately the company embarked on an 'Effectiveness Program', at the heart of which was its 'Business Process Improvement (BPI) initiative':

> Launched in the summer of 1993, BPI is revolutionizing the way we work. Using small, carefully chosen cross-functional teams we are not

only tackling processes in urgent need of improvement but also over-coming the biggest barrier to change – attitude. No longer is it sufficient that something had always been done a certain way. Each stage of a process must now demonstrate measurably that it adds value. Steps that fail the test are discarded or changed.

(Nova Scotia Power, 1994a)

It soon became clear, in words and in deeds, that far from maintaining the integrity of the previous culture, re-engineering represented a new mindset and new practices that, in many ways, contradicted the established ways of working. It was indeed revolutionary and for those committed to the estab-lished culture the introduction of re-engineering was 'the beginning of the descent into hell'.[16] Certainly numerous official statements linked the new initiatives to the Culture Change programme. If nothing else the previous focus on cultural values provided a reference point for establishing a plau-sible account. But the framework was now different and provided very different cues and different meaning to existing cues. Valuing employees, the province, the environment and the customers found voice in formal state-ments but their meaning had changed. The Effectiveness Program, for example, is presented as an increased interest in, rather than a changed perception of, effectiveness:

Turning up the burners on effectiveness

Nova Scotia Power's Effectiveness Program is not new. Between 1989 and the beginning of 1993 it produced modest annual gains. This year we set ourselves an ambitious goal – reducing expenditures to avoid a 1994 rate increase, and establishing a long-term change in the way we work.

Starting in February we eliminated non-essential positions and estab-lished generous voluntary early retirement and voluntary separation programs to stimulate an immediate reduction in overall workforce numbers while causing the minimum internal disruption. By the August cut-off date 238 employees had taken advantage of these optional programs that either bridged financially the period to a planned retire-ment date, or allowed employees to explore new mid-career directions. In just 10 months, without layoffs, we have reduced positions by 400 and increased overall productivity by 18%. With just a two-year payback, this initiative will result in a $10 million annual saving in payroll costs.

(Nova Scotia Power, 1994a)

For one thing, this gave new meaning to the term 'we value our employees'. In the President's Address to Shareholders at the 1994 Annual Meeting, Louis Comeau made it clear that effectiveness was linked to competitiveness, productivity and profitability:

> Two things were particularly clear to everyone in the Company through-
> out the past year. One . . . was the need to gain the confidence of the
> Canadian financial community and investors everywhere. . . . The other
> clear challenge was the continuous need to reach new levels of effective-
> ness and productivity in our operations. . . . Well, I can tell you that every
> part of the Company, every person in the Company, is involved is some
> way in making your Company more competitive. Infrastructure, opera-
> tions, systems, internal and external communications, purchasing, office
> routine, compensation – all of these and more are among the areas we are
> addressing in keeping rates down and building productivity up. Over the
> past 18 months or so, we have implemented an effectiveness program to
> do just that and under the program all job functions have been evaluated,
> some positions eliminated, other new ones created.

The Effectiveness Programme was developed in four phases. In the first phase,
termed 'immediate opportunities', budget expenses for the year were reviewed
to distinguish between the 'must have' from the 'nice to have' items, with
the latter being eliminated. In the second phase – 'vice presidential initiatives' – all six vice presidents were required to produce 'plans for reducing
expenses that would not require altering current activities' (Crawley, 1995:
34). The third, 'other initiatives', phase examined 'projects of a lengthier
nature that would require changes to the way that work was performed'
(Ibid.). A list of twenty operating areas 'with potential for improvement' was
established and from this four areas were selected for an initial trial, 'based
on their potential for saving money, reducing bureaucracy and successful outcome' (Nova Scotia Power, 1994a). The fourth phase, 'business process
improvement', involved an examination and then improvement of selected
overall work processes. In each case 'process teams' were established to review
a specific problem area. One team was assigned the task of 'decreasing bureaucracy and reducing cycle time approvals' (Nova Scotia Power, 1994a). A second team, of mechanics, was focused on the company's hydraulic equipment,
'contracting routine servicing to outside suppliers' (Nova Scotia Power,
1994a). A third pilot team involved the development of a call centre in
Halifax, offering customers 'one stop shopping': 'Under this new system,
account representative will assume the responsibilities of several existing separate groups and process service inquiries, make adjustments and collect
accounts' (Nova Scotia Power, 1994a).
    A fourth team was engaged in a 'six-month multi-task job pilot':
'Working out of mobile offices in their homes, field workers combine functions such as field collection, meter reading and installation, each previously
performed by different individuals' (Nova Scotia Power, 1994a).
    Over the next three years, the process of re-engineering was not without
its problems. As we shall see later, the changes tested the morale of employees
as they went through one change based on concern for employees, to another
focused on effectiveness and profitability. The idea of the centralized call

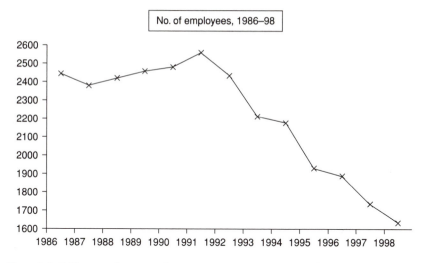

Figure 2.3 Falling employee numbers at Nova Scotia Power, 1986–98

centre made the company appear removed from the local community. The concept of the Customer Service Field Representative (CSFR) ran into numerous difficulties in its complex mix of skills (requiring anything from clerical to electrical knowledge) and emotional labour (combining the friendly service orientation of the field collector with the serious authoritative tone of the bill collector). And the company emphasis on the valuing of employees came under serious scrutiny as employment fell from well over 2,500 to around 1,900 in the period 1991–6 (see Figure 2.3).

When the company eliminated 250 jobs in July 1995 Louis Comeau commented that 'sacrifice was needed to keep company profits up'; the jobs were being eliminated so that Nova Scotia Power could maintain its profit share and make the company more 'competitive and customer-driven': 'We are making these major changes, and making the difficult decision to reduce the number of employees at Nova Scotia Power to help improve our competitive position' (Louis Comeau, quoted in Conrad, 1995). This was a far cry from Comeau's statements on employees five years earlier.

Despite various problems, numerous company accounts proclaimed re-engineering a success. Focusing on selected outcomes, various corporate documents were able to present a plausible account of Nova Scotia Power's successful BPI initiative:

A number of highly creative ideas came forward from employee groups and individuals during the year. Virtually all of them had strongly positive effects on the Company's finances. . . . Other examples are found throughout the Company, many of them as a result of the Business Process Improvement (BPI) program. BPI fosters interactive thinking in a group of people so that any solution they reach is new, fresh, often unconventional and quite likely effective.

(Nova Scotia Power, 1995a)

Nova Scotia Power Inc. turned to re-engineering to improve the quality of customer service, revitalize corporate culture and keep the competition at bay. . . . Nova Scotia Power Inc. is one company that successfully turned adversity into advantage by transforming itself, and its culture, one process at a time. The story of how NSPI made this transition provides lessons for other companies that want to focus on their customers and increase value for their shareholders.

(Crawley *et al.*, 1995: 33)[17]

Nonetheless, not everyone was convinced that re-engineering was a success. One former director expressed doubts to me, not only about the outcomes but the process itself. Commenting on the fact that Nova Scotia Power invested first in an extensive culture change programme and then in an equally extensive, and often contradictory, process of re-engineering he stated that: '[Nova Scotia Power] will jump on any train running through town . . . sometimes two or three at the same time' (Anonymous Interviewee, 1995).

Beyond BPI: background to the David Mann era

Between 1988 and 1992 culture change moved from a central theme in the activities and images of Nova Scotia Power to something that was marginal; in part ignored, in part rejected and in part reinterpreted as a focus on BPI took centre stage. In the period 1993 to 1998 BPI suffered a similar fate, becoming a central theme for a short period of time before taking a back seat to new, emerging trends. A changing emphasis on BPI can be seen in the company's annual reports over the period. The 1993 annual report captures something of the revolutionary fervour of re-engineering and its adoption by the company: 'To be the best we can at what we do is Nova Scotia Power's corporate mission' (Nova Scotia Power, 1994a). 'To Be The Best' was the new slogan of the company[18] and appeared throughout the 1993 annual report and other corporate documents. Under the header 'BPI Launched' the company's adoption of re-engineering was centrally featured. The 1994 annual report captured the on-going progress of BPI in a central and direct way:

Largely through the Business Process Improvement (BPI) program that has involved hard-working employee–management teams throughout the Company, we have discarded many of the traditional approaches to service that have long been the norm among most public utilities . . .

One of the most exciting initiatives taken under the company-wide drive is the Call Network currently being introduced . . .

In another push toward new highs in service quality, three field service functions were folded into one during the past year. After a highly successful pilot project confirmed the soundness of the concept, the new function of customer service field representative (CSFR) was created.

(Nova Scotia Power, 1995a)

In the 1995 annual report, references to BPI are less direct – the word BPI is not used once – but still very much in evidence. Discussion of BPI is more subtle, viewed more in the language used rather than in any overt references as Comeau develops images of 'customer value', 'team-work' and, above all, 'creating more with less':[19]

Over the past year, Nova Scotia Power has concentrated on a single, primary goal: to create even greater value for our customer in the delivery of electricity.

Across the province, communities faced their own challenges on the road to success. We recognize their imagination and spirited teamwork. Their efforts – in fields as diverse as the arts, small business, the information highway and community health care – reflect the core of the Nova Scotia character. Drive, determination and perseverance. And, above all, a focus on the future.

In working toward our goal of creating customer value, your company, too, exemplifies that character.

(Nova Scotia Power, 1996)

It is interesting to note that Comeau embeds the language of BPI in a story that references the previous cultural values of community concern and, in the process, lends an air of plausibility to the account.

The 1995 annual report was the last under the direction of Louis Comeau. Comeau retired from the company in April 1996, to be replaced by J. Gerald Godsoe, QC, a senior partner with a prominent law firm and a former president of the provincial Liberal Party. However, eight days after being appointed, Godsoe died of complications from leukaemia, on 11 April. Board member Tom Hall, a consultant with Marble Mountain of Nova Scotia, took over as interim president on 17 April and David Mann, a well-known Halifax lawyer, took over as company president on 22 July 1996[20] and is still President in 2002.

In Mann's first annual report there was a new vision. Much of the language of BPI was gone as the focus shifted to 'the introduction of a new strategic plan for the company'. Within the company those who zealously continued to advocate BPI become known, disparagingly, as 'the revolutionaries'. A new, simpler, vision was taking hold: 'Our vision is simple: to be the customer's choice in energy and services. While we have work to do, our experience during 1997 and our prospects for 1998 convince us that this straightforward vision remains the right one' (Nova Scotia Power, 1998a).

Corporate structure Prior to 1 January 1999

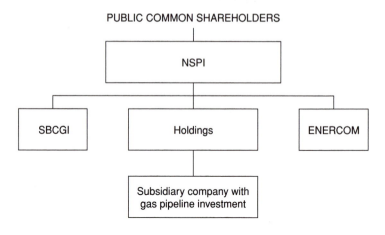

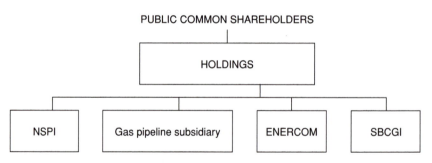

Figure 2.4 The restructuring of Nova Scotia Power, 1999

Source: Adapted from Nova Scotia Power, 1999b

Note: SBCGI = Stellarton Basin Coal Gas Incorporated

Mann went on to outline a series of strategies for achieving the new vision:

> We set four strategies: to develop employee commitment; to build custo-
> mer loyalty; to cut costs; and to build our business. Implicit in these
> strategies are two predominant values: the safety of our employees and
> our customers, and the protection of our environment.
>
> (Nova Scotia Power, 1998a)

Reflecting the new strategies the company slogan was changed to 'Partnerships for Success' and the annual report, in something of the feel of the original
Culture Change programme, outlined a series of partnerships 'with our customers', 'with businesses', 'with our employees' and 'with our community'.

In 1998, the company went through a major process of restructuring that involved the company in a creation of a holding company structure (see Figure 2.4). Following restructuring of the company the renamed Nova Scotia Power Incorporated (NSPI) became part of a corporate structure whereby 'the regulated utility business of NSPI [was] held in a corporation which is separate from any other business activities. [NSPI continues] to carry on its regulated electric utility business and ... is the principal subsidiary of NS Power Holdings Incorporated' (Nova Scotia Power, 1998b). By the time the 1998 Annual Report was in print the company was now operating under the umbrella of a holding company. There were still references to 'Employee Commitment' and 'Community Involvement' but this was in the context of a more central theme of 'reorganization to a holding company' and the importance of the company's 'core business' as 'a powerful foundation' of the new business. In the meantime employment in the company reached a new low point of 1,634, just over three-fifths the size of the company at the height of its Culture Change programme and approximately three-quarters of its size when it embarked upon re-engineering (see Figure 2.3). In 1999 employee numbers fell again to 1,588, but began to rise again the following year.

The balanced scorecard

By the late 1990s the structural changes to NPSI had placed it in a new operating environment and, once again, senior managers sought new management strategies. In this context David Mann introduced 'strategic business units' (SBU) but was also 'looking around' for management formulas to help him manage the SBUs:

> In late 1998 NSPI was separated from non-regulated energy enterprises and placed within a newly established holding company Nova Scotia Power Holding Inc. NSPI could not increase its prices for electricity despite internal and external cost pressures. Working with a strategy consulting firm Mann's senior management team had formulated a new strategic plan but Mann wanted a measurement system to guide and gauge the success of the plan. In addition, NSPI had recently reorganized into SBUs and Mann felt the need for a tool to unite the plans of the SBUs so they would all be working towards the same overall goals.
>
> (Kaplan and Norton, 2000: 121)

In response, Jay Forbes, the Company's vice president and chief financial officer, proposed that NSPI adopt the 'balanced scorecard' approach.

The balanced scorecard was an approach that was developed by Kaplan and Norton (1992) as a way of measuring performance. It was soon repositioned as a management strategy in its own right. In brief, it combines measures of financial performance with measures on 'the drivers, the lead indicators, of future financial performance' (Kaplan and Norton, 2000: 3). Part of its attraction for companies is that the balanced scorecard combines elements of management by objectives, culture change, and total quality management. Thus, for example, Kaplan and Norton argue that 'new strategies [require] that the entire organization adopt a new set of cultural priorities' (2000: 4). They go on to contend that, 'the balance scorecard is perfectly consistent with TQM principles' (Kaplan and Norton, 2000: 376).

Given NSPI's history of adopting change programmes it is not surprising that Forbes' application of the balanced scorecard approach looked remarkably similar to various elements of previous change activities:

> The scorecard was based on the four strategies in the NSPI plan:
>
> > Cut costs (revise to 'manage costs in 1999')
> > Build customer loyalty
> > Build the business
> > Develop employee commitment.
>
> > > (Kaplan and Norton, 2000: 121)

Like the introduction of culture change training a decade earlier, 'personal scorecards were developed only for senior executives and sales accounts managers' but were eventually extended to other employees. While the culture change found its champion in Louis Comeau and BRP found its champion in Wayne Crawley, Jay Forbes took on the cause of balanced scorecards with the same fervour. Forbes and Paul Niven, the company's Business Performance Analyst 'went to countless meetings and forums, any agenda [they] could wiggle [their] way on to, to try to help people understand the scorecard. [They] plastered the scorecard everywhere [they] could' (Forbes, quoted in Kaplan and Norton, 2000: 220).

Forbes joined the company in 1993 as corporate controller and must have been well aware of the major organizational changes that Nova Scotia Power had been through since 1982. Nonetheless, the zeal with which he embraced the balanced scorecard (BSC) clearly blinded him to past events when he declared that to sustain commitment to the new approach you need 'to avoid the 'flavor of the week' problem [by embedding] . . . the BSC into everything else you do' (quoted in Kaplan and Norton, 2000: 220).[21]

3 Strategic sensemaking

Choosing the sensemaking model

My initial study of culture change at Nova Scotia Power faltered in the face
of different interpretations of the programmes involved, and an inability to
pinpoint an adequate or appropriate measure of 'success'. Thus, for example,
while studying culture change one manager told me that he found the new
corporate values too vague and confusing. As far as he was concerned the
corporate values encouraged employees to look for what they could get out
of the system: 'These values are terrible . . . anything can be a values issue.
They [the employees] only think of values to the employee. They have become
a negotiating tool' (Senior Manager).

Louis Comeau, on the other hand, was very clear about the values, as was
Jim Woods, Director of Human Resources. Comeau believed that the corporate values were about leadership. He expected managers to instigate change
and encourage employees to 'live the values'. Indeed, for Comeau, 'so much
of the change depend[ed] on individual members of management and their
style of managing': 'In human resources, we have shown leadership. Our
productivity improves, our values and culture change programs are evidence
of this' (Nova Scotia Power, 1991c).

For Jim Woods the 'cultural change program centred around Corporate
Values . . . [emphasized] the importance of positive behaviours and attitudes,
mutual trust and respect, individual control and accountability': 'With all
of [the] programs that have come about as a result of our culture change
efforts, the bottom line is to make Nova Scotia Power a better company, a
more effective organization, and a better place to work' (Nova Scotia Power,
1991c).

For other employees, however, the introduction of the new corporate values
met with a variety of contradictory responses, from that of a clerk from Cape
Breton, who told me that the values made no difference to him ('I've always
been company oriented. Eastern Light and Power was always customer
oriented'), to a thermal plant shift supervisor, who 'changed [his] perception
of what's really important'.

These and many other differences in perception left me with a number of
questions about the role of sensemaking in organizational change. I began

to wonder just how far the acceptance and implementation of a change programme depends on how individuals make sense of it.

This line of questioning deepened as I attempted to come to terms with an apparent switch in direction from a focus on 'the employee' to a focus on customer service and efficiency, as the company moved from culture change to re-engineering (see Table 3.1). I was particularly perplexed by the decision of senior management to move away from an apparently successful culture change to a programme of re-engineering which seemed to contradict the previously established values (see Chapter 2).

This raised questions about the process of adopting and implementing organizational change. For instance, I began to reflect on what had contributed to management's decision to initiate cultural change. My first impression was of a senior management concerned with employees, the environment, customers and voters. It was easy to believe that the introduction of cultural change was inspired by a principled commitment to definite values, including a concern with employee well-being. No doubt those values and initiatives were sincerely expressed, yet within two years a concern with employees had given way to a concern with efficiency (Table 3.1).

As I reflected on the dramatic turn-around in corporate thinking, questions were raised about what influenced each change process. What factors contributed to the adoption of a Culture Change programme? What factors contributed to the adoption of re-engineering? What, if anything, was different between the two decisions? What, if anything, was different in employees' responses to the different change programmes? What was the connection between disparate understandings of the change process and the problems of local realities, which I had witnessed in some locations? Was the negative reaction to the culture change by employees in one location the result of a habitual response to ideas put forth by management and, if so, why? These questions were encouraging in me a need to find answers in a social-psychological framework.

Once I had collected the data for both phases of the changes at Nova Scotia Power, I realized that I had an incredible amount of material, which supported a 'differentiated perspective' of culture (Martin, 1992). Yet, I did not have an adequate explanation for what had occurred, or a clear framework for understanding the processes which caused the fractures in the organization. Contradictions between what I had read and understood about culture and change and what I saw at Nova Scotia Power made me want to look beneath the surface. I wanted to understand what was driving the need to implement different change programmes and what caused different responses among employees. Had changing the culture arisen out of a commitment to certain ideals or was it a response to perceived external environmental threats facing the company? Did senior management attach certain expectations to the notion of culture change, or was this part of a pattern to continually reinvent the organization with no thought to long-term consequences? For me, what needed explaining was why Nova Scotia Power appeared to move from the dedicated goal of changing the culture, to an increased interest in change for the sake of change.

My interest in psychology fuelled my need to make sense of these issues and patterns of behaviour. In my search for answers I was taken with Karl Weick's work on sensemaking. In particular, his notion of 'organizing as a social psychological phenomenon that results from sensible interlocking behaviours' (Weick 1979: 3), and his approach to organizational sensemaking (Weick, 1995) with its focus on meaning and identity, captured my interest. Over time, I came to feel that this notion of organizational sensemaking could provide a framework with which I could analyse some of the fundamental questions that had been raised in the course of my research; questions which, for me, traditional models of culture and change did not answer.

I had started out at Nova Scotia Power by looking for predictors of events, which could flag problems for companies undergoing change, but eventually I became more interested in what was driving organizational members' behaviour to follow through with a particular course of action. Weick (1990a) suggests that understanding the processes that lead to certain organizational situations (such as crises) can help circumvent potentially disastrous outcomes. Using this approach I was able to revisit my observations of employee behavioural responses to the introduction and implementation of change programmes. My aim was to focus on trying to make sense of issues surrounding the process of change and exploring the events that 'triggered' sensemaking occasions for change at Nova Scotia Power.

Weick (1995) cautions that 'organization sensemaking' differs from 'everyday sensemaking'. Nonetheless, it can act as a frame for understanding the process of organizational change and the behaviours of individuals who are creating and responding to the changes. At the organizational level, sensemaking can offer an explanation for understanding the management of change, while at the individual level it serves up an explanation for understanding the management of meaning (Smircich and Morgan, 1982). The tension between 'everyday sensemaking' and 'organizational sensemaking' can provide insight into why some programmes are accepted over others, why employees accept or reject these programmes, and how expectations differ according to location.

Through a focus on 'the properties of sensemaking' Weick (1995) offers a framework for explaining (a) individual differences in the way events are understood, (b) how/why those differences are translated into 'sensible interlocking behaviours' (Weick, 1979) and (c) the relationship between identity construction and organizational outcomes. Thus, using Weick's (1995) properties of sensemaking as a framework, I set out to analyse the process of change at Nova Scotia Power by attempting to answer the following questions:

1   What factors contributed to a perceived need for change and how did they influence the change process?

Table 3.1 Employee vs efficiency: contrasting foci at Nova Scotia Power 1990–3

Culture change and the employee	Re-engineering and efficiency
I believe in people, in the sense that you achieve your goals through people, and people only produce those results when they feel good about their work. Over 25 years in management, that's been my experience. And everywhere it's the same. (Louis Comeau, Nova Scotia Power, 1991c)	Ensuring long-term strength and viability for the Company means adopting clear business strategies to address all areas in which we may ultimately become vulnerable. In this regard, our company is reviewing both its cost effectiveness and its revenue opportunities. Through improved productivity, aggressive production management and successful debt refinancings, we have been able to realize cost reductions. To complement this strategy of cost effectiveness we are planning to make the most of our diverse customer base through a market-driven approach to seeking new revenue sources. . . . A lot of change has taken place. Bureaucracy was examined, processes were reviewed, accountabilities were strengthened, and the workforce was reduced. (Louis Comeau, Nova Scotia Power, 1993f)
It was a great year for enhancing employees' work environment. (Nova Scotia Power, 1990a)	
Nova Scotia Power's Human Resource Objective is: To have the right number of people, with the required skills, at the right places, when needed, doing meaningful and necessary work, safely, at a high level of productivity and motivation . . .	We believe that having a satisfied shareholder depends on satisfying customers first. (Nova Scotia Power, 1993f)
The total number of Corporation employees has grown by only 13% (about 300 new jobs) over the past 16 years despite a 50% increase in the number of customers, 1,100% increase in electrical load and substantial growth in the amount of generation, transmission and distribution plant. . . . Maintaining these gains and establishing through employee development the foundation upon which further gains can be made are the motivating factors behind the Corporate cultural change program. (Corporate Plan, Nova Scotia Power, 1991b)	All Vice Presidents have presented ideas allowing for expenditure reductions which would not significantly alter how we do business. . . . [Reductions include 'Cancellation of budgeted vacant positions. Travel. Training']. (Effectiveness Update, March 31, 1993)

Table 3.1 (continued)

Culture change and the employee	Re-engineering and efficiency
We've worked very hard to make this company a more humanistic company. . . . [This] change to a more people-centred approach has . . . allowed us to develop and implement initiatives like the Employee Assistance Program, job sharing, modified hours of work (or 'flex time' as it's often called). (Jim Woods, Nova Scotia Power, 1991c)	Process improvement refers to work processes within the Company that will be analyzed on a cross-divisional basis to ensure the efficiency of the activities *and the right number of employees for the work to be done*. (Effectiveness Update, March 31, 1993: my emphasis)
[We] will be doing a lot more in the areas of empowerment and teamwork. We've got to delegate more decision-making authority to the front-line employees. . . . The vast majority of Nova Scotia Power people are bright, well educated and responsible. Not only should we empower them as individuals, but we should be doing more to help them to work together in teams. (Jim Woods, Nova Scotia Power, 1991c)	We are well aware that many employees are deeply concerned with job security. This is an unpleasant but apparently unpreventable result of the Effectiveness Program. (Effectiveness Update, March 31, 1993)
[Culture change] will make the Corporation a better company, more productive because employees will enjoy their jobs more and be challenged. (Jim Woods, Nova Scotia Power, 1991a)	Business Process Improvement (BPI) is a major part of our total Effectiveness goals which are to achieve a minimum of $25 million in savings in Divisional costs and continuous improvement throughout the organization. . . . Obviously, changes in the way we do business could result in redundant or unnecessary positions. Thus, layoffs may be necessary. However, every effort will be made to retrain or transfer employees before layoffs are considered. (Effectiveness Update, May 14, 1993)

2   How did senior management reconcile re-engineering to the culture change?

3   How do individual versus organizational values influence the outcomes of change?

4   What are the implications of the social construction of change on the nature of change?

5   What is the relationship between pre-packaged change problems and local realities?

6   How did competition and privatization impact on the change process?

Defining the sensemaking model

There are several key aspects of Weick's (1995) sensemaking approach that are important to the framework of analysis developed in this study. To begin with, there is the question of whether it can be seen as a theory of organizational behaviour or something less grand. Second, is the notion that people discover their own invented reality. Third, there is the distinction between organizational sensemaking and everyday sensemaking. Fourth, there is the notion of 'shocks' as occasions for sensemaking. And, fifth, there are the 'properties of sensemaking'.

Sensemaking and theories of organization

Although Weick's notion of sensemaking has become more refined over time, its origins are rooted in his initial criticisms of more traditional approaches to organizational analysis and a concern for process over outcomes. Since the late 1960s, dissatisfaction with traditional approaches to organizational analysis increased as a number of organizational theorists began to criticize the dominant organizational paradigm that viewed organizations as hierarchical, rational, goal driven structures (Burrell and Morgan, 1979; Corman and Poole, 2000). This gave rise to a number of emergent paradigms, including the work of Silverman (1970) who focused on the actor's 'action frame of reference' but within an existing understanding of organization structure. In a similar vein, Weick drew attention to the social-psychological aspects of behaviour in organizational contexts but, unlike Silverman, Weick's approach consisted of a fundamental critique of hierarchical notions of organization. Weick's understanding of organizations as loosely coupled systems led him to explore the social-psychological linkages, rather than focusing on coping with, or reproduction of, hierarchical behaviour. Indeed, Weick helped to shift attention away from 'organization' towards an understanding of the process of 'organizing'. This approach has made him one of the most influential proponents of a 'new orthodoxy' (Mangham, 1987). This contravention of the conventional North American social-psychological approach, suggests that Weick's work shares more of an affinity to the European social-psychological tradition of Henri Tajfel (Tajfel, 1979; Tajfel and Turner, 1979) with its emphasis on social representation and identity. As such, Weick drew on existing social-psychological theories (which are discussed later in this chapter) to develop new ways of understanding organizational behaviour.

From a barely defined aspect of the social psychology of organizing in his earlier work (cf. Weick, 1969, 1979), sensemaking has taken centre stage as a framework for predicting organizational action in Weick's more recent work (cf. Weick, 1995). Thus, for example, in one of Weick's (1979: 133–4) earliest references to sensemaking he uses the term 'recipe for sensemaking' to describe the processes whereby the 'organism or group enacts equivocal raw talk, the talk is viewed retrospectively, sense is made of it, and this sense is then stored as knowledge in the retention process'. By 1995 the 'recipe' had been developed into a coherent framework for viewing organizations as sensemaking systems, a 'set of ideas with explanatory purposes' (Weick, 1995: xi). In its developed form, Weick's (1995) framework involves seven 'properties', consisting of social sensemaking, identity construction, retrospection, plausibility, extracted cues, on-going sensemaking and enactment.

The trajectory of the sensemaking model

Since the publication of *The Social Psychology of Organizing* in 1969, the trajectory of Weick's sensemaking model can be traced as it developed from a subset of ideas derived from a social-psychological analysis of organizing, to its present day status as a framework for making sense of organizational outcomes.

While Weick's research career has certainly been prolific and profound, including over 350 books, journal articles, book chapters and conference papers, it is his work on the social-psychological element of organizing, which focused much of his research and provided the foundation for the development of the sensemaking model. *The Social Psychology of Organizing* (1969) is important because it introduces discussion of what would later be termed sensemaking properties and vocabularies. More importantly, the book's significance lies in its focus on a micro, social-psychological analysis of behaviour, which draws attention to organizing rather than organization, and where process over outcome becomes the key issue. This approach drags 'people and the processes through which they interact back onto the organizational stage at the expense of more traditional and tangible fixtures like structure which are seen as reifications' (Colville, 1994: 22).

The social psychology of organizing

In 1969, Weick contributed to the field of organizational studies by challenging the dominant approach to organizational analysis, which suggested that organizations were stable and complex, differed according to size, and could be understood in terms of outcomes at a point in time (Weick, 1969:

1). Instead, Weick proposed a way of learning, looking and thinking about organizations that focused on the *process* of organizing. This perspective offered an alternative way of viewing organizing as a social-psychological process grounded in retrospection.

From the opening chapter – 'What Organizing Looks Like' – Weick moves us away from organization *per se*, to the processes of organizing. From the first paragraph he makes it clear that his purpose is not to tell the reader 'what organizations are' because 'organizations and their environments change so rapidly that it is unrealistic to show what they are like now, because that's not the way they're going to be later' (Weick, 1969: 1). For Weick:

> one gets the impression that first organizing occurs and then, *after* it is concluded, the reason for the organizing becomes apparent. It is as if people act so that they can eventually determine what it was that they had done. This sequence in which actions *precede* goals may well be a more accurate portrait of organizational functioning.
>
> (Weick, 1969: 8)

In this statement we can see an early exposition of the notion of retrospective sensemaking.

He contends that organization theory has 'often been stifled' through a managerialist approach (Mills and Simmons, 1999), which analyses organization 'using managerial concepts rather than psychological or sociological ones' (Weick, 1969: 22). In this form of (managerialist) analysis, key social interactions were being ignored and problems were being defined in terms of managerial concerns, rather than members' social interactions. Weick (1969) argued instead for an understanding of how socialization occurs in the organizing process, and suggested links between organizational behaviour and identity construction. It is through a critique of the mainstream focus on 'organization' that we begin to see some of the embryonic elements of Weick's sensemaking approach, in particular, the notions of retrospection, enactment, and, to a lesser extent, identity construction and on-going sensemaking.

Weick (1969: 22) develops his critique by arguing for a social-psychological approach whereby understanding can be advanced by removal of the symbols used by practitioners, and 'the phenomena recast into language that has psychological or sociological meaning'. For Weick (1969: 22) 'managerial talk carves up the world of the organization in a particular way. It isolates certain phenomena and certain implications'. In particular such 'talk' directs attention towards organizations as rational, goal seeking entities whose purposes are reflected in, among other things, their structures and organizational behaviours. In his search for social-psychological 'meaning' Weick does not simply set out to examine the micro processes that contribute to rational, goal directed behaviour but to question the very assumption of such phenomena as a framework of analysis.

Weick counters mainstream organizational analysis with two central ideas – retrospective sensemaking and enactment; essentially the notion that the idea of an organization is the enactment of a retrospective account of action. As we have seen above, Weick argues that 'organizing precedes the reason for organizing'. This notion of retrospective sensemaking is clear in the following example:

> The common assertion that goal consensus must occur prior to action obscures the fact that consensus is impossible unless there is something tangible around which it can occur. And this 'something tangible' may well turn out to be actions already completed. Thus it is entirely possible that goal statements are retrospective rather than prospective.
>
> (Weick, 1969: 8)

From this perspective a focus on '"organizational behaviour" serves no useful guiding function' in its implication that behaviour is shaped within organizational settings (Weick, 1969: 27). Instead, according to Weick (1969: 26), organization should be viewed as the sense that arises out of behaviour that 'is continuous with behaviour in other settings'. Here we can see the beginnings of Weick's notion of enactment, whereby organization is a form of enacted sensemaking. This brings us to Weick's (1969: 27) discussion of 'environment' where he argues that 'rather than talking about adapting to an external environment, it may be more correct to argue that organizing consists of adapting to an enacted environment, an environment which is constituted by the actions of interdependent human actors'. Later Weick defines what he calls 'several properties of an enacted environment':

> First, the creation of meaning is an attentional process, but it is attention to that which has already occurred. Second, since the attention is directed backwards from a specific point in time (a specific here and now), whatever is occurring at the moment will influence what the person discovers when he glances backwards. . . . Third, . . . memory processes, whether they be retention or reconstruction, influence meaning. Fourth, . . . an action can become the object of attention only after it has occurred. While it is occurring, it cannot be noticed.
>
> (Weick, 1969: 65)

Here the 'properties' are linked to enactment but focused on explanations of retrospective sensemaking. In Weick's later work, specifically *Sensemaking in Organizations*, he talks in terms of 'the properties of sensemaking', relegating his earlier notion of properties to a discussion of retrospection.

Within Weick's (1969) discussion of enactment and retrospective sensemaking we can find fragments of other sensemaking properties which, collectively, raise questions about the notion of organizations as stable, rational, goal seeking entities. Weick's critique is of particular interest for the developing debate around the issue of organizational change. Indeed, Weick contends that change, not stability, is the rule in any organization, and individuals continually live within streams of on-going events. It is through discussion of 'ongoing events' that Weick gives us insights into some of the key social-psychological factors associated with organizational change. To begin with, he argues that processes of organizing, 'create, maintain and dissolve social collectivities', and the ways in which 'these processes are continuously executed *are* the organization' (Weick, 1969: 1). According to Weick, by uncovering the social-psychological process that impacted on these interlocking behaviours, the elements of organizing would emerge (Ibid.: 43). Here Weick's argument contains the assumption that individuals try to make sense of their actions by seeking out cues to make plausible explanations for their behaviour, suggesting that 'behaviour can be viewed as responses in search of appropriate stimuli or excuses for expression' (Weick, 1969: 26). It should be noted, however, that at this stage he does not directly refer to 'cues' or 'plausibility'.

If organization arises out of the processes of retrospective sensemaking then, as Weick (1969: 36) contends, the 'processes involved in organizing must continually be reaccomplished'. Herein lies the potential for many of the problems associated with organizational change:

> At any moment in time, there are possibilities inherent in the information on which an organization operates which, if noticed and actualized, can undermine the workings of the organization. There are always mutations, which affect the workings of the organizational processes. These mutations occur continuously. Any process is always being diverted, modified, undone, simplified, or made less orderly. It is never true that a process simply unfolds time after time. Instead, in order for the process to unfold at any moment in time, its components must be reinstated, reaffirmed, and reaccomplished.
>
> (Weick, 1969: 36)

In statements of this type we can see the seeds of Weick's later notion of organizational 'shocks' or 'bursts' to explain breakdowns in on-going sensemaking and their links with organizational change:

> If change is so continuous, it becomes difficult for a person to make sense of what is happening and to anticipate what will happen *unless* he is able to make some of the events recur. . . . He has to stabilize some portion of the ongoing events.
>
> (Weick, 1969: 44)

This raises the question of how people manage to maintain an ongoing sense of a situation. Weick's answer is to introduce the notion of interlocking behaviour and the grammar of organizing. Simply put, interlocking behaviour occurs when two or more people inter-relate in a process of organizing. The transition from one person to two 'creates the basic unit of social behaviour', characterized by 'interdependence, reciprocal behaviour, and the necessity for accommodation to another person' (Weick, 1969: 24). In this way, behaviour of one individual becomes contingent on the behaviour of another, thereby defining action as collective rather than individual. Through a series of interlocked behaviours individuals are encouraged to reproduce a sense or organization due to control pressures of the 'collective structure', psychological pressures to provide 'structural assurances' to one another and to reduce uncertainty (or 'equivocality') from 'the informational environment', and a pre-existing vocabulary of 'regulative and organizational properties' that informs collective behaviours.

While Weick's emphasis on social-psychological processes reveal the limitations of traditional approaches to organizational theory (and change), it does not adequately deal with issues of power and control, and the 'institutional' and 'imaginative' aspects of those 'formative contexts' that inform vocabularies of action (Unger, 1987a). Instead, Weick (1969: 37) argues that control 'is accomplished by relationships, not by people'. That it 'is relationships and not people that impose control in an organization' (Ibid.). And he contends that 'principles of organization and relationship could not have evolved; they had to exist in some form from the beginning' (Weick, 1969: 62). As Unger would have it, 'social institutions come to appear less the outcomes of various political disputes and more as acceptable if, perhaps, imperfect approximations to the ideals of efficiency and good sense' (Blackler, 1992a: 281).

Organizations as loosely coupled systems

The next step in the trajectory of Weick's work represented something of a break with his previous (highly structured) notion of interlocking behaviour. In 1976, drawing upon data which studied organizational processes in education, Weick (1976: 1), challenged the notion that 'elements in organization are coupled through dense, tight linkages', i.e., that behaviours are linked together through consciously arranged tasks, descriptions, or structures of co-ordination and control. In contrast, Weick contends that the mainstream preoccupation with the notion of organizations as rational entities blinded researchers to the less tightly coupled events, which impact on organizational outcomes. Thus, he proposes, instead, that 'elements are often tied together frequently and loosely' (Weick, 1976: 1), i.e., interlocking behaviours can be characterized by such things as 'a relative lack of coordination. . . . (or) absence of regulation; planned unresponsiveness; decentralization', etc.

Arguably, Weick's discussion amounts to little more than a rehash of the debate around 'organic' and 'mechanistic' organization (Burns and Stalker, 1961) that expands little on sensemaking. Indeed, there is virtually no reference to processes of sensemaking. What it does add to his emergent sensemaking approach is new insights into the problem of interlocking behaviours, enactment, and organizational change. It does this by suggesting that not all elements of an organizing process are closely linked, and that some elements may be better able than others to develop novel solutions to problems, to adapt to local situations and to encourage member self-determination.

The social psychology of organizing revisited

The year 1979 saw the appearance of the second edition of *The Social Psychology of Organizing*. This edition expanded on the earlier concepts of enactment, and interlocking behaviours and began to cast them as key elements of a 'sensemaking recipe' for understanding the process of organizing. It centred on 'organizing as a process through which people make sense of their world by reducing equivocality' (Ibid.: 219), and defined organizing as 'consensually validated grammar for reducing equivocality by means of sensible, interlocking behaviours. To organize is to assemble ongoing interdependent actions into sensible sequences that generate sensible outcomes' (Weick, 1979: 3).

Although Weick uses the term 'sensemaking' sparingly and belatedly to describe the social-psychological processes of organizing, his focus on 'equivocality' gives primacy to the search for meaning as a way of dealing with uncertainty. The sheer number of ways that something can be understood triggers sensemaking activity whereby actors work to make something sensible and thus certain. For Weick, equivocality was especially important because it provided a link between interlocking behaviours, loosely coupled systems and the assemblage of these interdependent actions into 'sensible sequences that generate sensible outcomes'. Equivocal information, according to Weick, triggered organizing, which in turn involved the effort of two or more people to stabilize and give meaning to this equivocality. With equivocality offering an explanation for why sensemaking occurs, Weick returned his attention to enactment, described as 'efferent sensemaking' (1979: 159), as a key part of the sensemaking process. According to Weick (1969: 133), enactment is the action that produces the raw materials to make things sensible. Because sensemaking is retrospective, enactment produces events that can be made sensible. In other words, it is the vehicle for sensemaking.

Weick begins to link organizing to identity construction where he explains how self-reflection influences a retrospective account of attributional processes on behaviour. Yet at this point discussion of identity construction is overwhelmed by a focus on collective or social sensemaking. Structure becomes more closely equated to notions of enactment, interlocking behaviour and collective actions. We can also see a rudimentary discussion of plausibility where Weick discusses notions of interdependence as they are related to self-fulfilling prophecies.

Weick (1969: 234) described this book as being 'as much about organizational theorizing as it is about organizational theory' and he suggested that 'organizations are in the business of making sense' (1969: 250). These statements seemed to have paved the way for Weick's further research, where he translated the theory into empirical settings and further developed the sensemaking approach.

Sensemaking and empirical research

In reviewing Weick's empirical research, it is interesting to follow the refinement of what has become known as the sensemaking approach. By combining elements from his work on the social psychology of organizing, and his premise of organizations as loosely coupled systems, one can see how he has broken down the social construction of organizing into concepts that have later developed into sensemaking properties, organizational shocks and vocabularies of language.

Sources of order   This first becomes clear in Weick's (1989) exploration of the impact of new technologies on managerial sensemaking. By stating that 'technology' was analogous to 'equivoque', because of the various 'plausible' interpretations that made it 'uncertain', Weick then postulated that technologies would require 'ongoing' structuring and 'sensemaking' in order to be managed (Weick, 1989: 2).

The Tenerife disaster   In 1990, Weick applied a sensemaking approach to the Tenerife air disaster, in order to uncover the processes that set crises in motion, and to gain a better understanding of how small separate failures become linked (Weick, 1993b). Referencing other major disasters (i.e. Bhopal and Three Mile Island), he acknowledged the relationship between tightly coupled systems and the linkage of separate small events that amplify into unpredictable and inexplicable outcomes (Weick, 1993b: 174). But he suggested that what was missing from the previous analysis of these disasters was an understanding of the process that linked the series of separate small events into a major crisis.

Again, drawing upon the metaphor of organizations as a series of interlocking behaviours and habitual patterns of behaviour, Weick suggested that interruptions of important routines, regression to habitual responses, coordination breakdowns, and misunderstandings in communication occurring in tightly coupled and linear systems, increased the likelihood of these outcomes. He concluded that this type of analysis uncovered an inherent vulnerability in human systems, which had been previously ignored.

An examination of the cockpit tapes and the pilots' responses supported Weick's premise that crises typically involve an interruption of plans (1993c: 182) and, when systems break down, people revert to familiar scripts. In the case of the Tenerife disaster, a series of small interruptions to a planned course of action had dire consequences. While each on its own may not have resulted in a fatal outcome, Weick shows how interdependence, and sensemaking by the extraction of cues, lent plausibility to the actors' actions. Although not articulated, Weick was restating the basic tenet of sensemaking, which is that people make sense based on what they already know.

It is not, for example, uncommon for aircraft to be diverted because of fog or bomb scares, yet it seldom results in a fatal outcome. It is also not uncommon for air traffic controllers to reassign runway positions. But it wasn't an everyday occurrence at Tenerife airport, or for these pilots. In combination with time pressures and miscommunication, both pilots ignored the cues they were receiving and instead relied on habitual responses to bestow meaning on their actions. The novelty of this particular analysis lies in its ability to show the transformation of a series of loosely coupled events transformed into a series of tightly coupled events, which changed the nature of the process from simple and linear to a complex process filled with unexpected contingencies (1993c: 189). The value of this analysis lies in its ability to generalize the process to other accidents to show that blame is not necessarily attributable to one cause, but instead to a series of smaller events which tighten the coupling and increase the complexity of the system.

Mann Gulch   In 1993, Weick applied his 'sensemaking recipe' to the study of the disintegration of rule structure and sensemaking in the Mann Gulch disaster, in order to find out why organizations unravel and what could be done to make them more resilient. Weick maintains that faulty organizational sensemaking, not decision-making, is the reason organizations falter, and that sensemaking is about contextual rationality (Weick, 1993a: 636). In the Mann Gulch case, Weick set out to show how identity construction and habituated patterns of action gave plausibility, therefore meaning, to the fire-fighters' sensemaking, which in turn contributed to the disintegration of role structure when they were faced with contradictory cues.

Recognizing that organizations provide meaning and order, in the face of contradictory environmental demands (Weick, 1993a: 635), Weick uses the Mann Gulch experience to show how individuals use sensemaking to make events rational to themselves and others. Describing the organization as a 'role structure of interlocking behaviour' (1993a: 633), Weick shows how shocks (i.e., such as new leadership and inconceivable events), unravel existing interlocking routines, and break down habituated patterns of response, thereby causing a sudden loss of meaning associated with the event.

In this case, the fire-fighters, by ignoring the severity of the fire, created cues that contradicted the reality, but gave them a plausible, albeit inaccurate account of actual events, that made it difficult for them to socially construct the severity of the fire. In this way, the order to drop their tools contradicted both their identity as fire-fighters and their habitual pattern of behaviour, so that they were unable to deal with this sudden loss of meaning.

Weick acknowledges the main cause of events at Mann Gulch as the break-down of role structure and identity created by sudden shocks to the routine, but suggests that the disaster need not have occurred. He maintains that had the fire-fighters been able to recognize the influence of tradition and ideology on their scripts of organizing, and had they sought out alternate patterns of behaviour, the inaccuracy of the cues they had extracted might have been evident in their own social construction of reality.

The analysis of Mann Gulch is significant because of its practical appli-cation to organizational analysis, which forces us to consider the impact that interlocking behaviours and structure have on sensemaking and behav-iour. Here Weick not only incorporates the elements of sensemaking model into a framework of analysis but he questions the value of decision-making analysis as orthodoxy in organizational analysis. Yet it is important to note that both Mann Gulch and Tenerife are only snapshot studies. The case of Nova Scotia Power offers, not only the possibility of studying a long-term process of events, but a longitudinal study that is important for a full-scale examination of the strengths and weaknesses of the sensemaking approach.

Sensemaking in organizations

From his interest in the social psychological processes of organizing, through to his empirical work on large-scale accidents, Weick has developed the framework of what is now being accepted as an important method of studying organizations. The strength of Weick's (1995) work on sensemaking lies in its ability to bring together the various strands of his earlier research into a comprehensive framework for understanding the social-psychological and structural elements of organizing.

As an explanatory process, Weick suggests that sensemaking is unique because it is set apart from understanding, attribution and interpretation. For example, whereas interpretation focuses on text, sensemaking looks at how people generate what they interpret (Weick, 1995: 13). For Weick, that means that sensemaking is more about the invention than the outcome. And what sets it apart is its seven distinguishing characteristics, which he labels 'properties' (Weick, 1995: 17).

Weick claims that sensemaking is nothing more than a set of ideas that have explanatory possibilities (Weick, 1995: xi), not a theoretical framework, and he reiterates that sensemaking is not a body of knowledge, rather a recipe for analysis. Nonetheless, he provides a deeper level of analysis with his linkage of the vocabularies of sensemaking and the seven properties of sense-making. In this work, we begin to see the articulation of the properties into a description of sensemaking and as a heuristic for understanding organiza-tional processes.

The role of the sensemaking properties

At the crux of Weick's account of the sensemaking process are seven characteristics, or properties, which he describes as 'an observer's manual or a set of raw materials for disciplined imagination' (Weick, 1995: 18). Chosen because of their practical implications and frequent use in sensemaking literature, Weick maintains that each property 'is a self-contained set of research questions', each follows a rough sequence of events, and each relates to the other. Because of this, the importance of the properties lies in their ability to act as guidelines for telling us what sensemaking is, how it works, and where it can fail (Weick, 1995: 18). As such, the properties act as boundaries around the sensemaking model and answer Weick's question, 'how can I know what I think until I see what I say?'.

Practically speaking, the sensemaking properties provide the vehicle for incorporating action and research. On its own, each property has the ability to partially explain action, but the strength of the properties lies in their holistic ability to comprehensively dissect sensemaking events. What are the reasons for our behaviour when faced with situations of ambiguity and uncertainty? Why does the sensemaking differ, despite shared experiences? At this level, the properties can be understood as a template for making sense of our activity. The relevance of the sensemaking properties is that they provide answers to the question of what we need to look at if we want to understand why an outcome has occurred.

The substance of sensemaking and vocabularies

While the properties of sensemaking can be thought of as the engine that drives the sensemaking model, Weick argues that people get caught up in the process imagery and forget to look at what is being processed. In order to give substance to sensemaking, he states that there needs to be an understanding of the meaning of its content.

He suggests that a way to focus on the meaning of sensemaking, and give it substance, is by drawing upon different vocabularies that form the content of sensemaking. By working with an assumption that people draw upon frames of reference to cue their understandings, Weick explains how frames are derived from past moments of socialization, and cues are the result of present moments of experience (Weick, 1995: 111). He states that the way that the two are connected forms the content of sensemaking.

The importance of substance analysis in the sensemaking framework, according to Weick, is that by understanding what people draw upon to construct reality, we can gain insight into how to understand and change behaviours. By drawing attention to (six) different vocabularies that inform sensemaking, Weick is offering a preliminary link between the reasons for enactment that are revealed by the sensemaking properties and the intent that the content analysis uncovers. For example, words are pulled from vocabularies of society, organizations, occupations, coping, predecessors and sequence, and sense is made respectively with ideology, third-order controls, paradigms, theories of action, tradition and the use of narratives. This is a much more developed notion of vocabularies than that introduced in 1969 but arguably it still lacks explanation of how the institutional and imaginative aspects of organizational grammar are shaped and selected. As I shall argue later, the content of sensemaking needs to be explored through various levels of action, rulemaking, and formative contexts but ultimately hinges on Weick's more highly developed properties of the sensemaking framework.

In their current form the properties of sensemaking, as the primary analytic tool, broadly includes a map, which takes us to the content of sensemaking. Taken together, the properties of identity construction, plausibility, enactment and extraction of cues, guide us to an understanding of how sensemaking is shaped, scripted and enacted.

Sensemaking and future research

The detailed account of sensemaking that Weick presents in 1995 is important because it demonstrates the relevance of sensemaking as a heuristic for organizational analysis, and its generalizability to a number of organizational types and situations. And this is reiterated in Weick's proposal for the future of sensemaking.

Although Weick puts forward a number of different ways that the sensemaking model can be expanded upon, a common theme seems to focus on discovering why sensemaking can differ within the same settings. Because Weick understands organizations as a series of interlocking, loosely coupled systems, power is not a central issue in his analysis. But in the process, discovering how sensemaking becomes negotiated, power becomes evident as a factor, which demands further attention. For example, Weick (1995: 172) states that a key question in the future of sensemaking research centres on understanding how meanings and artefacts are produced and reproduced in complex and collective settings. He highlights areas, such as socialization, and policy making, where sensemaking activity can be clearly identified, and suggests a variety of qualitative approaches to the methodology that include grounded theory, interviews and critical incident analysis. Weick (1995: 18) considers this area particularly important, in order to offset a tendency to frame organizational sensemaking at the individual level of analysis.

Weick also notes that managerial activity utilizes elements of sensemaking, and acknowledges that the extension of these studies will advance the sensemaking model. He further notes that activities that fall within this category, such as the management of meaning, enactment and self-fulfilling prophecies, are all boundary conditions, which impact on the sensemaking process and require more investigation. Again, this implies a power relationship.

In a similar vein, Weick proposes that sensemaking in low-discretion conditions needs to be developed, in order to understand the avoidance and acceptance of certain sensemaking processes. Furthermore, he suggests that an analysis of the negotiation of multiple identities in sensemaking can be helped by an expanded use of the sensemaking properties.

By targeting some of the underdeveloped aspects of the sensemaking model and showing how it can be utilized to explore other organizational processes, Weick strengthens the value of the sensemaking properties as a heuristic for understanding a number of different organizational events.

In attempting to understand the management of change, we can see Weick's (1995) approach to sensemaking in organizations as a heuristic rather than a theory. As a heuristic its value lies in two key areas. At one level, it is a useful framework for making sense of the process of organizational change. Yet, at another level, the framework has implications for theories of organizational change in that it points to the importance of something called sensemaking. Arguably, this is the missing element in a number of different theories that guide the management of change, the management of meaning and the enactment of culture. It can be used to explain how/why particular change programmes are adopted in the face of evidence of their shortcomings, and why, despite every effort, some managers unilaterally reject such attempts at change. In short, sensemaking goes beyond being just a way to give meaning to situations; it helps to clarify the issues that allow for the holistic exploration of change. As Weick states,

> There is no such thing as a theory of organizations that is characteristic of the sensemaking paradigm. Nevertheless, there are ways to talk about organizations that allow for sensemaking to be the central activity in the construction of both the organization and the environments it confronts.
>
> (Weick, 1995: 67)

The antecedents of sensemaking

Weick's sensemaking model is premised on his earlier work, which challenged the traditional notion that organizations were rational, goal directed entities. For Weick, organizational 'plans were retrospective reconstructions or elapsed actions that had functioned earlier like blind interpretations' (Colville *et al.*, 1999: 138). This approach sees 'organizing as a process of sensemaking' (Ibid.), and builds on the work of Follett (1941) and others who understand organizing and organizations as a process rather than an outcome (Brown, 1992; Colville *et al.*, 1999). The value of this type of insight can be seen in Mintzberg's (cf. Mintzberg, Brunet, and Waters, 1986) work on strategy, which suggests that long-term organizational decision-making often emerges as a result of retrospection, rather than the outcome of deliberate planning.

As a starting point, Weick uses generative theory (Gergen, 1992) to explain why people question basic assumptions (Colville, 1994). Weick's framework also incorporates various strands of other social theories to explain the different properties of sensemaking. Social constuctionism (Berger and Luckmann, 1967) and interpretive interactionalism (Mead, 1962) underlie much of Weick's approach and, in particular, the respective properties of social sensemaking and identity construction (Colville, 1994; Weick, 1995: 41). This draws our attention to the role of the actor in the process of change. As John Child (1972) long ago suggested, the interpretations of the decision-maker can play a significant role in strategic choice. By drawing attention to the various ways that actors may understand a situation, Weick points out the potential source of the problem of acceptance and implementation that dogs traditional theories of organizational change. In particular, sensemaking theory goes beyond a focus on the actor to raise questions about the role of identity in the change process. As a number of recent commentaries have suggested, identity construction may be a central issue in the way that images of organization are constructed and maintained (cf. du Gay, 1994; Nord and Fox, 1996). For example, it could be argued that in order to understand the culture change of Scandinavian Airways (SAS) in the late 1970s, we needed to understand something about the unique identity of its CEO, Jan Carlzon.

The property of retrospection is rooted in attribution theory (Garfinkel, 1967) to explain how meaning is bestowed on an action, and Weick (1995: 11) draws on the concept of cognitive dissonance (Festinger, 1957) to show how 'outcomes develop prior definitions'. This raises questions about the relationship between descriptions of organizational outcomes and the context in which those descriptions are formed. For example, there is a need to explain the discrepancy between numerous reports of successful organizational change and a widespread perception of the failure of change programmes.

Garfinkel's (1967) work on juries forms the basis of Weick's (1995) plausibility property of sensemaking. He draws on Goffman's (1974) frame analysis and the work of James, to elaborate the notion of extracted cues (Weick, 1995: 49). This work brings into focus the psychological aspects of the evaluation of change. In contrast to traditional theories of organizational change that link successful outcomes to scientific method, a focus on plausibility draws attention to the role of psychological agreements, and contextual cues, in acceptance of something as 'successful'.

Weick's notion of the on-going nature of sensemaking borrows from Katz and Kahn's (1966) open systems view of organizations. This is useful in signalling the need to understand what triggers organizational change. Traditional theories often downplay this factor, focusing instead on a perceived need for change and the process of implementation. It may be that the source of organizational change is as important, if not more so, than the implementation process in understanding outcomes. For example, Hammer and Champy (1995) attribute the 'widespread failure' of re-engineering to its implementation, but fail to question whether each and all of the various companies involved actually 'needed' to introduce change and if re-engineering was appropriate in all cases. Others have suggested that the successful marketing of re-engineering (cf. Jackson, 2001) may be both an important source of organizational change and an explanation for a high level of failure.

Finally, Weick's enactment property shares similarities with Pfeffer and Salanik's (1978) management of environmental influences. By rooting much of this work in story telling, Weick builds on current interest in narrative (e.g., Mumby, 1993) as a way of linking cognitive maps to the property of enactment (Taylor and Lerner, 1996). Here we are reminded that organizational change results from the actions of decision-makers. From this perspective, we are not simply drawn to the position of the decision-maker, so much as the social-psychological processes, whereby organizational change is made 'sensable'. We know, for example, that Sir John King embarked on a culture change of British Airways in the early 1980s but that tells us little of how employees came to embrace the process. For that understanding, we need to know something of King's strategy. For instance, a closer look reveals that employee commitment was achieved through a series of events linked by the story of 'Putting People First', whereby employees were encouraged to see themselves as part of a customer-centred company (cf. Bruce, 1987).

Weick's phenomenology is similar to Silverman's (1970) interpretive focus (Clegg and Hardy, 1996: 2) and builds on interest in chaos theory and the garbage-can model of decision-making (Cohen *et al.*, 1972). This, among other things, encourages Martin (1992) and Hatch (1997) to describe Weick's approach as an example of a fragmented perspective, although the underlying notion of social constructionism seems to suggest more of an integrationist approach. Weick's contribution to the non-traditional group of theory researchers lies in its ability to tie together the different strands of social theories into a comprehensive model of processual analysis.

Invented reality

At the heart of Weick's (1995) approach is a crucial distinction between interpretation and invention of reality. According to Weick (1995: 15) 'people make sense of things by seeing a world on which they have already imposed what they believe'. Thus, sensemaking is not about interpreting what is going on, it is about discovering your own invention. For example, it could be argued that in 1988 Louis Comeau interpreted the results of an employee attitude survey as signifying 'low morale' and the need for culture change. However, there is evidence that Comeau, sensing low morale, commissioned a survey that would confirm that sense. There is also evidence that Comeau was already drawn to the idea of culture change prior to the completion of the attitude survey. A sensemaking interpretation would argue, then, that in finding low morale Comeau was in fact discovering his own invention.

From everyday to organizational sensemaking

There are two key divides in Weick's (1995) notion of sensemaking – sense-making *per se* (or 'everyday sensemaking') and 'organizational sensemaking' as a particular form of sensemaking. Weick (1995) explains everyday sense-making by reference to the processes (or 'properties') involved. At its simplest, sensemaking 'literally' means the making of sense. Active agents construct sensible, sensable events. They 'structure the unknown" (Weick, 1995: 4). This simple account suggests that people do something, engage in some process, to end up with a sense of understanding, a feeling that they 'know' what is going on. But how specifically do people make sense? In Weick's (1995) view sensemaking is generated by words that convey what we are experiencing. In other words, a person makes sense of a situation through thought or expressed words that convey what s/he is experiencing. In essence, everyday sensemaking involves a *frame*, a *cue* and a *connection*. A frame refers to a set of abstract words used to categorize data and label experiences, and a cue refers to less abstract words within the framework. Frames 'include and point to other less abstract words (cues) that become sensible in the context created by the more inclusive words' (Weick, 1995: 110). A connection refers to the fact that to be meaningful a frame and a cue are understood in relation to each other: 'Meaning within vocabularies is relational. A cue in a frame is what makes sense, not the cue alone or the frame alone' (Weick, 1995: 110).

According to Weick (Ibid.: 3), sensemaking is 'organizational' when it takes place and is part of 'interlocking routines that are tied together in relatively formal "nets of collective action".' This would appear to have two key aspects. First, at its most simple, organizational sensemaking is about making sense of events tied to the operation of an 'organization'. Second, and more complex in its implications, the operation of an 'organization' or set of 'organized' activities forms a particular framework within which sense is made. For example, organizations 'stay tied together by means of controls in the form of incentives and measures. . . . [They] also have their own languages and symbols that have important effects on sensemaking' (Weick, 1995: 3).

Thus, everyday sensemaking and organizational sensemaking are not identical. Organizational life, in contrast to everyday life, is taken for granted to a much lesser degree. Indeed, much of organizational life is 'fair game for continual negotiation, controlled information processing, and mindful attention [a need for reaccomplishment and a] pervasive . . . need for accounting, justification, and rationalizing' (Weick, 1995: 63).

The only thing that people in organizations do not do, Weick (1995: 63) concludes, is 'to take things for granted, which is what they spend most of their time doing everywhere else'.

At first sight it appears that Weick (1995) is suggesting that organizational sensemaking is less stable than everyday sensemaking, that accomplishments in organizations are far more the result of 'negotiated order' (Strauss *et al.*, 1963) than those in everyday life:

> [S]ensemaking in organizational life is distinctive because . . . organizations challenge everything and ask for explanations of everything including rationality itself . . . ; because socialization is shallower, more transient, and more easily upended by deviants and mavericks and less controlled by the elders . . . ; and because social competence tends to be office specific, local, narrowly defined, and nonpredictive of what will pass as competence anywhere else within the firm.
>
> (Weick, 1995: 64)

This element of instability may, in part, help to explain how it is that apparently unifying events (e.g., the introduction of culture change) come to be viewed in contrasting, sometimes contradictory ways, by different organizational members.

On the other hand, Weick uses the notion of the instability of organizational life to explain the relative stability of aspects of organizational sensemaking:

> One begins to wonder when work ever gets done and whether the whole reason routines seem so characteristic of organizations is that they free up the controlled processing necessary to make sense of the dilemmas that need to be managed before people can even get at the work.
>
> (Weick, 1995: 64)

In other words, Weick (1995) seems to suggest that such things as organizational 'routines' may actually serve to encourage and stabilize certain forms of sensemaking.

'Shocks' as occasions for sensemaking

The importance of organizational routines as sensemaking scripts is strengthened in Weick's (1995) discussion of 'occasions for sensemaking' where he refers to 'shocks' as the 'trigger' for sensemaking:

> Two types of sensemaking occasions common to organization are ambiguity and uncertainty. The 'shock' in each case is somewhat different. In the case of ambiguity, people engage in sensemaking because they are confused by too many interpretations, whereas in the case of uncertainty, they do so because they are ignorant of any interpretations.
>
> (Weick, 1995: 91–2)

Ambiguity and uncertainty are 'shocks' in so far as they are breaks or gaps in organizational routines. It is not so much that routines are a problem as when (as cognitive frameworks) they do not exist or are no longer able to deal with certain events.

Weick (1995) takes this a stage further by linking the ideologies involved in everyday sensemaking to institutionalized scripts within organizations.

Drawing upon Trice and Beyer's (1993) work on the cultural sources of ideology, Weick (1995) connects sensemaking with institutional theory to explain how ideology and institutional systems become the scripts that stabilize into meanings. The language of sensemaking, therefore, is based on past activities and story telling and cultural scripts. In other words, sensemaking in organizations is strongly influenced by cognitive frameworks in the form of institutional systems, routines and scripts.

Sensemaking properties

Weick's research on sensemaking developed out of his earlier research on 'enactment', i.e., the process whereby a particular reality is socially constructed (Weick, 1979, 1985a, 1985b, 1990a, 1990b). But how is it constructed? What is the basis of people's discovery of their own social construction?

In trying to make sense of the issues surrounding enactment, Weick articulated the notion of sensemaking through (a) a focus on 'occasions for sensemaking', and (b) the construction of sensemaking as a series of activities. The latter include 'such things as placement of items into frameworks, comprehending, redressing surprise, constructing meaning, interacting in pursuit of mutual understanding, and patterning' (Weick, 1995: 6). He then categorized the various activities into seven 'properties', or 'distinguishing characteristics that set sensemaking apart from other explanatory processes such as understanding, interpretation, and attribution' (Weick, 1995: 17).

Over time, Weick (1995: 17–62) has developed this framework of sensemaking properties, which have become the cornerstones of sensemaking and provide the analytic tools needed to understand the sensemaking process. None of the properties can be thought of as stand-alone elements of sensemaking, indeed, each is dependent on the other. However, some properties have greater or lesser relevance in explaining certain behaviours in particular organizational situations.

Sensemaking and identity

Weick implies that the sensemaking event is grounded in identity construction: 'sensemaking begins with a sensemaker' (Weick, 1995: 18). Indeed, as I shall argue later, identity construction is at the root of sensemaking and influences how other aspects, or properties, of the sensemaking process are understood. As Weick (1995: 20) expresses it, 'the establishment and maintenance of identity is a core preoccupation in sensemaking' (Weick, 1995: 20). People are concerned to promote self-enhancement, efficacy and consistency and this acts as a trigger for sensemaking activity. Sensemaking can be triggered by a failure to confirm one's self, or in the service of maintaining a consistent, positive, self-conception because 'people learn about their identities by projecting them into an environment and observing the consequences' (Weick, 1995).

For Weick (1995: 23) this has consequences for organizational sense-making in that 'people simultaneously try to shape and react to the environments they face. They take the cue for their identity from the conduct of others, but they make an active effort to influence this conduct to begin with'. Thus, a person makes sense of an event by asking what implications it has for who that person will be. For example, if negative images threaten a person's sense of self they may 'alter the sense they make of those images, even if this means redefining the organizational identity' (Weick, 1995: 21).

There are two paradigmatically different elements contained in this approach. Weick's (1995) notion of the 'individual' is very much modernist in tone (Calás and Smircich, 1992) yet his discussion of 'identity' has much in common with present day post-modernist accounts (Hatch, 1997). This is both a strength and a limitation. On the one hand, sensemaking contributes to the current debates concerning identity and organization (Aaltio and Mills, 2002; du Gay, 1996; Jacques, 1996; Townley, 1994), providing insights into the relationship between organizational outcomes and senses of self. In that regard, it is timely and important in providing a framework for under-standing the social-psychological processes that link identity construction with organizational realities. On the other hand, Weick's notion of 'the indi-vidual' is not always clear, at times suggesting the existence of an essential self and at times suggesting a 'parliament of selves'. This latter problem might well be accommodated as a condition of the search for identity. That is to say, that a sense of a fixed self is, in fact, a part of the post-modern condition of several selves, and helps us to understand the process whereby people seek to achieve a firm sense of self.

There are also two major dichotomies involved in Weick's (1995) account. First, it is made clear that sensemaking is an individual activity but it is also made clear that individual behaviour is influenced by the conduct of others. Second, Weick (1995) contends that a person's sense of a situation owes much to his or her efforts at identity construction but, on the other hand, he also argues that the 'situation' can determine which 'self' a person chooses to be: 'What the situation will have meant to me is dictated by the identity I adopt in dealing with it. And that choice, in turn, is affected by what I think is occurring' (Weick, 1995: 24). These two dichotomies capture the complexity of the sensemaker in action but also point up the limits of an approach that is overly focused on the individual. I will take this up later in a discussion on the role of formative contexts (Unger, 1987b) discourse (Foucault, 1979), organizational rules (Mills and Murgatroyd, 1991) and activity systems (Blackler, 1993a, 1993b).

Social sensemaking

Sensemaking is a social activity. Here Weick (1995) attempts to deal with the individual–social dichotomy. Basically, Weick draws our attention to the fact that:

1   we make sense for ourselves, drawing upon a common language and everyday social interaction (i.e., our individual thoughts are social in the language we use and the actions we engage in);

2   an individual's sensemaking is 'contingent on the conduct of others, whether those others are imagined or physically present' (Weick, 1995: 39). In other words, how a person makes sense of a situation will depend to some extent on how others react or are thought to be reacting;

3   we make sense for others. Part of the sensemaking process involves sharing ideas with others, influencing how they make sense of events. In other words, my expression of a sense of a situation is in part the outcome of how I see the situation and in part an outcome of how I want my expression to be received.

Here Weick is doing two things. First, he is basically reminding us that sensemaking is at one and the same time individual and social, that 'human thinking and social functioning are essential aspects of one another' (Weick, 1995: 38). But, second, he is arguing that, in the context of organizations, the social aspect of the process has important consequences for the individual and, consequently, the organization. Essentially, the individual's attempt to make sense occurs in the context of organizational routines, symbols, language and scripts.

To begin with, the individual is the final arbiter of his or her own sense of reality. As I drive my car, for example, the language and the rules of the road may bind me, but it will be my decision, based on personal experiences and preferences, on whether to take one route or another. Nonetheless, my individual sensemaking as a car driver cannot be divorced from the legal rules under which I drive.

Similarly, within an organization the individual's ability to make sense will rely to a large extent on certain rules, routines, symbols and language. To return to the driving analogy, the rules and language of the road – like organizational rules, routines and language – serve to take much of the thinking out of the process. I do not have to spend time making sense of why people on one side of the road are driving in the opposite direction to those on the other side of the road. I develop a habitual response to certain activities. It is where those 'social' aspects of sensemaking break down that the individual is likely to fall back on a more personal or habitual way of making sense. For example, a person who is driving around a rotary (round-about) has the legal right of way over those who are trying to enter the rotary. This law helps drivers to make sense of the action of others. In Halifax (Nova Scotia), however, an informal rule has developed around use of the city's largest rotary. Local drivers using the Armdale Rotary 'know' that people take equal turns at access. Thus, the person on the rotary will give way to allow another driver on, and each person, whether on or entering, will wait their turn to proceed. The stranger to Halifax will find that the situation at the Armdale Rotary does not make sense and will likely revert to previous experience when proceeding. This makes for a potentially dangerous situation every time a stranger approaches the Armdale Rotary.

In several studies Weick shows how such breakdowns lead to organizational crisis as individuals either cling to routines or fall back into a more personal way of making sense. Weick's (1990a) study of the Tenerife air disaster, for example, pointed to the vulnerability of human systems through the interruption of routines, regression to habitual responses, language and symbolic misunderstandings, and breakdown of co-ordinated activities. Using transcripts of the cockpit tapes, Weick (1990a) was able to show how the biggest commercial air crash in history arose out of interruptions to expected routines[1] which, coupled with ambiguous language,[2] led to a breakdown in the communication process and a crash that killed approximately 400 people. The pilots, disrupted from their expected routines and not understanding the response they received, reverted to their individual sensemaking to direct their responses. Like a kind of gestalt (Kohler, 1961), the pilots were unable to cope once the figure (e.g., the flight instructions) had been disassociated from the ground (e.g., the flight routine).

Similarly, Weick's (1996) study of the death of a group of fire-fighters points to a reliance of individual sensemaking on organizational patterns. In that study the fire-fighters, under a particular leader, had been trained to 'look after' their tools, to ensure, among other things, that they did not lose them. Faced with a crisis situation (an engulfing fire), and a new and untried leader, many of the fire-fighters died because they held on to their heavy tools as they attempted to escape the fire. In the face of uncertainty (a new leader who told them to drop their tools) and a crisis situation, many of the fire-fighters reverted to habitual action.

Thus, within organizational situations the conduct of the individual is contingent on the routinized or scripted conduct of others. Among other things, this involves a process of anticipating how others will react, using such things as routines as guides to sensemaking. When deviations from anticipated outcomes occur, it is usually when methods of guiding and co-ordinating social activity, such as use of symbolism and language, are misinterpreted, misread, or plain inappropriate (i.e., literally do not make sense to people). A prime example of this is the attempt by Nova Scotia Power to reduce the trappings of bureaucracy by changing their system of colour-coding hard hats. Under the old system managers in the Transmissions and Distribution Division wore white hard hats and their 'subordinates' wore yellow hard hats. The hats clearly signalled hierarchical status. Under the new 'culture' all employees – managers and subordinates alike – were issued with yellow hats. The new symbolism meshed well with the 'humanist, employee-centred' objectives of the culture change but failed, nonetheless, because it clashed with other habitual sensemaking. Many managers resented the new system because it cut across their sense of self. The previous white hats signalled their achievements in attaining the position of manager. This was a reaction grounded in identity. Other employees did not like the new system because they were no longer able to 'spot' managers and react accordingly. This was a reaction grounded in issues of control.

The relevance of sensemaking as a social activity in a managerial sense means that similar experiences can be understood in different ways and subsequent interpretation of a situation depends on what meaning is attached to the activity and what influence locally shaped values have on the situation. For example, Nova Scotia Power had hoped that the introduction of four corporate values would result in the creation of a unified culture. Yet the existence of different regional gestalts (Köhler, 1961) led to different outcomes. In Cape Breton, many employees, who were used to strongly divided class loyalties, made sense of culture change as yet another management attempt to manipulate, typify this. Faced with a new situation they made sense of it by reference to habitual practices.

Finally, sensemaking is social in that a person's sensemaking is public, i.e., they test out, and/or attempt to impose, their sense on others. This, as we shall see below, speaks to issues of enactment (creating a sense of what is happening), on-going sensemaking (speaking to a sense of something that is in progress), and plausibility (making sure that what is said makes sense to selected others). What this tells us is that the individual process of making sense takes its cues from the arena or context in which it is located. This suggests certain limits and possibilities for managers.

When Louis Comeau made sense of an employee attitude survey as signalling 'low morale' he was, at one and the same time, creating the impression of low morale and speaking to an on-going sense that morale was low. In other words, through his expression of 'low morale' Comeau was moving to the front a perception that was one of many in the company and making it into a more definite sense. That sense then served as a powerful cue for the next move, which was to introduce culture change. Here Comeau was enacting a sense of the company that built upon the developing sense of the company but went beyond it. Culture change was perhaps all the more plausible coming in the wake of an employee survey that signalled low morale.

Once the culture change programme was introduced and underway it established something that can be likened to political correctness in that it cued the way people subsequently made sense of events. For example, when I asked employees whether the new values had any impact on their daily routine (see Appendix B, Question 8) a senior plant engineer told me that there were no changes because culture change 'is a management style. It can't be taught. Sending people on courses does not work'. He was not rejecting the idea of culture change but instead made sense of management behaviour in reference to that idea. Within the framework of culture change he saw certain management styles as problematic. Both the senior plant engineer and I were engaging in a process of sensemaking that was rooted in a particular organization paradigm.

Sensemaking as a form of political correctness was particularly evident during the period of re-engineering. To begin with, the consultants and Nova Scotia Power's Re-engineering Project Manager attempted, through legal contract, to ensure that my research did not have anything critical to say about the company's BPI programme. This was an overt attempt at enactment that I successfully resisted. Some employees were less successful. BPI 'activists' or 'revolutionaries' as they came to be called, often complained about other employees who appeared to be less than enthusiastic. In this atmosphere it is not surprising that some people's public sensemaking played to the on-going story of re-engineering. This more extreme example of political correctness merely points out that sensemaking activity is often strongly influenced by anticipation of other's responses.

Sensemaking cues

Sensemaking is focused on and by extracted cues, which are familiar structures that individuals draw upon to 'develop a larger sense of what may be occurring' (Weick, 1995: 50). Cues are important in that they 'tie elements together cognitively': presumed ties are then given more substance when people act as if they are real (Weick, 1995: 54).

Cues are linked to a broader context of ideas and actions, which affects not only what is extracted as a cue but also how that cue is interpreted. For management, cues are important in the generation of 'a point of reference, against which a feeling of organization and direction can emerge' (Smircich and Morgan, 1982, quoted in Weick, 1995: 50). Indeed, it can be argued that 'control over which cues will serve as a point of reference is an important source of power' (Ibid.).

The study of Nova Scotia Power is rich in cues and the impact of those cues on events. A prime example is the use of the 'four values' as central cues in the introduction of culture change. Time after time senior managers referenced the four values in their discussion of culture change and improvements to the company's 'way of working'. Sometimes those cues worked where there was general acceptance of the culture change as a new and improved way of working (e.g., among the company's headquarters' staff). Sometimes those cues were counter-productive where culture change was viewed as a new form of management manipulation (e.g., among Cape Breton employees).

Cues can also prove problematic to later events. By 1993 and the introduction of BPI, the culture change programme was well under way and the four core values were firmly established as important cues. Part of the explanation of why some people resisted the new programme of re-engineering lies in the fact that the four core values were no longer front and centre, and a new set of cues (e.g., 'process', 'efficiency') were discordant in the supposed context of continuing culture change. In 1993–5 references were still being made to culture change but the new cues of BPI that were being used to redefine that change were often at odds with the notion of 'a humanistic company'.

On-going sensemaking

Weick (1995: 43) argues that 'sensemaking never starts', it is on-going. We are always in the middle of things. 'Flows are the constants of sensemaking' (Ibid.). People are constantly making sense. Yet, elsewhere Weick (1995: 91) refers to 'shocks' as the 'trigger' or 'occasion' for sensemaking. This suggests that sense is made of a situation, which is then in a constant process of reaffirmation, maintenance and modification. It is a process of sensemaking that, relatively speaking, is devoid of active feelings of emotion (i.e., '"arousal" or discharge in the autonomic nervous system', Weick, 1995: 45). Shocks, thus, are interruptions to the on-going flow of sensemaking and become the occasion for emotion-charged sensemaking (Weick, 1995: 45): 'The reality of flows becomes most apparent when that flow is interrupted. An interruption to a flow typically induces an emotional response, which then paves the way for emotion to influence sensemaking.'

How does this inform our understanding of organizations? Weick, who is primarily interested in organizational crisis (cf. Weick, 1990b, 1993a, 1996, 1997), discusses the link between on-going sensemaking and our understanding of the outcomes of breakdowns in organizational routines. He argues that procedures 'tend to become more tightly organized the more frequently they are executed' (Weick, 1995: 46) and are, thus, more susceptible to problems where they are interrupted: 'When interruption first occurs, there is redoubled effort to complete the original interrupted sequence. If there are many different ways in which an interrupted sequence can be completed, then arousal is not likely to build very much.'

Weick (1995: 46) goes on to argue that if we can describe the distribution of interruption in organizations, then 'we can predict where sensemaking will be especially influenced by emotional experiences'. In particular Weick is concerned with helping organizations to predict and thus avoid the onset of negative emotional reactions. Such reactions are likely to occur when (a) an organized behavioural sequence is interrupted unexpectedly, (b) the interruption is interpreted as harmful or detrimental, and (c) there is no means to remove or circumvent the interruption. Identifying and addressing the potential organizational breakdowns is made all the more important by the fact that they are more likely to encourage negative than positive emotions:

> First, people have little control over the onset or termination of interruptions. Second, over time people experience more rather than fewer interrupting stimuli in the form of regulations, deaths, competitors, takeovers, reorganization, and so on. And third, the achievement of plans in organizations is more often slowed than accelerated due to, for example, budget cutting, turnover, resignations, shortages, or currency revaluation.
>
> (Weick, 1995: 48)

Weick's account speaks directly to the issue of organizational change, suggesting that organizational breakdowns can occur where the sense of the interruption is not adequately addressed and negative emotions are encouraged to develop. When, for example, senior management at Nova Scotia Power inaugurated culture change training in their Cape Breton plants they actually increased the potential for conflict. Instead of addressing the on-going sense of class division that was strong in the region management inadvertently accentuated it by establishing a hierarchical system of training, with the provision of a four-day training programme for management and only a one-day training session for other employees. As a result many Cape Breton employees refused to attend the provided training session and some who did attend walked out in anger.

The Cape Breton example references another aspect of the significance of on-going sensemaking, and that is that people make sense within a 'flow' that, in large part, frames understanding and meaning. This means that managers, when introducing change, need to address some aspect of the existing flow of sensemaking.[3] A uniform training session (four days for managers and employees alike) may not have addressed established class animosities but it may have avoided exacerbating them.

Retrospective sensemaking

Retrospection is, for Weick (1995: 24), the single most 'distinguishing characteristic' of sensemaking. His basic argument is that people act and then make sense of their actions. Sensemaking is always retrospective because we are reflecting on what has occurred: '[The] creation of meaning is an attentional process, but it is attention to that which has already occurred' (Weick, 1995: 25–6).

Corporate statements are good examples of retrospective sensemaking. Reports of on-going company activities are, in fact, sensemaking accounts of something that has already occurred. This, as we shall see below, enacts a version of reality, placing a particular understanding on events. For example, Nova Scotia Power senior management's interpretation of the 1987 employee attitude survey made sense of events in terms of low morale. Low morale then became an important sense that people made of existing behaviours.

Retrospection, however, is not simply about reacting to past events but is very much influenced by what is occurring at the time: '[Because] the attention is directed backward from a specific point in time (a specific here and now), whatever is occurring at the moment will influence what is discovered when people glance backward' (Weick, 1995: 26). For example, 'improvements in productivity' were made sense of in the context of culture change as related to 'living the values', and in the context of re-engineering as related to changed processes. In a wonderful turn of phrase, Weick (1979: 202) characterizes this as 'believing is seeing'.

The situational context of an action also influences the choice of a 'plausible stimulus' to a response, which, in turn, 'affects the choice of what the action "means"' (Weick, 1995: 26). For example, at Nova Scotia Power an employee's lack of enthusiasm for certain tasks may have been judged as individual laziness in 1986, low morale in 1987, an inability to 'live the values' in 1988, and deliberate rebellion in 1993.

Weick brings his insights to bear on the problem of managing and, in the process, provides some valuable clues to the relationship between retrospective sensemaking and the management of change. Primarily, Weick's (1995: 30) aim is to make managers (and other organizational activists and educators) aware of the significance of retrospection in sensemaking so that they can develop a reflective approach to action: 'The dominance of retrospect in sensemaking is a major reason why students of sensemaking find forecasting, contingency planning, strategic planning, and other magical probes into the future wasteful and misleading if they are decoupled from reflective action and history.'

In outlining his approach to reflective action Weick (1979, 1995) touches on a number of the problems facing those charged with managing change. Centrally the problem confronting management is 'equivocality' (i.e., a situation that is fraught with the potential for multiple meanings). That is not to say that managers face an environment that 'is disordered, indeterminate, and chaotic' but one that 'is rich in the possible connections that could be imposed on an equally rich assortment of possible punctuated variables'. In short, 'it is the richness and multiplicity of meanings that can be superimposed on a situation that organizations must manage' (Weick, 1979: 174). But the problem is 'that there are too many meanings, not too few': it is a problem of confusion not ignorance (Weick, 1995: 26). It can be argued that senior management at Nova Scotia Power acted to achieve clarity when they reduced a number of organizational problems to an issue of 'low morale'. As their own employee attitude survey indicated, employees had a multitude of meanings for events (defined as problems) within the company. These meanings included paternalistic management style, lack of customer focus, an inappropriate company identity ('a construction company, rather than an electric utility'), and a failure 'to recognize the Corporation as an instrument of public purpose' (Nova Scotia Power, 1990b). Although these 'issues' were subsequently 'selected' for further attention a focus on 'low morale' helped to simplify the perceived problem at hand. Indeed, Weick suggests that oversimplification may be a useful strategy for managing meaning:

> [If] people want to complete their projects, if effort and motivation make a difference in completing those projects, and if *the* environment is malleable, then a reading of past indeterminacy that favors order and oversimplifies causality . . . may make for more effective action, even if it is lousy history.
>
> (Weick, (1995: 28–9)

People who are 'overwhelmed by equivocality . . . need values, priorities, and clarity about preferences to help them be clear about which projects matter' (Weick, 1995: 27–8). Indeed, 'the *feeling* of order, clarity, and rationality is an important goal of sensemaking' (Ibid.: 29). The focus on four core values, as a way of introducing Nova Scotia Power's Culture Change programme, was another example of how senior management attempted to reduce equivocality by literally establishing values, and a sense of priorities.

The problem is that equivocality confronts managers who, because of the pace of managerial activity, have little time to adequately 'clarify' situations. Where senior managers, such as those at Nova Scotia Power, do open up space to clarify situations, a failure to understand the retrospective nature of sensemaking can have long-term implications.

In the 'normal' course of events managers, faced with serious time constraints:

1   tend to 'enforce organizational routines because this reduces variety in the environment . . . and also shift lingering equivocality to someone else (supervisors handle odd cases)';
2   avoid taking time out to experiment with new developments because 'there isn't time to interpret equivocal enactments that would come from attempted tests';
3   invoke 'habit, tradition, and total crediting' to accommodate numerous demands for decision-making in limited time periods;
4   are usually only able to preserve a small, limited sense of a situation because they typically deal with 'smaller scraps of data at any one time', in an immediate fashion.

(Weick, 1979: 203–4)

Thus, once something like a culture change programme is underway its development is in the hands of numerous managers and supervisors who are operating with limited time and resources: clarity becomes a constant rather than a given. The development of habitual responses may characterize strength of a particular culture but it also contributes to a number of potential weaknesses where, for example, people fail to modify their behaviour to changed situations (Bate, 1994).

There is also likely to be a disjuncture between the thinking of those at the top and operational managers closer to the work processes, i.e., 'projects at the top and bottom differ dramatically, as do readings of the "same" event' (Weick, 1995: 27). Certainly my interviews during the culture change suggest that employees had a very different way of framing the notion of 'living the values' than did senior managers. At the top, 'living the values' was more likely to be understood as an overall strategy, which attempted to encourage greater output and customer care through improved concern with employee well-being. At the bottom, 'living the values' was more likely to encourage expectations of great respect from managers.

At the level of senior management the danger of an unreflective approach is that people start 'believing their own publicity'. They fail to understand that others may not share their sense of a situation, no matter how loudly or widely it is expressed. They may also fail to recognize that 'meanings change as projects and goals change' (Weick, 1995: 27). A classic work on this problem is Danny Miller's (1990) *The Icarus Paradox*, in which he shows how 'exceptional companies bring about their own downfall' by clinging to the factors that made them successful while ignoring new factors that may have helped them to maintain their success. At Nova Scotia Power it was not changing gears that was the problem but a failure to recognize that new projects opened up new meanings and that old meanings had a potential influence on how people made sense of the new projects. Senior managers at Nova Scotia Power had little difficulty in moving from a culture change programme to BPI. Where they did have difficulty was in understanding that previously created expectations of a 'humanistic' company were influencing how employees responded to re-engineering. For some employees the introduction of downsizing (in 1993 and 1995) was contrary to the expressed corporate valuing of employees and may have served to influence how sense was made of re-engineering. Senior managers and BPI activists, on the other hand, were prone to see negative expressions as individual acts of rebellion rather than problems with the way employees were expected to switch rapidly their sense of the company.

Thus, at all levels, managers' attempts to make sense of on-going situations are problematic and can have profound implications for future action. If they deal with equivocality in a piece-meal fashion they may fail to reduce an excess of ambiguity in their workplace. How they make sense of and characterize a situation at one point of time may come back to haunt them at a later stage. For example, whether a situation is made sense of as an opportunity or as a threat may 'influence sensemaking at an earlier stage' in that a dominating 'definition of a project' may 'influence what is extracted from elapsed experience' (Weick, 1995: 27). Also, the characterization of an outcome as a 'success' or a 'failure' can influence which antecedents are chosen to represent causal factors and relationships. If, for example, 'the outcome is perceived to be bad, then antecedents are reconstructed to emphasize incorrect actions, flawed analyses, and inaccurate perceptions, even if such flaws were not influential or all that obvious at the time' (Weick, 1995: 28).

Weick (1979, 1995) goes on to draw some interesting lessons from his discussion of retrospection. For one thing, he warns that, 'those people who do have time to reflect on occurrences and interpret them control the labels and definitions imposed by those who don't' (Weick, 1979: 204).[4] Reflection can also reveal the problems involved in assigning causes rather than sensemaking processes to outcomes. The *Challenger* disaster is a classic demonstration of the problem. Almost all commentators, classifying the situation as an obvious 'disaster', have set out to reveal the negative antecedents that played a causal role in the outcome. Structure, organizational politics, gender, psycho-dynamics, and communication failures are some of the various factors that have been singled out to 'explain' the disaster (McConnell, 1987; Maier and Messerschmidt, 1998; Messerschmidt, 1995; Schwartz, 1987; Trento, 1987). Diane Vaughan (1996), on the other hand, focusing on retrospective sensemaking, presents a different way of viewing the *Challenger* disaster (see also Weick, 1997). She argues that it is not so much discrete antecedents that are the problem but any search for antecedents that is divorced from reflective action. In other words, in failing to recognize that the reconstruction of events is a process of retrospective sensemaking we may (a) objectify those events, (b) give undue weight to some factors over others, (c) unduly assign a causal relationship to certain factors, and (d) ignore the important role of sensemaking in previous outcomes, as well as in the current project of seeking answers to an outcome. For example, part of the explanation for the *Challenger* disaster may not have been so much a breakdown in communications as unreflective understandings imposed on communications at the time.[5] At Nova Scotia Power the classification of people as 'rebels' by internal BPI advocates is an example of how some managers, concerned with failures of re-engineering, looked for simple causal relationships and ignored the role of (retrospective) sensemaking.

Plausibility

Weick (1995: 55) contends that sensemaking is driven by plausibility rather than accuracy. People act as if there is the possibility of correct or accurate information, or if there is a truth to be discovered. Yet, in most things, people make decisions based on incomplete (sometimes inaccurate, sometimes conflicting) information that they nonetheless feel certain enough about to act. In short, 'the sensible need not be sensable' (Weick, 1995: 55).

In the process of sensemaking, accuracy is secondary to plausibility because:

1   people 'need to distort and filter, to separate signal from noise given their current projects';
2   'sensemaking is about the embellishment and elaboration of a single point of reference or extracted cue';
3   'speed often reduces the necessity for accuracy in the sense that quick responses shape events before they have become crystallized into a single meaning';
4   where 'accuracy does become an issue, it does so for short periods of time and with respect to specific questions';
5   understanding of events are influenced by 'the interpersonal, interactive, interdependent quality of organizational life';

6 'accuracy is defined by instrumentality'. It is project specific and pragmatic;
7 'stimuli that are filtered out are often those that detract from an energetic, confident, motivated response'; and
8 'it is almost impossible to tell, at the time of perception, whether the perceptions will prove accurate or not'.

(Weick, 1995: 57–60)

Thus, faced with invariable situations of bounded rationality[6] (Mumby and Putnam, 1992; Simon, 1976) people rely, instead, on accepting and creating feelings of 'plausibility'. But what is plausibility? What makes something plausible? And how can the notion of plausible sensemaking add to our understanding of the management of change?

Weick (1995) does not define plausibility but rather suggests various cues. Plausibility is a feeling that something makes sense, feels right, is somehow sensible, and fits with what you know. A sensemaking outcome can feel plausible where: (a) pressures of time and the availability of different interpretations make it feel right 'under the circumstances'; (b) there are no better solutions forthcoming; (c) it concurs with the feelings or perceptions of others;[7] (d) it 'counteracts interruptions and facilitate(s) ongoing projects' (Weick, 1995: 59); (e) it appears to encourage an 'energetic, confident, motivated response' in others (Weick, 1995: 60); and (f) there is an, as yet, untestable belief in its accuracy. In summary, plausibility is strongly associated with 'pragmatics, coherence, reasonableness, creation, invention, and instrumentality' (Weick, 1995: 57).

What makes something plausible depends on the context in which a sensemaking 'story' is being told or made sense of. A good story is the essence of plausibility, the medium through which plausibility is created. To put it the other way round, to be plausible a good story has to be 'something that is reasonable and memorable. It should embody past experiences and expectations, resonate with other people, can be constructed retrospectively but also can be used prospectively, capture both feelings and thought, allow for embellishment to fit current oddities, and is fun to construct'.

> A good story holds disparate elements together long enough to energize and guide action, plausibly enough to allow people to make retrospective sense of whatever happens, and engagingly enough that others will contribute their own inputs in the interest of sensemaking.
>
> (Weick, 1995: 60–1)

Weick's (1995) analysis of managerial actions reveals that accuracy is rarely, if at all, attained, but contends that this is 'no big problem' because it is plausibility that achieves results. Thus, he continues,

[It] is less productive to follow the lead of behavioral decision theorists
. . . who gloat over the error, misperceptions, and irrationalities of
humans, and more productive to look at the filters people invoke, why
they invoke them, and what those filters include and exclude . . .

(Weick, 1995: 57)

The same could be said of success and failure (i.e., that it is not so much
interesting whether a person or an organization has been 'successful' so much
as how/whether they have constructed a plausible story of 'success'; and what
organizational managers do, or need to do, to create plausibility).

When Nova Scotia Power introduced culture change they developed a
story to explain why it was being introduced; in fact, they developed several
stories around the same theme. One such story was entitled 'Culture Change
at Nova Scotia Power' (Nova Scotia Power, 1990b). The plausibility of the
story was held in place by a number of elements. To begin with, by referencing the company's 'one hundred' year history of growth 'through
acquisition and amalgamation', the story draws on images of attachment,
emotional commitment, and success while, at the same time, suggesting an
underlying disunity that needs adjustment. When the story states that, 'By
the middle to late 1980s it became apparent that the "culture" of the
Corporation was unsuited to the times', it is creating a sense of objectivity
and accuracy. Although it is placed between inverted commas, culture is
presented as a well-known object that elsewhere numerous companies are
attending to. The story continues by providing four key examples of where
the culture of Nova Scotia Power is unsuitable. This is interesting because
the four selected examples match each of the four values that, elsewhere in
the story, appear as answers to the problem. Next, the story references the
employee attitude survey of 1986 and selects out comments about an
uncaring management. This aspect of the story builds plausibility out of
references to something that appears to concur with the feelings of employees
and addresses their central concern about how they are treated. Finally, much
of the remainder of the story reinforces the general theme and concludes with
an interesting comment that seems designed both to encourage action and
discourage doubts about accuracy: 'We are extremely encouraged with our
cultural change process to date although we have few hard facts to support
this feeling; rather, we hear of individual success stories that keep us buoyed
up and moving on.'

It might then be asked, 'Why wasn't this story seen as plausible to some
employees, who reacted against the culture change?' That is not an easy question. Clearly, it speaks in part to the problem of the notion of plausibility.
At what point is something deemed plausible: when everyone accepts it, a
majority, or just the key actors involved? Certainly that is a weakness in the
theory. But there is an argument that employees did not reject the idea of
low morale, or of an underlying disunity of purpose, or even management's
need to resolve the problem through culture change. What they did reject

was the underlying sense of their involvement in the process. Yet even here it was the selling of the story – four days' training for managers and one day for employees – rather than the story itself that people reacted against. Nonetheless, this issue raises some questions and limitations around the notion of plausibility.

Enactment

Finally, and crucially, Weick (1995: 30) argues that sensemaking is enactive of sensible environments. Once again this is a simple yet complex notion. At its simplest, enactment is another way of referring to the social construction of reality (Weick, 1979: 164). However, it differs from some understandings of social construction in that enactive sensemaking does not assume that there is an objective reality that is subjectively, and thus, imperfectly, constructed. At its more complex, sensemaking is about the relationship between acting, thinking, bracketing and retention.

In discussing enactment, Weick (1995: 30) is concerned with explaining 'the activity of "making" that which is sensed. Sensemaking is literally about making sense of action. Thus, enactment "is first and foremost about action in the world, and not about conceptual pictures of that world"' (Weick, 1995: 36). 'The concept of an *enacted environment is* not synonymous with the concept of a *perceived environment*. . . . If a perceived environment were the essence of enactment then . . . the phenomenon would have been called enthinkment, not enactment' (Weick, 1979: 164).

As people act they think about their action and, in the process, make sense of it. In particular through their actions and sense of those actions people select (or 'bracket') elements to focus on. By focusing on some elements to the exclusion of others a sense of the event is retained and sense is made of it. In the words of Weick (1979: 131), 'retention involves relatively straightforward storage of the products of successful sense-making, products that we call *enacted environments*'.

Weick is not arguing that the process of sensemaking is completed independent of the action it purports to make sensible, nor that people are independent of their environments. On the contrary, he contends that people create their own environments and these environments then constrain their actions. People are 'very much a part of their own environments. They act, and in so doing create the materials that become the constraints and opportunities they face' (Weick, 1995: 31). 'When people act they unrandomize variables, insert vestiges of orderliness, and literally create their own constraints' (Weick, 1979: 164).

While there is some recognition of the role of power in the process of sensemaking, Weick's cues are ambiguous and his focus on individual sensemaking tends to obfuscate the issue. In one place Weick (1995: 38) concedes that 'power privileges some meanings over others'. In another place he argues that 'it is not some impersonal "they" who puts these environments in front of passive people . . . [It] is people who are more active' (Weick, 1995: 31). And in yet another place he argues that managers 'construct reality through authoritative acts' (Weick, 1995: 30–1).

In summary, a key part of Weick's notion of sensemaking in organizations is 'enactment' which refers to the construction of social reality through action that is then (retrospectively) made sense of by the actor or actors involved. People act in one way or another, and in so doing come to make sense of their actions in ways that constrain and also provide opportunities for future actions. How people come to construct social realities through enactment is influenced by the 'ongoing' nature of sensemaking, the 'enacted cues' that people use to build a sensible story around the situational and 'social' contexts in which 'retrospective' understandings occur, the need for 'plausibility' in story construction, and the impact of sensemaking activity on 'identity construction'.

The choice of both culture change and re-engineering demonstrates how Nova Scotia Power's senior management enacted an environment that reflected their interests and at the same time set the stage for how they expected employees to behave within those constraints. The interesting thing for study is not that they enacted a sensible environment but how they enacted that environment and what influence it had on subsequent events.

Projective sensemaking

Enactment led me to suggest another type of sensemaking, which I have termed 'projective'. Unlike the Freudian 'defence mechanism', which assumes we project aims and wishes we cannot accept in ourselves (Bohart and Todd, 1988), 'projective sensemaking' assumes subjectivity by those desiring specific outcomes and not by those involved directly in the process. While Weick (1995: 23) contends that, 'people learn about their identities by projecting them into an environment and observing the consequences', he does so in a way that downplays the role of more powerful actors. Although focused on 'action', much of Weick's theory centres on the imposition of ideas on situations that have consequences for those beyond the primary sensemakers. This is at its clearest where Weick references managers as sensemakers who 'construct, rearrange, single out and demolish many "objective" features of their surroundings' (Weick, 1979: 164). Thus, while it may be true that everyone can be said to engage in sensemaking, it is far from clear that everyone is more or less equal in the process, or is equally interested in enacting realities that come to dominate others' sensemaking, or in the creation of ordered understandings of reality.

Projective sensemaking assumes that (a) one constituency can project their sensemaking process onto another; or (b) one constituency will predict the sensemaking behaviour of another. Douglas (1986: 91) has said that institutions are built by 'squeezing each other's ideas into a common shape so that we can provide rightness by sheer numbers of independent assent'. When different constituencies made sense of the need for change and the change process, they were not only basing their judgement on their own values and beliefs, they were projecting this belief system to anticipate the other constituent's sensemaking. This form of sensemaking is particularly problematic because it does not control for perceptual biases, individual differences and the group norms.

For example, Nova Scotia Power's management wanted the culture change to be a success and their measure of success was to assume everyone would agree upon and embrace the four cultural values they had defined. According to Weick (1995) we discover our own inventions. In this instance, we are assuming that our vision is shared and forms the basis of another's sensemaking. Management assumed that everyone would embrace the idea of culture change because they would all go through the same sensemaking process. But we can also 'invent' our notion of how we think others will make sense of a situation. This occurred when management assumed that employees would see a blurring of the boundaries by the elimination of different coloured hard hats for management and staff.

The importance of understanding how change is managed and understood through sensemaking, by those extracting the cues (rules) and those enacting them, at what stage in the management of meaning that sensemaking occurs and how it moves from invention to interpretation, underlies the importance of projective sensemaking in this instance. What I have termed projective sensemaking drives the implementation of the change process because it assumes that change is understood and accepted equally by everyone in the organization and when that appears not to be the case, the blame is associated with non-compliance, rather than misunderstanding.

Conclusion

Sensemaking has been described as 'a new fundamental unit for organizational analysis' (Nord and Fox 1996: 157). By applying sensemaking to organizational theory, Weick has offered a way of thinking about organizations that deviates from the mainstream approach (Calás and Smircich, 1992). The main strengths of sensemaking lie in its ability to tie together strands of various social theories into a comprehensive framework, its ability to conceive of organizations as processes rather than outcomes (Colville, 1994; Ferguson, 1994), and its revelation of the role ambiguity and uncertainty play in organizing (Gherardi, 1995). Nonetheless, with rare exception (e.g., Taylor and Lerner, 1996), Weick's theory of sensemaking has yet to be utilized by others as a framework for making sense of organizational outcomes. Just as rare have been critiques of Weick's approach. While numerous studies have utilized aspects of sensemaking, as of yet, it has not been the subject of critical debate.

The limited criticism of sensemaking centres on questions of rationality, gender and its viability as a working 'conversation'. Reed (1992: 224), for example, agrees with (Ferguson, 1994), that analysis of organizations as processes allows us to ask, 'how does it come to be?', rather than, 'what is it?', but warns that one must also be wary of overly discarding the role of rationality in organizational processes and outcomes. By downplaying its role in organizational action, we are ignoring the power and control that rationality has over the decision-making process, even when sensemaking differs. On the other hand, Calás and Smircich (1992) are concerned that Weick's work is ultimately embedded within modernist notions of rationality that privilege theorists over persons, rationality over emotionality, and, perhaps, men over women. By re-writing parts of Weick's text, they show how 'organization theory discourse is sustained . . . by previous discourses of knowledge and reason' (Calás and Smircich, 1992: 247) and therefore becomes gendered. What is also interesting is that Calás and Smircich (1992) seem to have unintentionally challenged a major premise of Weick's work, which contends that sensemaking is done without prior knowledge. This is particularly relevant when looking at issues of intersubjectivity and motives for different behaviours. By revealing the modernist framework of patterns of thought, Calás and Smircich (1992) suggest that perhaps we do know before we think.[8]

At a different level, criticism has been levelled against Weick's sensemaking for its cryptic advice to managers (Colville, 1994: 22), use of language, superficial treatment of narrativity and systematic lack of explanation for the basis of narrative development (Taylor and Lerner, 1996: 259–60).

While sensemaking provides a useful framework in which to place the data gathered from the study of Nova Scotia Power, it is important to note that the study has been limited by (a) the inherent weaknesses and limitations of the sensemaking model to fully explain the change process at Nova Scotia Power; and (b) the type of data collected. The use of this approach with the existing data will in no way overcome the limitations of the actual data collection. It merely serves to offer an analytic tool for the existing material. However, I believe that the novelty of this study and the rich insight it gives us to an organization that has continually undergone change will compensate for these limitations and strengthen our knowledge of the process and its impact on organizational culture.

4 The story of organizational change

[S]tories are powerful stand-alone contents for sensemaking. . . . First, stories aid comprehension because they integrate that which is known about an event with that which is conjectural. Second, stories suggest a causal order for events that originally are perceived as unrelated and akin to a list. Third, stories enable people to talk about absent things and to connect them with present things in the interest of meaning. Fourth, stories are mnemonics that enable people to reconstruct earlier complex events. Fifth, stories can guide action before routines are formulated and can enrich routines after those routines are formulated. Sixth, stories enable people to build a database of experience from which they can infer how things work. And seventh, stories transmit and reinforce third-order controls by conveying shared values and meaning (a script is a second-order control that works like a standard operating procedure . . .).

(Weick, 1995: 129)

Introduction

In this chapter the phenomenon of organizational change is examined. In particular it attempts to account for the widespread acceptance of an imperative of organizational change, and the equally widespread appeal and 'failure' rate of pre-packaged change programmes such as Total Quality Management (TQM), organizational culture change, business process re-engineering (BPR), Six Sigma and the Balanced Scorecard.

It is argued that, within management thought and practice, the notion of organizational change has changed in significance over the last two decades, from one of many potential strategies of managing to a key influence on organizational effectiveness and survival. The focus has shifted from the strategic choice (Child, 1972) of the actor to one of incontrovertible external forces that managers need to anticipate, react to and manage. It is contended that organizational change as imperative has become an important management discourse (Foucault, 1979) that can be witnessed in the discursive practices of companies throughout North America and Europe (Cooke, 1999).

To make sense of the continued power and influence of the change discourse, this chapter will explore the links between management practice and management theory (including the business school and the business text), the popularizers of management practice (including the best-selling 'how to' books, management gurus and consultants), and the socio-political environment (particularly the advent of Thatcherism in the UK and Reaganism in the US). It is contended that the development and continued popularity of a discourse of organizational change owes much to a story-line which: (a) features simplicity, realism, threat, opportunity, uncertainty, globalization, popular narrative and the image of the wise, or good, manager; (b) is transmitted and fuelled by a multi-billion dollar education industry consisting of business education, management gurus, popular 'how to' trade books, and consultants; and (c) is given legitimacy to the extent that it appears to reflect socio-political realities and received knowledge.

The chapter concludes that an imperative of organizational change is a social construction that is not well understood as such. It is contended that a failure to understand that organizational change is a social construct, that different actors make sense of in divergent ways, has several consequences for managers and the process of organizational change. To that end, Weick's (1995) sensemaking approach is advocated as a framework for taking account of the social constructionist core of organizational change.

Nova Scotia Power and change: background to the problem

When I began my research of Nova Scotia Power in 1991 my initial impression was of a company where many of the planned culture changes were working: 'The past 12 months represent a period of significant change within Nova Scotia Power – progress that will have a positive impact on our customers' (Louis Comeau, Nova Scotia Power, 1991c). I was impressed by the fact that corporate statements were stressing the company's commitment to its 'core values' of concern with employees, customers, the environment and the province of Nova Scotia:

> We work together safely . . . make effective use of modern technology and innovation . . . recognize employee contributions through timely feedback, fair and equitable rewards, opportunities, and compensation. Our goal is customer satisfaction. We provide our customers with quality, responsive service in an efficient, courteous and cost-effective manner.
>
> We will continue to broaden our understanding of the environment and be considerate of potential impacts resulting from our activities.
>
> We are proud to belong to the Nova Scotia community, and to be a major contributor to its economic and technological development . . . to be a leader in the energy sector . . . to conduct ourselves in a manner that is responsive to and respectful of community needs.
>
> (Highlighted comments from the 1989/90 Annual Report, Nova Scotia Power, 1990a)

Further study, however, changed my perception, as it became clear that employees and management held different opinions of what culture change was, and what the intended outcomes were supposed to be (see Chapter 2). My changed perception was strengthened as I studied the impact of re-engineering on the culture of Nova Scotia Power. At first I was mystified that managers, who two years earlier were extolling the notion of the 'humanistic' company, were now almost exclusively talking in terms of efficiency and competition (see Table 3.1). But I came to the view that it was not culture change, but change *per se* that was at the forefront of thinking within the company: 'The world in which we operate is not only changing faster than ever before but also tending to change direction more abruptly' (Nova Scotia Power, 1994a). 'Look what's going on today. Deregulation, satellite technology, fibre optics, interactive systems, integrated data systems. These and other factors have changed the way business is done' (President's address to shareholders at the 1994 Annual Meeting, Nova Scotia Power, 1994c). Culture change was hardly mentioned any more and, as I looked back to the previous era (1988–91), I began to feel that the Culture Change programme was itself more about an imperative of change than about any particular change programme.

As I looked closer into the issue of change what I found was a company that was continuously engaged in change. In each case consultants were employed, a change programme introduced, and senior management enthusiastically embarked on a campaign of support for the new programme. If there was a common theme in company documents and the statements of managers and employees, it was change – the need for change, the introduction of different change programmes, responses to change programmes, and the outcomes of change programmes. If we look closely at many of the company's statements on change, we can see that they are expressed as imperatives rather than choices:

> The Corporation cannot choose to operate in a vacuum, indifferent to, or ignorant of *external factors* that can impact not only on our business, but on the lives and businesses of all our customers. These external factors influence economic growth in Nova Scotia with consequent impacts on the nature of demand for electricity. External factors also influence the opinions and expectations of our customers and other stakeholders and hence dictate business direction for Nova Scotia Power. It is incumbent upon the Corporation to consider these influences.
>
> (Meeting Customer Expectations into the 21st Century,
> Nova Scotia Power, 1991b; emphasis in the original)

> NSPI is preparing for the prospect of a competitive market, having organized into business units . . .
>
> (Notice of Special Meeting to Common Shareholders to be held
> Wednesday, December 2, 1998, Nova Scotia Power, 1998d)

As I reviewed my observations on the culture change and re-engineering, it occurred to me that these change programmes were the outcomes of a deeper process at work, namely a management discourse on organizational change. A closer look at some of the statements on culture change, for example, reveals referencing to an underlying theme of change: 'Recognizing that Nova Scotia must compete in a business environment having external factors that are increasingly global *dictates* that the Corporation have a global view of its role . . .' (Meeting Customer Expectation into the 21st Century, Nova Scotia Power, 1991b; my emphasis). 'On the threshold of the 21st century, power utilities are operating in a world of change that is changing faster than ever before' (1992 Annual Report, Nova Scotia Power, 1993f). Similarly, statements about the introduction of re-engineering were prefaced with references to a broad vision of change:

> Success in today's business environment *demands* corporate attributes scarcely understood a decade or so ago. Stimulated by technology and changing attitudes, commodities such as information, capital and human resources are more mobile than they've ever been before. One of the most *powerful driving forces* is global competition among nations and states, provinces and towns for sustainable, profitable industry to assure their economic futures. Fitting ourselves to thrive in the new world market-place is both a goal and a responsibility.
>
> (1993 Annual Report, Nova Scotia Power, 1994a; my emphasis)

The more I reflected on the difference between my current and earlier perceptions the more I felt that my initial approach had been a reproduction of a script of change management. I had read the stories of culture change and had gone out expecting to find aspects of the story being enacted. My initial reading of the 'successful' progress of Nova Scotia Power was, in part, influenced by the underlying change story that I had bought into.

In short, I was encouraged to rethink the focus of my thesis. It was no longer centrally about organizational culture but rather focused on the process and management of organizational change. My inquiries led to a number of questions that became focal points of the thesis. In particular I wanted to understand what encourages an organization to undergo a programme of change; how different understandings of change impact the choice and implementation of a change programme; and what can we learn from the implementation of pre-packaged programmes?

The more I studied Nova Scotia Power the more I felt that existing models of organizational culture did not explain the underlying assumptions that appeared to fuel the organization's need to continually engage in change. As such, the study of culture at Nova Scotia Power became secondary to the process of change, which continually re-invented it (Weick, 1995).

Pre-packed programmes: perceptions of popularity and failure

In order to argue that the notion of organizational change, and particularly the pre-packaged change programme, has acquired something of the status of a discourse, it is important to demonstrate its widespread acceptance. That is not difficult.

Since the mid-1970s there has been a rapid growth in the number of English-language books (see Figure 4.1) and scholarly journal articles (see Kieser, 1997) on organizational change, in particular specific models of change (Figure 4.2). For example, Jackson (1995) estimated that between January 1994 and February 1995, 1,264 articles were published on re-engineering, and Kelemen (1999: 163) estimates that between January 1994 and February 1996 there were 1,078 articles published on TQM. A 2002 website search on change indicates that there were just under 2,000 articles published on the subject in the last five years (see Chapter 1).

In practice, that means that a vast number of companies have adopted one or other major change programme since the beginning of the 1980s (see Appendix A). By the onset of the 1990s, 80 per cent of Canadian companies were planning or had implemented TQM programmes (Field and House, 1995: 606). In the US, a 1993 survey of more than 300 electronics companies, sponsored by the American Electronics Association, indicated that 73 per cent had a TQM programme underway (Schaffer and Thomson, 1998: 192). Between 1990 and 1995, ISO 9000 registrations (which arose out of the TQM movement) grew at a tremendous rate worldwide (Figure 4.3). In terms of re-engineering, 70 per cent of the largest US corporations had undergone a process of re-engineering by 1994 (Walston and Burns, 1998). A 1994 survey of 621 companies, representing a sample of 6,000 of the largest corporations in North America, indicated that 69 per cent of American-owned and 75 per cent of European-owned companies based in North America had adopted a re-engineering programme and a further 50 per cent of the remaining companies were thinking of adopting such a programme (Champy, 1995: 2). Yet by 1995, re-engineering had reached its peak, and by 1997 a survey of 4,137 respondents in fifteen countries indicated that its use had dropped from 78 per cent to 64 per cent (Jackson, 2000).[1]

A further sign of the powerful influence of such popular change programmes can be seen in their spread from the private sector to the health-care system.[2] In Canada almost 75 per cent of all hospitals had implemented a form of TQM or Continuous Quality Improvement by 1993 (Baker *et al.*, 1993). In the US, over 60 per cent of hospitals had been re-engineered by 1995 (Walston and Burns, 1998). Not only have numerous companies adopted culture change, re-engineering, TQM and other change programmes, but their actions have been reported widely throughout the business and business education media.

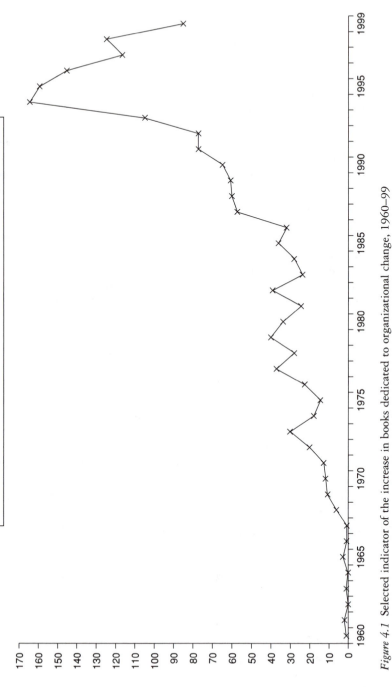

Figure 4.1 Selected indicator of the increase in books dedicated to organizational change, 1960–99

Source: Figure compiled from book titles that include the words 'organizational' and 'change' in the US Library of Congress catalogue, July 1999

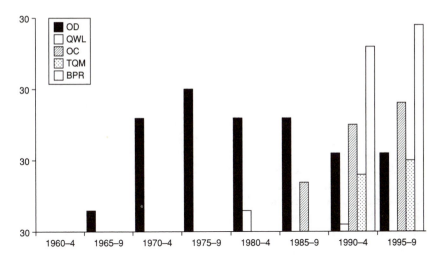

Figure 4.2 The growing popularity of selected change programmes as reflected in the increasing publication of change books listed by the US Library of Congress, 1960–99

Source: Figure compiled from 1,972 books on 'organizational change' listed in the catalogue of the US Library of Congress, July 1999

Notes: OD = Organizational Development; QWL = Quality of Work Life; OC = Organizational Culture; TQM = Total Quality Management and other quality management programmes; BPR = Business Process Re-engineering and other re-engineering programmes

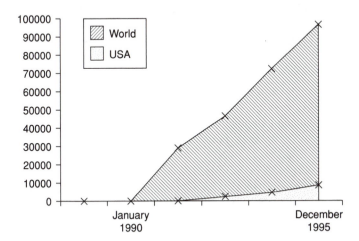

Figure 4.3 Growth in ISO 9000 registrations, 1990–5

Source: Adapted from Uzumeri, 1997: 27 (see Hatfield and Mills, 1997)

Explaining the popularity of organizational change in sensemaking terms (Weick, 1995), it can be argued that change has become a conventional management practice, developed and sustained (i.e., cued) through a powerful management discourse, whose 'on-going' character influences the decision-making of large and small companies, profit and not-for-profit companies alike. Whether or not the adoption of a particular programme of change is the right course of action for some companies doesn't seem to matter. Decisions to implement change programmes, as I will argue later, are based on 'plausibility' rather than 'accuracy' (Weick, 1995).

If, indeed, some notion of 'accuracy' (i.e., 'evidence' that application led to desired outcome) was prevalent in the decision-making of major corporations senior managers might have been expected to take note of the perceptions of failure associated with pre-packaged change programmes. The warning signs were out there. By the late 1990s, there were clear indications of widespread disquiet with TQM and re-engineering. Choi and Behling (1997) provided one of several accounts of the problems associated with TQM:[3]

> The 1990s have not been good to TQM: A survey of 500 executives in US manufacturing and service firms indicated that 'only one-third believe that TQM made them more competitive'; a survey of 100 British firms that had implemented quality programs found that only one-fifth believed that their programs had a 'significant impact'; an American Electronics Association survey revealed that use of TQM by member firms dropped from 86 percent in 1988 to 73 percent in 1991 and that 63 percent of the firms reported that TQM failed to reduce defects by 10 percent or more, even though they had been in operation for almost two and one-half years on average; McKinsey and Company found that two-thirds of the TQM programs it examined had simply ground to a halt because they failed to produce expected results.
>
> (Choi and Behling, 1997: 37)

There have been similar stories about re-engineering. According to one source, by 1993 re-engineering had experienced a 70 per cent failure rate (Stewart, 1993)[4] and by 1995, the rate had risen to 87 per cent (Holland and Kumar, 1995). Indeed, James Champy (1995) himself has stated that:

> Re-engineering is in trouble. It's not easy for me to make this admission. I was one of the two people who introduced the concept.
>
> *Re-engineering the Corporation* has sold nearly two million copies worldwide since it was published in 1993, an astonishing success for a business book. But it's *your* bottom line, not ours, that ought to measure the success of any set of management ideas. And by that measure, there's much more re-engineering to do. . . .
>
> On the whole . . . even substantial re-engineering payoffs appear to have fallen short of their potential. . . . Although the jury is still out on

71 percent of the ongoing North American re-engineering efforts in our sample, overall, the study shows, participants failed to attain [re-engineering] benchmarks by as much as 30 percent.

(Champy, 1995: 1, 3)

Despite widespread and prominent critiques of pre-packaged change programmes companies continue to adopt them, spending millions of dollars in the process. To understand why change programmes remain popular, we need to explore the various key elements that contribute to a management discourse of organizational change. In particular we need to understand something of the formative context (Unger, 1987b) in which such a discourse has developed. But first we need to know something of the contours of the discourse itself.

The discourse of change management

Prior to 1980, within business texts, organizational change as a management technique was either not mentioned at all (cf. Steers, 1981), or was limited to discussion of group dynamics and employee resistance to change (cf. Davis and Scott, 1964; Filley and House, 1969; Herbert, 1976, 1981; Huse and Bowditch, 1973; Klein and Ritti, 1980). The notion of organizational change in the late 1970s and early 1980s, developed from learning theories and an action research approach to organizational problems (Hendry, 1996). Drawing on behavioural and cognitive theories, organizational development (OD) techniques were used to redesign jobs. For example, management and supervisory training was used to promote leadership abilities.[5] Various models focusing on quality of working life, socio-technical theory, autonomy and job enrichment were employed to improve working conditions, where typically the emphasis was on rewarding and reinforcing particular behaviours (cf. Cherns, 1976, 1987; Hackman and Oldham, 1980; Kelly, 1982; Trist and Bamforth, 1951; Walton, 1975).

Over time, the emphasis on change programmes has switched focus from ways to improve employee satisfaction to a goal today of customer-driven corporate effectiveness. But something more than a change in focus has occurred. The notion of organizational change has taken on new meaning. Since the early 1980s, it has become an imperative rather than a technique to be considered at appropriate times, a holistic rather than a piecemeal approach to organizational effectiveness.

Over the last two decades managers have increasingly been confronted with the notion that 'change' is a global phenomenon that is tangible and inevitable, yet understandable and manageable. In this tale 'change' is, at one and the same time, a threat and a challenge. Managers ignore change at their peril and there are numerous books and articles willing to argue that managers need to master (Chang, 1994), plan (Clark, 1995), implement (Lippitt *et al.*, 1985), control (Harvey and Wehmeyer, 1995), manage (McLennan, 1989) or ride the whirlwind of change (Annison, 1993).

Over time, popular arguments on the importance of change and change management have cohered into a powerful set of ideas and practices that inform new generations of managers. Todd Jick (1993) captures something of the growing managerial concern with change:

> 'Change,' in its broadest sense, is a planned or unplanned response to pressures and forces. Hence there is nothing new about change or the need for it. Technological, economic, social, regulatory, political, and competitive forces have caused organizations to modify for decades – if not centuries. Change is such a potent issue these days, however, because simultaneous, unpredictable, and turbulent pressures have become the norm. When this is broadened to a global scale, the forces multiply, some might argue, exponentially. Competition intensifies, more complex relations with other firms are established, strategic choices increase, adaptation is needed for survival. . . .
>
> Ultimately, the pressures that provoke change can be considered obstacles or challenges, threats or opportunities. They can elicit despair or mobilize energy. The reactions depend on how an organization interprets the forces surrounding it, and what it does with them.
>
> (Jick, 1993: 1)

Jick's statement is an example of how organizational change is presented as something that is 'real' and pressing. It is a typical story of change that simultaneously encourages the belief that actors can play a role in managing events but can do little other than react to 'forces' of change beyond their control. It is a story that, with some variance, is repeated throughout the change management literature. Selling the idea of re-engineering, for example, James Champy (1995) contends that:

> *Nothing is simple anymore.* Nothing is stable. The business environment is changing before our eyes, rapidly, radically, and perplexingly.
>
> Now, whatever we do is not enough. Incremental change is what we're used to: the kind we could manage gradually, with careful planning, broad consensus-building, and controlled execution. No we must not only manage change, we must create change – big change – and fast . . .
>
> *Everything is in question.* The old ways of managing no longer work. The organization charts, the compensation schemes, the hierarchies, the vertical organization, the whole tool kit of command-and-control management techniques no longer work.
>
> *Everyone must change.* . . . Not just their sense of the task, but their sense of themselves. Not just what they know, but how they think. Not just their way of seeing the world, but their way of living in the world.
>
> (Champy, 1995: 10–11, italics in the original)

Wilkins (1983) uses similar language when arguing a culture change approach:

[People] have felt an increased need to understand problems that seem to relate to concepts of culture. The current interest in organizational culture can be attributed in large measure to two major factors affecting contemporary U.S. business: (1) economic turbulence that has led to major changes in organizations and (2) recent writings about Japanese industry and management.

Economic turbulence . . . has resulted in major strategic changes, new acquisitions, or attempts to improve innovation, [moving] companies into unfamiliar areas where what was previously taken for granted no longer works.

The focus on Japanese organizations has . . . had the effect of high-lighting the culture of U.S. organizations, but in a more generic way. Viewing the prototypical Japanese organization . . . has allowed us to focus sharply on the contrast with how we Americans 'do organization'. Before the contrast was highlighted, we just did what came naturally.

(Wilkins, 1983: 24–5)

And the same is true in Cherrington's (1994) description of the Organizational Development approach:

Organizations live in an ever-changing environment and their survival depends on their ability to adapt to new demands and opportunities. Organizational development is a series of planned systematic changes introduced into an ongoing organization. These changes typically referred to as interventions, are designed to improve the effectiveness of the organization and help it respond to a changing environment. Organizational development (OD) includes a wide range of change-inducing activities that may be targeted for individuals, groups, or the entire organization . . . to facilitate organizational renewal. . . . Because organizations exist in a world of rapid change, they must be innovative and creative to maintain their vitality.

(Cherrington, 1994: 713)

For the executive contemplating change Heifetz and Laurie (1998) leave little doubt about its pressing character: 'Leaders today face adaptive challenges. Changes . . . around the globe are forcing them to . . . learn new ways of operating.'

And for the next generation of managers, currently making their way through the North American business schools, numerous texts, such as that by Gibson *et al.* (1997), serve to 'educate' students in the new discourse of organizational change:

As managers contemplate the futures of their organizations as the 21st century looms they can't escape the inevitability of change. . . . Change is certainly among the most frequently used words on the business pages of every newspaper in the world. Not only have entire countries and empires gone through dramatic and wrenching changes, but so have great companies such as IBM, General Motors and Ford. The USSR no longer exists, but neither does Pan-American Airlines. . . . Effective managers must view change as an integral responsibility, rather than as a peripheral one.

(Gibson *et al.*, 1997: 453)

Within the broad framework of an organizational change discourse there has developed the notion of the pre-packaged programme or change technique. Beginning with Organizational Development (OD), a number of approaches have developed – including Organizational Culture, Total Quality Management (TQM), Business Process Re-engineering (BPR), the Learning Organization, Six Sigma and the Balanced Scorecard – which promise practitioners techniques for dealing with change. Each approach draws upon received knowledge that change is inevitable and must be managed if the organization is to be successful.

I would argue that it is the existence of an underlying notion of an imperative of change that encourages managers to seek out specific packaged solutions. In Weick's (1995) terms, the on-going character of the discourse of organizational change provides the framework for the salience of change programmes as significant sensemaking cues.

Programmatic change as part of the broader discourse

Within the broad framework of a discourse of change, a new and recurring theme has been the need to adopt a coherent or programmatic approach (e.g., OD, TQM, culture change, BPR), with an emphasis on customer service and the use of 'expert' knowledge to implement change. In the following examples, academics and professional managers provide a feel for how new programmes of change were, respectively, sold and accepted. Introducing his book on managing corporate cultures Stanley M. Davis (1984) sells the idea that 'corporate culture is real and powerful', that culture change is 'popular', and that, handled expertly, corporate culture can be managed to deal with turbulent change:

> During the past five years I have worked extensively with senior managers of several large companies in their efforts to understand and manage their corporate cultures. My goal was to assess whether and how the culture met the company's needs, and to assist in changing it where it did not.
>
> Immense changes in the economic environment and a radical increase in competitive pressures have put a premium on strategy and a company's capacity to implement it. . . . To tap this advantage, corporations have

to be able to act fast. Perhaps the single most promising catalyst . . . has come to be recognized as corporate culture.

(Davis, 1984: 1–2)

For the senior manager, culture change is made attractive, not only through reference to the on-going link between organizational change, threats and benefits, but to the identity of the individual manager and his/her potential to avoid being seen as regressive:

We are operating in a post-industrial, service-based economy, but our companies are managed by models developed in, by, and for industrial companies. . . . It is no coincidence that corporate culture has become a useful concept at a time when management concepts and approaches are being roundly criticized as rigid and anachronistic. . . . Corporate culture offers a contrast to mechanistic approaches, an antidote to the rigidity of previous models, and a return to knowing one's fundamentals.

(Davis, 1984: 2–3)

In both regards, as indicated by testaments on the back cover of the book, Davis (1984) was able to strike a cord with senior managers:

Stan Davis lays out a method for managing corporate culture . . . and it can be applied almost immediately by the thoughtful manager.

(Samuel Armacost, President and CEO, Bank of America)

It is important to be perfectly clear about your culture, so that new employees, customers, and shareholders know who you are and what you stand for. Stan Davis's book is an excellent first-hand guide for others about how to manage their corporation's culture.

(John Cunningham, President, Wang Labs, Inc.)

Most corporation will have to make major strategic shifts to be prepared for the post-industrial future. Changing a corporation's culture is essential to implementing such strategic change, and Stan Davis writes lucidly, from practical experience, about how to do so.

(William Woodside, Chairman and CEO,
American Can Corporation)

Examples of a similar type of thinking can be found within Nova Scotia Power in the mid- to late-1980s. Explaining 'culture change at Nova Scotia Power' employees are told the story of a company where 'morale was low', and 'management appeared aloof and uncaring' but where a new senior management team, aided by a consulting firm, saved the day by introducing a Culture Change programme:

The Executive Committee (President, Vice Presidents) made the initial decision to make an organized effort at changing our culture in March 1988 and chose a consulting firm specializing in culture change to provide their expertise. This firm . . . deserve a tremendous amount of credit for the success of the change process.

(Nova Scotia Power, 1990b)

Culture change was the first of several programmatic approaches to organizational change and was closely followed by TQM and BPR. The introduction of each new programme was premised on the idea that previous programmes were somehow inadequate and perhaps even harmful (Grint, 1994). Indeed H. James Harrington (1991) goes so far as to suggest that culture change and, to some extent, TQM are 'exotic' failures. Harrington (1991) does not argue against an imperative of change, far from it, he suggests that things are worse than anyone imagined. Nor does he argue against the notion of programmatic change, he knocks down one set of ideas in order to substitute his own.[6] In any event Harrington (and other apostles of BPR) reinforce the idea of an imperative of change and its resolve through an organizational change programme:

America is in trouble, there is no doubt about it. . . . There are many theories as to why America's economic standing is declining, but no one would argue against the idea that it has something to do with the way we've grown accustomed to doing business. . . .

Business Process Improvement offers a no-nonsense blueprint for re-structuring our antiquated 'business-as-usual' approach. It's not about automating processes that already don't work. It's not about importing some exotic Japanese management technique that only serves to further confuse everyone. It's about effecting a major change in the way we manage our organizations by applying new approaches to the business community as a whole, particularly service industries.

(Harrington, 1991: inside front cover)

When Nova Scotia Power introduced BPI into the company in 1993 the previous Culture Change programme was not disparaged but, rather, largely ignored through a re-conceptualization of events and developments.

In the early part of the 1990s, Nova Scotia Power took every opportunity to link corporate success with the introduction of a Culture Change programme. Culture change was linked to 'significant progress' and a 'financially . . . good year' in 1989–90 (Nova Scotia Power, 1990a); 'significant change and accomplishments' and the development of 'pro-active leadership' in 1990–1 (Nova Scotia Power, 1991c), and a 'gratifying . . . operational and financial performance' in 1991–2 (Nova Scotia Power, 1993f):

We are extremely encouraged with our cultural change process to date . . .

(Nova Scotia Power, 1990b)

[Culture change] will make the Corporation a better company, more productive because employees will enjoy their jobs and be challenged. It will make the company a highly respected organization in the province. It will allow us to be more responsive to customers and allow us to truly be environmentally sensitive.

(Jim Woods, Director of Organizational and Employee Development, Nova Scotia Power, 1991a)

Cultural change is directed at team building, conflict resolution, communications, building trust and commitment, empowering others, recognition, decision making and performance management. All are important in a business environment where the pace of change is rapid and individual responsibilities are increasing.

(Nova Scotia Power, 1991b, emphasis in the original)

Nonetheless, by 1993, the company was downplaying the benefits of culture change in the face of strong arguments for a new programme of re-engineering: 'Nova Scotia Power Inc. turned to re-engineering to improve the quality of customer service, revitalize corporate culture and keep the competition at bay' (Crawley *et al.*, 1995: 33).

It was the same old story of turbulent change with attendant threats and benefits to the company but this time the argument for programmatic change substituted BPI for culture change, and with customer service, rather then employee well-being, as the subject:

It's no secret that Canadian companies have recently had to face a seemingly endless catalogue of woes, ranging from dwindling demand and increased competition to employee burnout and outdated processes. In many instances, the changes needed to bring these companies into the reality of the 1990s have been expensive and painful. While consultants herald the advantages of re-engineering, line staff must embrace the resulting changes. . . . When re-engineering is done properly . . . the result is not just a leaner corporation, but a better one. The corporate focus shifts to the customer, where it belongs.

(Crawley *et al.*, 1995: 33)

From 1993 company references to corporate culture were, by and large, made to serve a focus on BPI, not the other way round: 'Nova Scotia Power Inc. is one company that successfully turned adversity into advantage by transforming itself, and its culture, one process at a time' (Crawley *et al.*, 1995: 33).

The rhetoric of change management

It has been argued that the popularity of pre-packaged change programmes has achieved the status of a fad (Macdonald, 1993) or fashion (Abrahamson, 1996; Jackson, 2000). Keiser (1997) and Macdonald (1993) have, respectively, detailed the time span and different forms that management fads take. For example, by 1996 TQM and re-engineering had gone from being the hottest management trend to a fad, whose day has come and gone (Jacques, 1996). It was not a coincidence that both culture change and re-engineering were at their peak of popularity (see Figure 4.2) when they were implemented at Nova Scotia Power.

Abrahamson (1996: 255) refers to the trend of adopting the latest management ideas as 'theories of management fashion'. He argues that they are shaped, not only by 'organizational performance gaps' opened by technical and economic environmental changes, but by 'socio-psychological forces', including 'aesthetic tastes, childlike excitement, mass conformity, and even something akin to manias or episodes of mass hysteria'.

While reference to fads and fashion helps to characterize the popularity of change programmes it does not explain that popularity. As Rüling (1998) puts it:

> As a concept in its own right, 'management fashion' . . . lacks conceptual clarity. Whereas some authors build on an everyday understanding of 'fashion', others discuss the specificity of management fashion either in terms of formal properties, e.g., its cyclical nature (Kieser, 1995), or other attributes, e.g., associated claims for rationality and progress (Abrahamson, 1996).
>
> (Rüling, 1998)

What is needed, according to Rüling (1998), is an approach that 'combines institutional and discourse analysis': 'Fashion is created and mediated through institutions, rules and routines present in a field. On the other hand, it is primarily linguistic in nature . . . and thus relies on constant reproduction through individual actors.'

To begin with, the latter analysis of the rhetoric used to argue for models of organizational change indicates a story line that succeeds because it:

1   is simplistic in style
2   is philosophically realist/functionalist
3   references mythical forces, that engender a sense of uncertainty and fear
4   builds on/creates a notion of on-going reality
5   offers unique solutions to organizational problems and
6   is optimistic in tone, encouraging the notion of the good manager and the cutting edge organization.

Simplistic

Most popular accounts of the management of change paint a very simple picture that contains equally simple solutions. Global forces beyond the reach of individual managers and companies are causing uncertainty. These forces, however, can be managed and turned to the advantage of the company. Managers who recognize the inherent dangers and opportunities can succeed in creating effective organizations, particularly where they adopt a particular approach (e.g., BPR) to deal with the problem (cf. Harrington, 1991).

References to the complex nature of global and organizational realities do often appear in such stories but they are invariably reduced to a few simple problems. Choi and Behling (1997: 37), for example, reduce an apparent widespread failure of TQM programmes to the 'underlying, often unspoken, orientations [of top managers] toward time, market, and customers'. Similarly, James Champy (1995) reduces the problems of re-engineering to the attitudes of managers:

> The results are in: Re-engineering works – up to a point. The obstacle is management. The only way we're going to deliver on the full promise of re-engineering is to start re-engineering management . . . [To change] managerial work, the way we think about, organize, inspire, deploy, enable, measure, and reward the value-adding operational work.
>
> (Champy, 1995: 1, 3)

Champy (1995) goes on to provide a template, or script, for achieving the desired changes.[7]

The simplistic nature of the storyline is, of course, not new. From Lewin (1951) onwards organizational scholars and practitioners have been proffering techniques that are simple to execute, and therein lies much of the appeal. As Table 4.1 indicates, a large number of books on organizational change proffer the idea that change can be dealt with through fairly simple, straight-forward solutions. In the largest number of cases, it is argued that 'organizational change' can be managed, mastered or controlled. Beyond that, key aspects of managing include developing strategies that include an emphasis on changing employee behaviour through training, learning, team building and empowerment.

Despite the development of more sophisticated theories of change over the years, many of the simplistic elements can still be found at their core. For example, despite the development of theories of culture (that take a more complex look at the organization as a whole) the notion of shared values and understandings still persist (Schein, 1985). As well, the notion of change as an entity has been enjoined by the notion of culture as an entity (Smircich, 1983).

It is surely easier to buy into the notion that change is more real than perceived, and that it can be addressed by manipulation of an existing rather than a metaphorical culture.

Table 4.1 Top ten change adjectives in the titles of organizational change books in the
US Library of Congress, 2001

Adjective (year term first appears in title) {number of books using the term}

1	Managing (1969), Mastering (1976) and Controlling change (1990) [174]
2	Strategies for change (1968) [72]
—	Training (1973), Learning (1975), Team Building (1977) and Empowering (1990) [72]
4	Techniques of change (and associated terms*) (1973) [69]
5	Leadership of change (and associated terms**) (1977) [63]
—	Change as Transformation (and associated terms***) (1985) [63]
7	Planned change (and associated terms⁺) (1968) [41]
8	Change Agents (and associated terms⁺⁺) (1974) [27]
10	Confronting change (and associated terms⁺⁺⁺) (1963) [13]

Notes:
* Other terms include Diagnosing (1969), Monitoring (1974), Guidelines (1975), Correctional applications (1976), Manual (1977), Assessing (1979), Handbook (1981), Models (1982), Casebook (1985), Pragmatic (1987), Practical (1988), Blueprint (1994), Formula (1994), Checklist (1995), Tools (1995), Skills (1995), Tool kit (1996), Translating (1996), Programme (1999].
** Other terms include Visualizing (1973), Creating (1974), Preparing for change (1979), Intervention (1979), Implementing (1981), Initiating (1985), Manufacturing (1989), Imaginization (1990), Mobilizing (1994), Facilitating (1999).
*** Other terms include change as organizational Life Cycle (1980), Transition (1994).
⁺ Other terms include Design (1972) and Redesign (1995).
⁺⁺ Other terms include Consultants (1974), Coaches (1979) and Practitioners (1981).
⁺⁺⁺ Other terms include Challenge (1973), Riding the waves of change (1988), Riding the whirlwind of change (1990), Adapting to change (1993).

From my study of Nova Scotia Power, it became clear that people did indeed treat change as if it was an imperative and organizational culture as if it materially existed in time and space. Objections appeared to be whether change should be responded to in a certain way and whether it was right or appropriate to change the culture, not whether it was a heuristic to effect change. It was also evident to me that perceptions of change, of culture, and of the changes being made were far from shared, in fact or in potential. People made sense of things in different ways and this seemed to have a bearing on organizational outcomes. Thus, I was led to the idea that an adequate theory of change needed to account for the way that people made sense of things and how conflicting sensemaking outcomes affected people's perceptions of the success of change programmes.

When Nova Scotia Power was in the process of buying a Culture Change programme, it was the simplicity of the adopted programme that appealed to senior management. The consultant's programme, which reduced culture change to four key values, was the most simple and straightforward of the models offered by competing consulting agencies.

Realist

The term realist is meant in two senses: first, the ontological sense of a material reality (Burrell and Morgan, 1979), and second, the 'common sense' notion, predominant in the business community, of a 'real world'. Organizational change stories appear to succeed where they reference 'reality' such as 'globalisation' and 'change' and focus on 'real' problems such as organizational effectiveness, growth and/or profitability. In the former regard globalization and change are presented as tangible things that exist apart from individual actors. It is that which lends itself to notions of uncertainty and fear and a need for managerial intervention. Schein's (1985, 1987) distinction between clinical and ethnographic research captures (and subsequently furthers) the significance of a realist approach to organizational change by suggesting that the value of the clinical approach is its link to 'real' organizational concerns. As we have seen in previous quotes, Nova Scotia Power was not immune from the realist themes of globalization, change, and the need for business development and growth. In the process the company contributed to the on-going discourse in words and in practices.

Realist methods – drawn in large part from natural science thinking – also play a role in organizational change stories where measurement is emphasized as the ultimate arbiter of the success of a particular programme. Yet, ironically, as Schaffer and Thomson (1998: 189) lament, in many cases managers fail to draw a direct link between a programme of change and 'achievement specific, measurable operational improvements'. This is less true in the case of re-engineering where measurement is an essential element of the process. The realist character of organizational change stories has been strengthened by links with apparent scientifically testable results.

Nova Scotia Power has always included some element of linkage between activity and outcomes. In the culture change era the link was only referenced in the broadest sense but reveals the problem of trying to measure the outcome of specific activities: 'The Corporation's positive operating income is the result of productivity improvements, an approved rate increase, as well as the impact of favourable market factors' (Nova Scotia Power, 1990a). With the introduction of re-engineering, the company's concern with measurement became more sharply, more directly, focused, with dollar estimates being linked to process outcomes:

> Process improvement refers to work processes within the Company that will be analyzed on a cross-divisional basis to ensure the efficiency of the activities and the right number of employees for the work to be done. ... It is estimated that with more efficient systems in place that is potential for cost savings of approximately $5 million within these interdivisional processes.
>
> (Nova Scotia Power, 1993c)

Mythology

Myth is an essential part of the organizational change story line (Clark and Salaman, 1996; Grint, 1994; Kieser, 1997). The primary myth is the idea of irresistible forces that compel change. Sometimes the myth is embedded in references to forces of change and sometimes in the notion of globalization:[8] sometimes (as in the Pierce and Newstrom, 1990 quote below) its functionalist roots show through:

> *Environmental Forces of Change: Organizations cannot control the environment; nevertheless*, astute managers identify the external factors for change and respond appropriately to them.
>
> (Cherrington, 1994: 716, emphasis in original)

> Canadian organizations are rapidly changing as they face an increasing global marketplace.
>
> (McShane, 1998: 392)

> *Global economy* [refers to] the recognized and emerging interdependency among the economic systems of all global nations.
>
> (Pierce and Newstrom, 1990: 344, emphasis in original)

It is this myth that is new to the idea of organizational change and which anchors much of the discourse. It is a myth of organizational change as an imperative and it has only developed within the last two decades. Essential features of the myth include an association of uncertainty and fear with irresistible forces. Its influence on the actions of managers can be glimpsed in the corporate statements of Nova Scotia Power (see, for example, previous quotes above).

Ongoing reality

Perhaps the most interesting aspect of organizational change stories is how they manage to simultaneously suggest that selected models of change are unique and that they are widely accepted. There was undoubtedly a point when certain organizational change stories were more about the construction of reality, but fairly soon such stories took on the appearance of reflecting on-going reality. The typical change story speaks to 'what everyone knows' (e.g., that the world is rapidly changing in terms of technology, values, and politics; that the 'average' company has undergone, or is undergoing, some form of organizational change, and that a specific change programme is the latest trend among 'leading' companies). Reading such stories the individual manager quickly gains the impression that s/he is being let in on the secret and should join the growing trend. Certainly Nova Scotia Power's senior

Table 4.2 Reflection of change myths and language in the corporate statements of Nova Scotia Power

What the 'experts' say	What Nova Scotia Power says
Culture's current popularity results from a major search for new management models. . . . We are operating in a post-industrial, service-based economy, but our companies are managed by models developed in, by, and for industrial corporations. . . . Corporate culture offers a contrast to mechanistic approaches, an antidote to the rigidity of previous models . . . (Davis, 1984: 2–3).	By the middle to late 1980s it became apparent that the 'culture' of the Corporation was unsuited to the times (Nova Scotia Power, 1990b).
	Since the mid-1980s our corporate culture has been undergoing a radical change. Through our values and cultural change programs we have become strong believers in participative management (Nova Scotia Power, 1993f).
Thousands of companies large and small have undertaken the mission of re-engineering, sparking a transformation in millions of working lives. The principles of re-engineering necessarily require not only a sea-change in the ways people work, but also a radical new approach to management (Back cover of James Champy's, 1995, *Re-engineering Management*).	Why BPI? This initiative is essential if Nova Scotia Power is going to be the best . . . The President has stated: 'Companies today cannot survive by simply doing what they have always been doing in the past. It's just too competitive. We've got to consider the '90s customer' . . .' BPI is an essential part of Nova Scotia Power's continued success (Nova Scotia Power, 1993d).
We must dramatically improve business results, now, and do it while earning the hearts and minds of our people. To make things still more difficult, 'now' has no traditions, no precedents, no time-tested formulas. Now has never been seen before (James Champy, 1995: 9).	Launched in the summer of 1993, BPI is revolutionizing the way we work (Nova Scotia Power, 1994a).
	It's no secret that Canadian companies have recently had to face a seemingly endless catalogue of woes, ranging from dwindling demand and increased competition to employee burnout and outdated processes. In many instances the changes needed to bring these companies into the reality of the 1990s have been expensive and painful. While consultants herald the advantages of re-engineering, line staff must embrace the resulting changes. . . . When re-engineering is done properly . . . the result is not just a leaner corporation, but a better one (Crawley *et al.*, 1995: 33).

management bought into the idea that they needed to deal with uncertainty and fear by adopting the newest, popular change techniques (see Table 4.2).

Unique solutions

Another key myth involves claims of uniqueness, newness, or radical difference in regard to the solutions offered to globalization and the forces of change. From culture change to BPR, advocates have claimed that the approach is new, different or even revolutionary (see the quotes of Champy, 1995; Davis, 1984; and Wilkins, 1983 above; see also Table 4.2).

Coupled with the idea that change is an imperative that has not been adequately dealt with in the past, claims of uniqueness appear attractive and offer not only a 'real' solution but also a strategy for putting the company and its managers on the cutting edge of business practice. Eccles *et al.* (1992: quoted in Kieser, 1997) contend that these aspects of management rhetoric can be positive in helping to energize employees and managers alike:

> Much of the current hysteria over labels, such as 'the new organization' and 'empowerment' can be seen as an attempt to lend new energy to the collective enterprises. . . . In their daily language, individual managers use such labels and concepts as they see fit as part of their ongoing use of language to coax, inspire, demand, or otherwise produce action in their organizations.
>
> (Keiser, 1997: 69)

Grint (1994: 198), on the other hand, contends that such theories are not unique and that while the lack of novelty does not imply that it will fail 'novelty is no guarantee of success'. Nonetheless, Grint (1994) concedes that it is not uniqueness or inherent rationality that make theories such as re-engineering popular but the ways in which 'the purveyors of such theories manage in and through their accounts to construct a series of sympathetic resonances or compatibilities. The idea and the language of uniqueness certainly appear to have resonated with 'internal accounts' (Grint, 1994) within Nova Scotia Power (see Table 4.2).

Optimism and the 'good' manager

In addition to offering unique solutions to the problems of change, organizational change stories often appeal to a manager's sense of self. At one level the notion of organizational change can be seen to appeal to what Weick (1995) refers to as an act of social sensemaking. The individual manager is led to believe that he or she is part of an on-going process of action in which others will judge his/her reactions. For example, if it is believed that there really is a 'major search for new management models' (see Table 4.2) then the individual manager may be inclined to feel that he/she must join that search or be judged incompetent or 'behind the times'. At another level, how the individual manager feels that he or she is positioned in regard to the thinking of other managers may speak to identity construction. For instance, an important element of the organizational change story is an implicit, often explicit, image of the 'good manager' as one who is able to grasp the underlying problematic and take appropriate action.

The image of the 'good manager' has, I would argue, always been implicit within much of management and organizational theory[9] but is stressed in a dramatic fashion in the change story. For example, in *Out of the Crisis*, W. Edwards Deming argues for the 'transformation of the style of American management', suggesting '14 steps management must take' (see Gartner and Naughton, 1990). Deming's fourteen steps turn out to be as much about the notion of what a good manager looks like as techniques of good managing. The steps to becoming a good manager include, the creation of 'constancy of purpose toward improvement of product and service', a ceasing of 'dependence on inspection to achieve quality', ending 'the practice of awarding business on the basis of the price tag'; the driving out of 'fear', breaking 'down the barriers between departments' (ibid.: 314–15). In almost every case, there is a strong suggestion that existing practices, and thus ways of managing, are outmoded and inefficient.

Deming is not alone in this appeal to the 'good manager'. As Thompson (1998) expresses it:

> The leader's actions in making TQM work are critical to its success. The TQM leader must be a cheerleader and supporter of quality and fully cognizant that the employees are the ones who need to be empowered to bring quality to the organization. The TQM mentality will not occur through an edict by management. The leader must set forth the antecedent conditions that allow a quality mentality to happen. In addition, the leader must focus on quality, support it, and work with others to ensure that the culture of the organization moves towards a TQM mentality.
>
> (Thompson, 1998: 257)

In this particular story the onus is on the manager to achieve the successful translation of the principles of TQM into action. In several other accounts the success or failure of a particular programme is laid at the door of the manager (see for example, Champy, 1995; Choi and Behling, 1997). Thus, while stories of change are located within a framework of optimism that encourages managers to feel that problems can be solved it also draws on a well of fear by offering dark images for the company and the bad manager who fail to grasp the nettle.

At Nova Scotia Power, no less than at many other companies, threat, opportunity and the construction of the ideal manager can be found throughout corporate statement (see Table 4.2 above). A classic example comes from the Seventy-First Annual Report of the company, which was laid out in Q and A style. Instead of the usual outline of the year's events and achievements written in the first person, the reports of the President (Louis Comeau), the Vice President of Engineering and Production (Gerry Lethbridge), the Premises Manager (Dave Driscoll), the Vice President of Planning and Environment (Terry MacDonald), and the Director of Organization and Employee Development (Jim Woods), were presented as answers to questions.

Comeau, for example, is asked the question: 'In the statement of our four corporate values, we say "We strive to be a leader in the energy sector . . ." What exactly does that mean?' In answering, Comeau presents himself as a pro-active leader: 'Leadership is about vision, being pro-active, leading the way. When you're talking about leadership, you're not talking today – it's looking ahead to where you'll be in 10 years, in 25 years. It's about being the best' (Nova Scotia Power, 1991c).

A different question, on concern for employees, allowed Comeau to locate the advent of the Culture Change programme as part of his identity as a manager. Here he is asked: 'Human resources has always seemed a primary focus of yours. Why is that?' To which he replies:

> I believe in people, in the sense that you achieve your goals through people, and people only produce those results when they feel good about their work. Over 25 years in management, that's been my experience. And everywhere it is the same.
>
> (Nova Scotia Power, 1991c)

The format is similar for Gerry Lethbridge who is asked: 'One of our Corporate Goals is to make effective use of advanced technology and innovation to produce quality results. Are we achieving this goal?' This allows him to locate his management style among those on the cutting edge:

> Certainly. We have been, and continue to be a 'state-of-the-art' utility in several areas. . . . We don't know of anyone else who's [doing some of the things we are doing], and our work in this area has been getting a lot of attention.
>
> (Nova Scotia Power, 1991c)

These, and other, company statements capture the essence of a management that is responding to an imperative of change by seeking out 'innovative' management ideas. As in the following example, this results in stories that paint Nova Scotia Power's senior managers as on 'the leading edge' of organizational change in the face of turbulent times:

> We . . . wanted to demonstrate that our employees were capable of responding to the new challenges of the marketplace. These challenges helped to shape the corporate agenda for 1993. . . .

The world in which we operate is not only changing faster than ever before but also tending to change direction more abruptly. Ten years ago we started evolving from a reactive to an anticipatory organization. In 1993 we accelerated that process. By redefining our company to meet the future now, we can do what is necessary on *our* terms. This redefinition is an essential process if our company is to thrive in the years ahead. . . .

To be the best we can at what we do is Nova Scotia Power's corporate mission. . . .

The creation of the Nova Scotia Power Commission in 1919 launched what has become a tradition of technical advancement, hand-in-hand with development by Nova Scotia's industries and communities. It is a tradition of which we are very proud – a tradition that continues to inspire our innovative thinking and our efforts in building a strong future.

(Louis Comeau, Nova Scotia Power, 1994a)

If we look at various corporate statements we see that various managers at Nova Scotia Power reproduce all of the key elements of the change story – global, real, inevitable yet manageable – in one way or another. The 'global' nature of change is mentioned in several references. There is little doubt that change is real or inevitable: it is a 'driving force', an 'influence', something that managers 'cannot choose' to ignore, it 'dictates' action, and it moves with 'the times'. Change is, however, something 'incumbent' on Nova Scotia Power managers to 'prepare for', 'respond to', 'adapt to' and 'organize' for.

In the 'typical' change story, change presents management with a tremendous challenge, providing opportunity to skilful managers and threat to weak managers. Again we can read this storyline in the narratives of Nova Scotia Power. On the one hand, change is seen as threatening in its 'abrupt' turns, with political (e.g., 'deregulation'), and technological (e.g., 'satellite technology, fibre optics, interactive systems, integrated data systems) change altering 'the way business is done'. On the other hand, change provides managers with the potential for a 'positive impact on customers', adapting to the 'thinking of the customer', moving with 'the times' (see quotes above).

Making sense of the popularity of change programmes

Many managers and employees in hundreds of organizations have experienced the struggles, successes, failures, and frustrations that go along with changing the way business is done. Innovations involving production quality, customer service, re-engineering, right-sizing, culture, and teamwork follow a regular pattern: introductory fanfare, followed by tough times of implementation, ending with something less than complete success, just in time for the next major change to begin.

(Reichers *et al.*, 1997: 48)

The introduction of change programmes has become a major phenomenon throughout North American businesses and not-for-profit organizations. New institutional theory provides one level of explanation for the popularity of specific change programmes, namely, that if certain activity appears successful in one organization it is likely to be mimicked by other organizations (DiMaggio and Powell, 1991). But that does not explain the process whereby mimicking occurs. 'In order to explain the recent popularity of change programmes, it is necessary to understand what drives the sense-making process of those who buy the programmes, and how those who sell the programmes act upon this sensemaking' (Ibid.).

Business practice

A discourse draws its strength from its links to practice (Foucault, 1979; 1980). It is not merely what people say but the fact that the words are rooted in action that makes the ideas appealing and influential. For example, Nova Scotia Power's interest in industry leader Florida Power & Light (FPL) was due not simply to their commitment to TQM but because of their application of that programme and what they were thought to have achieved from it. It is the institutional practices of organizations that encourage mimicry. DiMaggio and Powell (1991) argue that a 'startling homogeneity of organizational forms and practices' is due to a process of 'isomorphism', or 'a constraining process that forces one unit in a population to resemble other units that face the same environmental conditions'. They argue that there are three major forms of isomorphism – 'coercive', 'mimetic' and 'normative'.

Coercive isomorphism refers to pressures to conform that stem from political influence and problems of legitimacy. In the case of Nova Scotia Power that political pressure took two major forms. Prior to the appointment of Louis Comeau, in 1983, the government of the day 'sensed' that the corporation was out of touch with 'political realities' and appointed a president who could make the company feel like it was in touch. As Comeau was to state, as he later reflected on his appointment: 'The utility, in 1983, was not in very good shape. From the basic point of government relations and public and community relations, it was a disaster' (Bruce, 1991: 31). Comeau addressed the political pressures, in large part, by reproducing corporate culture practices that were in vogue in other companies (see Table 4.3).

The second, and more direct, political pressure[10] came in the form of privatization. Less than a year before the company was privatized Comeau stated that:

> In the 1986–87 fiscal year, all the subsidies were removed. We took three years . . . to get rid of them. So now we are completely on our own and we're now trying to build the equity of the company to make it more in line with private sector structure. But as a Crown corporation,

we should not have all the ratios of the private sector. *A Crown corporation has public purposes.*

(Bruce, 1991: 31, my emphasis)

As part of the public purposes of the corporation Nova Scotia Power had an extensive programme of culture change that emphasized concern for employees, voters, customers and the environment.

Once the company was privatized in 1992 new political pressures were evident, including a new emphasis on efficiency and competitiveness. A 1994 headline in the local newspaper, *The Chronicle-Herald*, sums up the change: 'Nova Scotia Power privatization a success – Comeau. Competitiveness driving force behind company':

> A word never spoken before at NSP has become a catch phrase – competitiveness. 'In the past, . . . we at Nova Scotia Power had little reason to think very much about competitiveness. . . . We think about it today for sure. In fact, it dominates our thinking,' [Comeau] told a business crowd recently.
>
> Mr Comeau said NSP must become more competitive to keep existing customers and to attract new businesses from other provinces . . .
>
> The company has reduced its training and travel budgets by $600,000.
>
> In the fall of 1991 the company launched an 'effectiveness program' and since then, overall productivity has increased 18 percent and 400 jobs have been eliminated through early retirement, attrition and voluntary separation, he said.
>
> 'We could have done a lot of this as a Crown corporation, but there's no question that the fact that we are an investor-owned utility we focus on a market-driven company,' Mr Comeau said.
>
> (Myrden, 1994)

The ending quote sums up the changing pressures within the company. Those changes could be seen from the beginning in Comeau's first annual report following privatization:

> *New Environment, New Challenges.* We cannot . . . be complacent. The future brings with it many challenges. First of all electricity in Nova Scotia is not as competitive as it can be. We must continue the progress made in productivity so that electricity becomes a more cost-effective choice for our customers.
>
> We must also become more aggressive in the way we run our business . . .
>
> As a public company we can now strengthen our financial status by investigating new opportunities in a competitive marketplace.
>
> (Nova Scotia Power, 1993f:
emphasis in the original)

Table 4.3 Selected organizational change programmes in Nova Scotia, 1985–96[1]

	Re-engineering	Culture change	Empower-ment	MBO	TQM	ISO 9000	Team circles	Origin of programme
Bank of Nova Scotia	—	—	—	1994	—	—	—	No information
Bank of Montreal	—	1995	—	—	—	—	—	Influence of other banks, senior management and consultants
Canadian Forces	—	—	On-going	—	1989–93	—	—	Consultants
Dept of National Defence	1992	—	—	—	1990–91	—	—	Consultants and internal management
DND – Marland, Ha Marine Atlantic Headquarters – Halifax	1993– on-going	Mid/late 1980s– on-going	Mid 1980s– early 1990s on-going	—	mid 1980s onwards	mid 1980s onwards	—	Consultants and internal management
Diesel Division, GM of Canada Ltd.	—	1995-6	—	—	1995-6	—	—	Consultants and internal management
Equifax Canada	1995-6	1995-6	1996–	1994– onwards	—	—	—	Consultants
Federal Govt DND – Ship Repair Unit Atlantic	1991– onwards	1991 onwards	—	—	1991 onwards	—	1991 onwards	Internal management
GE Capital Fleet Services	1995-6	—	—	—	—	—	—	Internal management

Table 4.3 (continued)

	Re-engineering	Culture change	Empower-ment	MBO	TQM	ISO 9000	Team circles	Origin of programme
Halifax School Board	—	—	—	—	—	—	—	Consultants
Halifax Shipyard Ltd.	—	1993	—	—	—	1994	—	Other shipyard; Consultants
Guarantee Company of North America, The	—	1989–94	1995–6	1989–94	—	—	—	Consultants and internal management
Maritime Medical Care	1994	—	1994	—	—	—	—	No information
MT&T	—	Late-1980s	—	—	—	—	—	No information
Northwoodcare Incorporated	—	1997	—	—	1995	—	—	Senior management
Petro-Canada	1991–ongoing	1993–ongoing	1992–4	1988–91	1991 ongoing	—	—	No information
Public works and Govt Service Canada	1990–96	1990–96	1990–96	1990–96	1990–96	—	—	Consultants and internal management
Registry of Motor Vehicles	1994–present	—	1994–present	—	—	—	—	internal management
Stora Port Hawkesbury Ltd.	—	—	—	—	—	1996	—	Other pulp companies; senior management
Wal-Mart Canada	—	unspecified period	—	unspecified period	—	—	—	Internal management

Notes: [1]Information based on surveys of local companies, part-time (mature/employed) students from two MBA and two undergraduate commerce classes at Saint Mary's University, Fall, 1996, and material from local newspapers and local informants.

A central part of the change process was finding a programme that could help the company conform to its new political reality and that is where re-engineering became attractive: 'At the heart of the Effectiveness Program is our Business Process Improvement (BPI) initiative' (Nova Scotia Power, 1994a).

Mimetic isomorphism refers to activities that result from standard responses to uncertainty. In a world of uncertainty companies often adopt those practices that appear popular and widespread if not successful. A good example of this is Louis Comeau's use of an attitudes survey, in 1987, to identify problems in the company. Comeau at that time was faced with a number of uncertainties about how to deal with perceived problems within the company. He dealt with the problem by a practice – the use of an attitude survey – that was 'normal' and well established.[11] By this means he was able to inject a level of certainty into the process. A few decades earlier that would not have been the case. Managers in the 1950s and certainly prior to the advent of Organizational Development theory (cf. French and Bell, 1972) sought very different methods of identifying and dealing with organizational problems (Bendix, 1974; Rose, 1978).

When Comeau was faced with 'evidence' of low morale it is interesting that he did not seek a solution aimed at dealing with specific problems (e.g., lack of performance feedback)[12] but instead sought ways to change the overall 'culture' of the company. Once again he was choosing a 'typical' and prominent management strategy of the day. The decision to introduce a Culture Change programme was not the only choice before Comeau but it was the most popular management change technique of the day. Comeau did not really have to 'look around' for a particular answer; he was already aware of culture changes in industry leader Florida Power & Light (FPL) and the powerful provincial telephone company Maritime Telegraph & Telephone (MT&T). Indeed, FPL and MT&T were just two of the many national, industry-wide, and local examples of companies that were receiving press for 'successful' engagement in one or other change programme at the time (see Appendix A and Table 4.3). Canadian no less than American companies are heavily involved in the process of major change (Hatfield and Mills, 1997; see Appendix A). Locally, throughout Nova Scotia and within Halifax itself, numerous companies have undergone culture change, re-engineering (and various other changes) prior to, and since, the changes made within Nova Scotia Power (see Table 4.2). Indeed, not only were they aware of the changes but the senior management at Nova Scotia Power sought direct help and advice from MT&T.

While it might appear that the company chose culture change and re-engineering because they targeted specific organizational problems, it is more likely that they were selected because of the powerful nature of the discourse of change. It can also be argued that Nova Scotia Power's problems were made to fit the solution, which happened to be the management fad at that time.

The same process was at work in 1993 when, faced with a perceived need to become more 'competitive' and 'efficient', Nova Scotia Power senior managers again turned to a highly popular and widespread programme called 're-engineering'.

Normative isomorphism refers to the standardization of ideas and values through the process of professionalization. In the modern world this is achieved through the education and socialization of managers in business schools, in-house training programmes, professional associations (e.g., accounting bodies) and business organizations (e.g., Rotary Clubs,[13] the Chambers of Commerce, etc.).

Examination of management training at Nova Scotia Power provides clues to the influence of normative isomorphism and its reproduction. In 1992, for example, the company initiated a 'Leadership Development Program' that was held at its Corporate Training Centre at the company's headquarters. In an accompanying booklet participants are, from the beginning, encouraged to think of change as an imperative that needs to be managed:

> The key to becoming a 'master manager', or achieving managerial excellence, is the manager's ability to apply an appropriate set of **ASK's** (Attitudes, Skills, and Knowledge). . . . The important question managers must answer . . . is 'what constitutes an appropriate set of management attitudes?' . . . By session's end, participants will be able to:
>
> * Articulate managerial attitudes appropriate to the 1990s and explain why each attitude is necessary;
> * Select personal behaviours which are consistent with appropriate attitudes for the 1990s, and
> * Explain what attitudes and behaviours fit the need of Nova Scotia Power.

The booklet goes on to outline a series of training topics that include, 'empowerment and productivity', 'building a winning team', 'stress management', 'effective interpersonal negotiating skills', 'goal setting', 'dealing with organizational conflict', 'communication skills', 'time management', and 'managing innovation and change'. These topics are presented as 'normal' aspects of management training. There is nothing to suggest that 'empowerment', 'communication skills', 'teams' and 'innovation and change' are relatively new aspects of management thinking. Examination of the company's 'innovation and change' training indicates how certain notions (or folklore) of managing are created, maintained or 'passed on' within Nova Scotia Power:

> The next decade will likely be a period in which managers are frequently called upon to fulfil the role of innovator and change agent within their own department. Such role responsibilities are being thrust upon the manager because of the increased rates of change at all levels of society.

In fact, the statement 'Change and adapt quickly or cease to be competitive,' is quickly becoming the battle cry of the 1990s.

(Employee Development, training booklet,
Nova Scotia Power, 1992)

But it is not enough for managers to respond to the 'battle cry' of innovation and change. They are to be trained to encourage employees to 'buy
into' the same thinking:

However, with every action there is often a reaction within the organizational system. In this case, the reaction to innovation and change may
be employee resistance. Failure of employees to be personally creative,
or buy into and support planned change can result in a stagnant, or even
regressive, organization. Managers must therefore learn to manage innovation, change, and the potential for employee resistance.

To prepare managers for this responsibility, this session will focus on
manager behaviours intended to stimulate employee innovation and overcome employee resistance.

(Employee Development, training booklet,
Nova Scotia Power, 1992)

It very much seemed that, in adopting programmes of change, senior
managers at Nova Scotia Power were working through and enacting an established script. It was as if a dominant set of compelling ideas, empowered
through their appearance as 'knowledge' (Walkerdine, 1990), was acting as
a script for managers to follow.

Normative isomorphism and business education

If not the originator, the university business school has contributed much
by way of an acceptance among managers of an imperative of organizational
change. Part of the development of organizational change, as an imperative,
was its inclusion as a key topic in the mainstream North American business
text (Mills and Hatfield, 1998). In recent years, culture change, TQM, and
BPR have become key discussion points within discussions of organizational
change and topic areas in their own right. For example, McShane's (1998)
organizational behaviour textbook devotes separate chapters to TQM, organizational change and development and organizational culture. The chapter
on 'Organizational Change and Development' includes reference to BPR:
'Some writers now argue that companies need more 're-engineering'
(quantum change) rather than incremental tinkering to survive in this rapidly
changing environment.'

A recent analysis of 138 North American business textbooks, published
between 1960 and 2000, found that re-engineering was discussed in 60 per
cent of all relevant textbooks (i.e. those published since the advent of the

programme), TQM was discussed in 47 per cent, Organizational Culture in 69 per cent, and Organizational Development (OD) in 67 per cent (Mills, 2001).

Not only do business textbooks introduce students to the topic of organizational change, but also do so in a way that encourages commitment to the process of change in the future. They do this by linking discussion of change to 'real life' examples drawn from the business world, with the successful application of selected programmes being illustrated by reference to actual companies.[14] In reflecting existing business practices the process can be described as 'order affirmation' (Meyer and Rowan, 1983).

Meyer and Rowan (1983) sum up the role of the modern university as personnel-certifying agencies, maintainers of societally agreed-on rites, institutions of instruction and socialization, producers of education for society as opposed to individuals and families, the central agency defining personnel for the modern state and economy, a central means of incorporating citizens into the political, economic, and status order of society, and an institution that is composed of a set of standardized public credentials used to incorporate citizen personnel into society. The production of the business textbook can be seen as a reflection of that broader framework (Mills and Hatfield, 1998), helping to legitimize through a process of normalizing certain ideas on organizational change.

While some aspects of the change discourse are relatively new (e.g., change as imperative, the service focus, the advent of the change package), most have always been part of organizational change theories (e.g., tangible, inevitable, universally understandable). What is significant is not the contours of the discourse itself but the fact that it has become a discourse; that organizational change has moved off of the margins of the business textbook into the thinking and practice of large numbers of managers and business educators; and that it acts as an imperative rather than a dusty theory. To understand that fact we need to explore the process by which theories are accepted into practice.

It has been suggested that management education and trends in business schools are guided by the needs of managers and that this material is being written specifically for managers (Galt, 1996). Managers are cued to choose a change programme, which often has its roots in academia but has gained popularity because of the way it has been marketed by gurus and consultants. These 'merchants of meaning' (Czarniawska-Joerges, cited in Alvesson and Berg, 1992) are playing on the plausibility and retrospection properties of sensemaking by creating a need for their solution in the minds of managers.

Increasingly over the years business schools have attempted to blend with their 'business environment', focusing on 'practical business applications' and utilizing the language of the business world. This has allowed business 'gurus' to play an ever significant role, acting as a bridge between management practice and theory (Huczynski, 1993). Arguably, it is the so-called gurus who are playing the lead role in defining new ideal forms of organizations and problem-solving tactics for managers (Gerlach, cited in Clark and Salaman, 1998). But we must also examine the role of the business press and the consultancy firm.

Educators, prophets, and missionaries

Apart from the normalizing and legitimating processes of business education and management practice, there are other aspects of the process that help to encourage and 'inform' managers of the benefits of certain programmes. At one level, there are the business publications, in particular the business magazines (e.g., *Fortune*) and the 'how to' business trade books. These publications help to 'educate' managers to popular practices. Within that framework there is the so-called business 'guru' who serves to encourage and energize managers to adopt a particular change strategy. And then there are the consultants who offer their 'expertise' in the implementation of selected change programmes. To draw an analogy with religious practice, we might see the myths of organizational change as being carried forward into the heart of management thinking by educators, (i.e., business publishers), prophets (i.e., gurus) and missionaries (i.e., consultants).

Educators   Trade or business journals have become popular means to transmit the latest business education trends, e.g., the numerous books written on TQM (Deming, 1986; Juran, 1988; MacLeod, 1994; Walton, 1990). For example, in the mid-1980s a number of companies introduced culture change programmes, including Scandinavian Airlines Systems (SAS), British Airways (BA), International Business Machines (IBM),[15] and many others, and their 'successes' were heralded throughout the business press and management education. While these publications have contributed to a feeling that certain change programmes are widely practised, it is the 'how to' books (cf. Hammer, 1995; Hammer and Champy, 1993; Kanter, 1983, 1989; Kaplan and Norton, 2000; Peters and Waterman, 1982; Senge, 1999) that have been responsible for encouraging managers to engage in certain practices in the first place.

The successful adoption rate of culture change, TQM and BPR can, in part, be attributed to the marketing of such programmes through a focus on 'practical' solutions, rather than detailed theory and research findings (Alvesson and Berg, 1992). Certainly when Nova Scotia Power was reviewing bids for their culture change programme they rejected one consulting company because their proposal was too complicated. The selected consulting company was chosen, in large part, because they offered a very simple solution to the company's problems.

Prophets   Once a manager is convinced that change is an inevitable process that needs to be managed we can speculate that s/he is perceptible to plausible claims of expertise from business writers and consultants. In other words, the individual manager is cued to look for someone with the right expertise to help him or her deal with organizational change concerns. Now and then someone comes along with a theory of change that, for some reason or other, captures the imagination of a large number of practitioners. When sufficient numbers of companies have hired that 'theorist' as a consultant, when sufficient 'success' stories surface, and when large numbers of copies of his/her book have sold, that person often takes on the status of a guru. In short, it can be concluded that the business guru is someone whose works (words) are widely known, accepted and revered throughout the business community.[16] It is likely that the appeal of any particular guru lies in his/her ability to establish a plausible account of his/her achievements and to appear to speak to on-going realities. I would surmise that plausibility is established through publication (which lends an air of legitimacy), the establishment of a number of prominent consultancies (which provide normalcy, further legitimation, an association with success, and a link to both on-going and social sensemaking) and publicity (which simultaneously brings them to the attention of a wider audience and suggests that s/he is a key element within the wider reality). As Jackson (2000: 13) suggests, guru status is a social creation but it is difficult to explain what it takes to be one, or how many there are.

Arguably the sensemaking of certain change programmes was predetermined by the business gurus who made the selling of the ideas of culture change, BPR and TQM easier for the consultants through the validation of their popularity. As Legge (1996) puts it, the gurus create and redefine existing organizational problems for which they have pre-packaged solutions.

Jackson (1996) contends that gurus have played a critical role 'in expanding, shaping and legitimating the management consultancy industry'. Using simplification, gurus convince managers that change can easily occur through suggested change programmes (while not admitting that *how* change is managed can vary widely and ultimately impact on the long-term success of the programmes).[17]

Not only have these gurus made the public more aware of management ideas and organizational improvement programmes (i.e., TQM, Business Process Re-engineering, the Learning Organization) but, Jackson (1996; 2001) maintains they have generated increased business for the consultancies. These gurus have become known because of the media attention focused on them. The popularity has, in turn, made them part of the sensemaking process. Indeed, as Uzumeri (1997: 21) points out, 'managers around the world are witnessing the spread of meta standards for evaluating managerial practices' (see Table 4.3): 'ISO 9001, the meta standard document in the ISO 9000 family of quality standards, is arguably the most influential single meta standard so far'.

The elevation of these change programmes, and subsequently their founders to guru status, depends on several factors (Jackson, 2001). One, as different contexts affect the need for different types of change, the media will seek out solutions that are familiar and address the current problem (e.g., when the economy creates the need for a tightening of the corporate belt the business press searches for change techniques that will address the issue). Two, as a shift in the economy causes 'formative contexts' (Unger, 1987b) to be redefined, new change techniques gain popularity. For example, culture change was popular in the early 1980s because change was driven by a perceived need to create participative, value-laden organizations. By the mid-1980s, concepts such as TQM and re-engineering gained popularity because of a shift in the economy caused by increased privatization and competition. Three, if enough people interpret the potential of a new fad as the current panacea for organizational problems, the result will be the social construction of the guru and myths surrounding the programme.

The result of convincing organizations of the merits of a particular technique of change is interpreted as collective sensemaking (Weick, 1995), and delivers to the managers a 'processed product' ready-made and proclaimed a successful 'hot fad' (Jackson, 1996; 2001). Managers are not required at this stage to interpret the programme as successful or not, but at the individual level the organizational decision-maker (a) decides which (predetermined) hot fad is right for his or her organization, and (b) is responsible for the continuing success or failure of the fad, contingent on how it is managed and made sense of within each organization.

The managerial role, defined as the process by which one person tries to define the reality of another (Smircich and Morgan, 1982), depends on the past experience of each manager and can be similarly compared to the role of guru: 'The situation is not one where gurus *impose* meaning on managers; it is one of negotiation where gurus' success lies in reflecting and modifying managers' meanings' (Clark and Salaman, 1998: 151).

It has been suggested (Clark and Salaman, 1998; Huczynski, 1993) that the gurus' appeal is based on persuasive communication. Specifically, Clark and Salaman (1998) offer three explanations for managers' acceptance of gurus which appeals to their sensemaking process:

1   The type of work managers are doing makes them receptive to guru ideas. Managers are painted as being on the front line of change and often are compelled to seek answers from the broader environment. As Clark and Salaman (1998) state, satisfying the psychological need to predict and control makes managers more receptive to gurus' ideas. What managers often fail to see is that the same constituencies that sold them the idea of change as an imperative in the first place are the ones offering the solutions.

2   The public performances of the gurus make them attractive to individual managers. As I have argued above, fame creates its own image. Retrospective sensemaking is likely to see the prominence of a person in one context as evidence of a wider prominence in other contexts.

3   The way ideas are re-framed to make them meet the expectations of their audience. Again this is in line with my argument above that gurus are successful where they manage to frame their ideas to meet the needs of individual managers.

Whether a specific guru influenced Nova Scotia Power managers is not clear. Certainly the adopted Culture Change programme of the consulting company had no obvious association to any of the leading theorists or advocates of culture change. The company's choice of Business Process Improvement (BPI), however, can be linked to the work of H. James Harrington. The link is not direct but Harrington was, at the time, the 'International Quality Advisor' for Ernst & Young, the consulting company that introduced re-engineering at Nova Scotia Power. BPI, as opposed to BPR and the more generic 're-engineering', is Harrington's term and is used almost exclusively in Nova Scotia Power's corporate statements, as is much of the language found in Harrington's (1991) book *Business Process Improvement*, which could be found on the shelves of Nova Scotia Power senior managers. For example, Harrington (1991: 133: emphasis in the original) states that: 'Improvement of a process means changing a process to make it more effective, efficient, and adaptable. *What* to change and how to change will depend on the particular focus of the PIT [Process Improvement Team] team and the process.'

Compare this with a statement in Nova Scotia Power's second 'Effectiveness Update' newsletter (1993c):

> Process improvement refers to work processes within the Company that will be analyzed on a cross-divisional basis to ensure the efficiency of the activities and the right number of employees for the work to be done....The project team has looked at many processes and decided to concentrate initially on a few specific areas.
>
> (Nova Scotia Power, 1993c)

The jacket of Harrington's (1991) book indicates how the business guru carefully establishes plausibility. First, fear and concern immediately hit the reader: 'America is in trouble, there is no doubt about it. . . . Needless waste, impenetrable layers of bureaucracy, and circuitous routes to company goals are killing the American spirit of innovation and achievement.' Second, managers are made to feel personally responsible for the problem: 'In a nutshell we have fooled ourselves into believing that being the world's best problem solvers makes us world-class, while all it really means is that we've had the most practice, because we create the most problems for ourselves.' Third, managers are offered a simple, easy to understand and apply, solution: 'Business Process Improvement offers a no-nonsense blueprint for restructuring our antiquated "business as usual" approach.' Fourth, the solution is sold as practical: 'BPI is not an untried theory; it is a proven process.'

Fifth, the solution is sold as widely used and successful: 'Companies such as IBM, Corning Glass, and Boeing have already embraced this new approach – and seen some startling improvements.' Sixth, the company (and, by implication, Harrington) is painted as well established and successful: 'BPI is . . . a proven process developed by Ernst & Young, the world's leading professional service firm, with over 80,000 employees around the world.'

Missionaries   Consulting firms are playing an increasing role in the selling and application of change programmes (Averett, 1999; Harrington, 1991; Jackson, 1996; Kay, 1996; Schuler, 1991; Steele, 1975). It is a multi-million dollar industry that makes its living by selling expertise to companies. Consulting firms can often make tens of millions of dollars for their intervention. For example, Symmetrix, a Lexington, Massachusetts consulting firm, was paid $24 million dollars by TransAlta (an electricity company in Alberta, Canada) in the mid-1990s to help them to re-engineer the company (Kay, 1996).

Managers, having been sold on the need to initiate wide-reaching change, may feel a need to employ the expertise to help them with their project; either they are overwhelmed with other tasks or they are, in part, driven by the notion that unique solutions need unique knowledge. Abrahamson (1996) describes the techniques associated with successful consulting:

> To sustain their images as fashion setters [management consultants and educators] . . . must lead in a race (a) to sense the emergent collective preferences of managers for new management techniques, (b) to develop rhetorics that describe these techniques as the forefront of management progress, and (c) to disseminate these rhetorics back to managers . . . before other fashion setters. Fashion setters who fall behind in this race . . . are condemned to be perceived as lagging rather than leading management progress, as peripheral to the business community.
>
> (Abrahamson 1996: 264)

The idea of ready-made, available and proven successful assistance will surely be attractive to managers faced with a barrage of information convincing them of the need to initiate organizational change.

At Nova Scotia Power in the mid-1980s it was not a question of being influenced by consultants, senior managers were already convinced to pursue culture change. It was a different matter in the early 1990s with re-engineering. The company had moved into the 'Effectiveness Phase' of their Culture Change programme but, since 1989, had achieved 'only modest annual gains' (Nova Scotia Power 1994a). The company's new auditors, Ernst & Young, convinced senior management to adopt a more 'ambitious goal' (Nova Scotia Power, 1994a) by introducing BPI. Ernst & Young then acted as consultants to the new programme, being involved in several stages of development:

During February and March 1993, the executive took the first step – an assessment by a joint NSPI/Ernst & Young team of the alternatives available to reduce costs and increase organizational efficiency throughout the utility. . . . The assessment team included members of the executive, a full-time project manager, two Ernst & Young consultants, a human resources specialist and dedicated communications support. . . .

After evaluating the alternatives, the executive engaged Ernst & Young Consulting to work with the utility on the initiative. . . . As well as offering general advice during the project, Ernst & Young was to provide an independent perspective on the necessary cultural changes and the utility's progress throughout the transition. . . . Ernst & Young provided project management assistance for the initiate and facilitators for each ['cross functional'] team.

(Crawley *et al.*, 1995)

As we can see from the quotes from Harrington's (1991) book above, Ernst & Young's approach is very much in line with Abrahamson's (1996) outline of the successful technique for selling change programmes.

Theories of change and formative contexts

Roberto Unger (1987a) has developed the notion of 'formative contexts' to frame our understanding of broad socio-political influences on events. For Unger, a formative context is 'an accepted set of pragmatic (and potentially, compulsive) institutional and imaginative assumptions that guide the ways in which interests are defined and problems are approached' (Blackler, 1992a: 280). Unger contends that 'the origins of social arrangements lie in past social conflicts and the institutional and imaginative arrangements, which followed their resolution. [That such] 'formative contexts' are deep seated and pragmatic in their effects on everyday life [and] provide an implicit model of how social life should be led' (Blackler, 1992a: 283).

This means that people are influenced by structural arrangements (e.g., hierarchy) and associated ideas (e.g., the 'right' of managers to manage) that serve to frame how they make sense of a situation. For example, Champy (1995: 9–10) provides an excellent illustration of the relationship between formative context and managerial action when he states that: 'The old ways of managing no longer work. The organization charts, the compensation schemes, the hierarchies, the vertical organization, the whole tool kit of command-and-control management techniques no longer work.'

Within this statement, such things as organization charts and compensation schemes can be seen as the 'imaginative' accounts of hierarchies and command-and-control institutionalized arrangements.

Using Unger's (1987) notion of formative contexts, I would argue that the discourse of organizational change could be viewed as imaginative accounts of changing institutional arrangements. Culture change and TQM can, to a certain extent, be traced to US reactions to Japanese competitive business pressures, and re-engineering can be linked to the Thatcher–Reagan revolution and the demise of the Soviet Union.

Culture change, total quality management and Japanese competition

A lot has been written on the renewed interest in organizational culture at the beginning of the 1980s. Although interest in studying organizations from a cultural perspective started in the early 1970s (cf. Eldridge and Crombie, 1974; Pettigrew, 1979), culture change really gained widespread acceptance and interest not from the research of the academic community, but with media attention. The 27 October 1980 issue of *Business Week* played an important role in the development of an organizational culture focus by devoting a cover story to the issue. A series of best-selling books followed, including studies of Japanese culture and lessons for the US (Ouchi, 1981; Pascale and Athos, 1982).

Turner (1990) suggests several reasons for this resurgence of interest in culture, including, (a) disillusionment with rational models of formal organizations, (b) crises in Western business organizations, (c) an interest in qualitative methods of inquiry; and (d) the success of Japanese styles of management.

Towards the end of the 1970s it was becoming clear to US business leaders and educators that not only was America losing its edge as the world's leading industrial power but that the Japanese were strong competitors to US supremacy. Existing ways of managing were no longer working as well as they had. The Japanese, who were hitherto regarded with disdain in regard to their ability to produce quality goods, were out-competing US companies in the North American market. As a result of the new competitive situation, a number of US business leaders and educators perceived the Japanese as a threat and sought to understand the 'secret of their success'. They were now primed to seek out different clues to the nature of organizational success. And those clues indicated a link between organizational culture and corporate effectiveness (Ouchi, 1981).

A holistic focus on the development of employees and their sense of organization meshed with developments in Organizational Development (OD) and the Quality of Working Life (QWL) movement that gained momentum in the 1970s.[18] Drawing upon experience from Japanese firms, Ouchi (1981) proposed the idea of culture change programmes that mesh with American realities; theory 'Z' as he called it, a hybrid of Japanese practice ['type J'] and American cultural, or imaginative, arrangements ['type A']. This, among other works, contributed to the development of a range of theories of organizational culture[19] and their enactment by numerous companies (see Appendix A).

As a result of the interest in Japanese management style, attention turned to some of the outcomes of culture change, specifically issues of 'quality'.

With the 'discovery' that W. Edwards Deming, an American business educator, played a leading role in the development of Japanese techniques of quality management, US management practitioners and educators were literally able to discover their own invention! This may have helped the plausibility of the new TQM movement.

By the time Nova Scotia Power introduced a culture change programme it had become a home-grown idea, but there were indirect links with Japanese management. Nova Scotia Power was drawn to the successful changes at Florida Power & Light, and FPL, in turn, was influenced by changes made by Kansai Power in Japan[20] Some of the cues of success were drawn from FPL's winning of 'Japan's prestigious Deming Prize for Quality' (Choi and Behling, 1997: 37).

Re-engineering

If culture change and TQM were, in large part, imports that built on existing, on-going frames of sensemaking, re-engineering owes more to changing meta-discourses and practices in the US, Britain and Eastern Europe.

Thatcherism in the UK and Reaganism in the US contributed to a climate of ideas, which shifted value away from welfarism and social ownership to an enhanced focus on profitability and privatization. The collapse of the Eastern bloc gave further 'evidence' of the vitality of capitalism and the profit motive and added fuel to the idea of a global (capitalist) economy. New communication technologies added to the idea of 'globalization', as people became aware of world events almost as they happened. And if managers failed to get the point there were plenty of management educators, gurus, and consultants to warn them of the need to develop the skills of change management for the new era.

Grint (1994) argues that, despite its own claims of uniqueness, much of re-engineering is not new:

> Clearly, some of the 10 aspects involved in re-engineering are more novel than others but . . . few, if any, are actually innovations, least of all radical innovations. . . . Some of the aspects, like job enrichment, have been tried and found wanting before. Others, like team-based organizations, have been tried and appear to have had some success.
>
> (Grint, 1994: 191)

This leads Grint to ask, '[Why] should an amalgam of relatively unremarkable ideas prove to be such a winner – at least for the re-engineering consultants if not for all those firms that have been, or are being, re-engineered?' He goes on to comment that, 'In effect . . . since all the elements have been around for varying amounts of time the issue is not so much whether the elements are novel but whether the packaging, and selling of the package, is what makes re-engineering different.' Thus, according to

Grint (1994: 192), we need to concern ourselves 'less with whether the *content* of re-engineering is radically different and demonstrably superior to anything that went before (which it appears not to be . . .), and rather with *why* the package is effective in its particular envelope of space and time.'

Answering his own question, Grint (1994: 193) anticipates Weick (1995) in arguing that, 'ideas and practices have to be read as plausible by those at whom they are targeted, and for this "plausibility" to occur the ideas most likely to prevail are those that are apprehended as capturing the *zeitgeist* or 'spirit of the time".'

Grint (1994) posits that the successful selling of re-engineering rest on its ability to resonate with three crucial aspect, or 'resonances' of the times – 'cultural and symbolic resonances', 'economic and spatial resonances', and 'political and temporal resonances'. The first refers to the ability of re-engineering advocates to build on the myth of 'the American dream' while addressing the cultural fears of Japanese superiority:

> Re-engineering isn't another imported idea from Japan. . . . Re-engineering capitalizes on the same characteristics that made Americans such great business innovators. . . . Business Re-engineering, unlike management philosophies that would have 'us' like 'them', doesn't try to change the behaviour of American workers and managers. Instead, it takes advantage of American talents and unleashes American ingenuity.
>
> (Hammer and Champy, 1993, quoted in
> Grint, 1994: 194)

The second set of resonances refers to 'the recent surge in global developments that has prompted many people to question the power of the nation-state . . .' (Grint, 1994: 195). In this context

> re-engineering offers not a single solution to the problems facing business, based on developing a competitive edge in a discrete area, but a multiple solution grounded in a complex and heterogeneous strategy incorporating a whole array of ideas and materials compounded into hybrid networks.
>
> (Grint, 1994: 196)

In particular 'the alliance of supporters . . . must also include other stake-holders who were previously muted – or at least ignored. Hence, contemporary corporations must look to their employees, their customers, their suppliers and their natural environment rather than just their share-holders' (Ibid.).

The third set of resonances refers to the match between the 'radical' rhetoric of re-engineering and the rapidly changing political world that includes the fall of Soviet communism and the rise of powerful trading blocs, from an enlarged European Union, the development of the so-called Asian 'Tigers' and the advent of the North America Free Trade Agreement (NAFTA). Thus, according to Grint (1994),

> [The] fall of the 'evil empire' has freed some of the language of change, such that 'radical' change no longer implies shifts to the political left, and talk of giving power to the employees no longer embodies the failure of management and capitalism. Hence, where several prior attempts at organizational change have concentrated upon partial and very specific aspects of the organization: total quality or human resources, etc., re-engineering gains strength from its radicalism. Where they have been tried and found wanting or, even more appropriately, found wanting because they are not just partial solutions but *foreign* partial solutions, then the time is ripe for radical overhauls.
>
> (Grint, 1994: 197, emphasis in the original)

In this last regard, Grint focuses on the stance of Presidents Bush and Clinton, but we also need to look at the presidency of Ronald Reagan (and along with him, the ideological leadership of Margaret Thatcher in the UK). It was Thatcher in Britain and Reagan in the US who fundamentally changed the face of consensus, social-democratic politics that had ensued since, respectively, the first post-war Labour government in Britain, and Roosevelt's 'New Deal' era in the US (Hobsbawm, 1994). Both Thatcher and Reagan were seen as 'radical' conservatives who inflicted a major onslaught, not only on welfare state politics, but also on welfare state thinking. In short, over time they encouraged a new discourse of 'anti-state, anti-welfare self-reliance'. As Margaret Thatcher was to express it, 'There is no society, only individuals' (quoted in Hobsbawm, 1994: 337).

The new discourse, with its emphasis on efficiency and profitability, and a stress on global competition, encouraged change across business and within the health system and government service agencies. In the UK this was accompanied by widespread 'privatization' in which employees and managers in state-owned companies found themselves facing new challenges and pressing changes. In the US a series of 'deregulations' forced a number of companies into new, uncertain areas of competition (e.g., the airline industry).

In many ways the language of re-engineering resonated with the new discourse by challenging long-held notions about the workplace, particularly the notion of job rights and tenure. In the new, re-engineered workplace the focus is on the process rather than the personnel. The new workplace has to be retrained or replaced. This is captured well in Michael Champy's (1990) phrase, 'Don't automate, obliterate'. Re-engineering certainly fit the new discourse with its language of radical change towards a new, more efficient capitalism.

Nova Scotia Power, Canadian sensibilities and the discourse of radical change

In Canada, while some of the elements of Reaganism/Thatcherism did not take hold, by and large Canadian businesses and not-for-profit organizations got caught up in influences from both the US, its powerful geographic neighbour, and the UK, one of its two founding nations. At the national level the signing of the North American Free Trade Agreement in December 1992 had a profound influence on the Canadian economy and business environment (Hurtig, 1992), fuelling the notion of global competition. In the process building up to the agreement, the Federal Government, and a number of provincial governments, took steps to privatize Crown Corporations, among them Air Canada at the federal level and Nova Scotia Power at the provincial level. A period of deregulation is still underway and many of the new business models (i.e., TQM, BPR) have been applied to a range of health-care (Armstrong *et al.*, 1997) and municipal organizations, including museums, libraries, etc. (cf. Townley *et al.* 1998).

Looking at Nova Scotia Power's decision to adopt re-engineering in 1993, it is not hard to see the 'resonances' with local realities. As a Canadian company, Nova Scotia Power certainly did not buy into any notion of an American dream, but the selling of its new image, following privatization and the introduction of re-engineering self-consciously linked competitiveness to Canadian images of excellence. For example, the 1993 Annual Report adopted the slogan, 'To Be The Best', and used the example of 'six of Nova Scotia's successful young athletes' to illustrate the company's philosophy and strengths (Nova Scotia Power, 1994a). The same feeling is generated by Crawley *et al.*'s (1995: 33) description of the adoption of re-engineering:

> It's no secret that Canadian companies have recently had to face a seemingly endless catalogue of woes . . . [But] Nova Scotia Power Inc. is one company that successfully turned adversity into advantage by transforming itself, and its culture, one process at a time.

In regard to 'economic and spatial resonances', the situation at Nova Scotia Power prior to re-engineering perfectly reflects Grint's (1994) comments about a perceived need for a focus on customers, employees, suppliers, and the environment. If that complexity of operation is indeed a prerequisite for re-engineering then Nova Scotia Power could not have been more receptive.

Finally, here was a company that had been a Crown Corporation for more than seventy-five years. In 1992, it was suddenly faced with privatization and a planned deregulation of the industry. It is no surprise that it was receptive to a model of change that promised radical change and the wherewithal to achieve competitiveness and profitability.

In brief, within the emerging discourse of radical change, managers in private and government-owned companies alike faced new emphases on their abilities to achieve high levels of efficiency and customer service. This was particularly dramatic in government-run companies unused to focusing on productivity, efficiency and the notion of the 'bottom line'. In case after case, management in these companies looked for appropriate mechanisms of change as they prepared for privatization and deregulation.[21] Utility companies like Nova Scotia Power were no longer guaranteed a monopolistic hold over electricity, and competition became more of a concern than employees' well-being. Consequently, the implicit assumptions of the earlier, piecemeal and employee-focused notion of change were no longer valid. Instead, companies sought solutions that promised them a way to overcome their problems.

Stories of failure

Examination of the popularity of change programmes suggests that managers are influenced in their enactive sensemaking by the formative context in which their companies are located ('ongoing and retrospective sensemaking'); isomorphic pressures that include the appearance of widespread acceptance of change programmes ('social sensemaking'); and the development, selling and rhetoric of change stories ('plausibility' and 'identity construction').

Examination of stories of why organizational change programmes fail suggests that a discourse of change, and the associated pressures, obscures the socially constructed character of change programmes and the role of sensemaking in their adoption and implementation. The problem of sensemaking is evident in most if not all of the major issues that have been identified as the key failings of organizational change programmes.

Leadership and top management attitudes

Choi and Behling (1997), among others,[22] root the failure of change programmes in the attitudes of top management. They argue that

> even though the most respected authorities on TQM have long argued that top management's leadership is key to TQM's success or failure. ... [It is] top managers' underlying, often unspoken, orientations towards time, market, and customers [that] affect the nature of their firms' TQM programs.
>
> (Choi and Behling, 1997: 37)

Using the three elements of time, market and customer orientation, Choi and Behling (1997) come up with three archetypes of management attitude – developmental, tactical and defensive. In their study of six US-owned companies that had 'implemented some TQM practices', Choi and Behling (1997) found that,

Of the 21 TQM-related practices we identified . . . about 15 were in use in the developmental orientation, compared with about five TQM practices in the company with the defensive orientation [and 6 to 14] at the companies with the tactical orientation. . . . Thus, the top managers with developmental orientation were associated with the most active TQM program, whereas those with the defensive orientation to TQM made the least use of TQM.

(Choi and Behling, 1997: 43)

Top managers are influenced by how they make sense of a particular change programme, and this can influence the outcomes. What Choi and Behling (1997) fail to see is that managers may not be able to reorient their thinking in order to successfully manage TQM or any other change programme; that change may require further analysis of the sensemaking framework and cues available. Certainly, to understand events at Nova Scotia Power we need, as I have argued above, to understand something about the sensemaking and the formative contexts of senior managers involved.

Change programmes and non-sense

Becker (1993) argues that one of the reasons for the apparent failure of change programmes is that some companies introduce 'poor substitutes' that are marketed under the label of TQM (or BPR). In a classic piece of circular logic, Becker (1993) argues that companies with successful TQM programmes 'are doing something right, something we call TQM. Those who fail are doing something wrong'. What appear to be failures of TQM, he contends, are often a mishmash of activities that a company has mistakenly called TQM.

It could also be argued, of course, that companies that are associated with successful implementations of TQM or BPR may also be doing something other than TQM and BPR. O'Mahoney and Newell (1998), for example, found that a number of British companies (successful or otherwise),

which claim to be implementing BPR have generally located their re-engineering package within a holistic organizational change programme [which include] quality standards, de-layering, training programmes, and a strategic shift [that] not only encompass and distort the process of re-engineering, but often are so incorporated with it, that it becomes impossible to identify the BPR programme in an unadulterated form.

(O'Mahoney and Newell, 1998)

One way or another, this suggests that how managers (and others) make sense of a series of activities can influence the outcome of their selection and implementation. When we analyse the change activities of Nova Scotia Power in the next chapters it should be clear that it is questionable whether they implemented either culture change or BPI, and this has implications for how the outcomes are judged.

Attitudes to change

Different types of attitude 'problems' are noted in the literature, including employee failure to change attitude, a gulf between expectations and reality, employee resistance, employee fear of layoffs and workplace disruption, differences in attitudinal direction and cynicism. Duck (1998: 55), for example, argues that, 'companies are full of "change survivors," people who have learned to live through change programs without actually changing'. The problem is 'that managers need a new way of thinking about managing change in today's knowledge organization'. She suggests that, 'Instead of breaking change into small pieces – TQM, process re-engineering, employee empowerment – and then managing these pieces, managers need to think in terms of overseeing a dynamic' (Ibid.)

Doyle (1992) contends that change programmes often fail because managers and employees alike may be led to expect results in a short space of time; and that when those results don't materialize as quickly as expected companies sometimes abandon the programme (in part or in whole). At Nova Scotia Power there was some recognition by management that culture change would take a long period of time to achieve, but that recognition was often missing from the comments of employees who appeared to expect faster results. Numerous people that I interviewed stated that even after three years they could not detect any change, and had clearly expected to do so. In some other cases, employees expressed the view that culture change was too long-term and thus not worth their time and effort. As one instrument technician expressed it: '[We're] not all convinced in change. [We've] spent years on courses teaching the complete opposite. Younger people will affect change.'

On occasion the sensemaking of a number of employees coheres into active resistance. According to one commentator, major change efforts often fail because 'executives and employees see change differently'. 'For senior managers, change means opportunity – both for the business and for themselves. But for many employees, change is seen as disruptive and intrusive' (Strebel, 1998: 139). Strebel contends that the solution lies in managers reconsidering their employees' 'personal compacts' or 'the mutual obligations and commitments that exist between employees and the company'. Strebel recognizes a gap in the sensemaking between managers and employees but makes the mistake of assuming that all managers concur in their understanding of events and that all employees concur in their viewpoint. As Choi and Behling (1997) indicate, managers differ in their orientations to time, market and customers. Certainly, at Nova Scotia Power managers differed among themselves, as did employees.

According to Reichers *et al.* (1997: 48), employee cynicism is often 'a response to a history of change attempts that are not entirely or clearly successful'. It is not really surprising in such cases that employees fear job loss (Doyle, 1992) and workplace disruption (Strebel, 1998). Despite arguments to the contrary, certain change programmes, particularly BPR, have become associated with downsizing (*New York Times*, 1996). At Nova Scotia Power a level of cynicism could be detected as people were first sold on the idea of an employee-centred culture and then asked to change gears as the company privatized and introduced a process and profit-centred re-engineering. The situation was not helped by a series of layoffs and a steadily reduction in workforce numbers.

All these studies of attitudinal problems, I would argue, point out the importance of sensemaking in the development of plausible change strategies. A failure to understand and deal with potential sensemaking differences can, with the introduction of change programmes, raise, rather than address, organizational difficulties.

Problems with application

Another major area of concern for the advocates of change programmes is the problems associated with design and implementation. Hammer and Champy (1993), for example, have argued that it is not their theory of re-engineering that has so patently failed but the way that managers have applied it. Schaffer and Thompson (1998: 189), argue that many programmes fail because 'management focuses on the activities, not the results':

> By initiating activities-centered programs, such as seven-step problem solving, statistical process control, and total quality management training, management falsely assume that one-day results will materialize. But because there is no explicit connection between action and outcome, improvements seldom do materialize.

The authors argue, instead, for a 'results-driven' programme.

Other theorists associate the failure of change programmes with such things as inadequate training (Holpp, 1989), a failure of management 'to appreciate the complexity of the changes involved or to understand the organization's missions, goals, and objectives' (Choi and Behling, 1997: 38).

Again, these issues speak to sensemaking. There is clearly a gap between theories and implementation of change programmes; between the theorists' vision of change and the contexts in which particular practitioners are operating. The 'theory' of culture change implemented by Nova Scotia Power was very much diluted by the way the idea was interpreted by the consultants and then, in turn, by the company's senior managers. The consultants were influenced by what had worked for previous clients. Nova Scotia Power managers were influenced by their need to deal with specific problems of low morale and political unpopularity. 'Success' and 'measurement', despite the view of Schaffer and Thompson (1998), are also sensemaking issues. In both cases, it can be argued that a focus on activities or on results can be linked to success or failure depending, in part, on the way either is defined. It is an issue of plausibility rather than accuracy. Nova Scotia Power managers were able to claim that their culture change was a 'success' by focusing on how well the key values were practised, and that re-engineering was a success by focusing on, at times, the processes, and, at times, the increasing ratio between employees and customers. In regard to training there is some evidence that the early culture change workshops were ill-thought out and nearly derailed the process in Nova Scotia Power's Cape Breton region. And, finally, the culture change phase at Nova Scotia Power is a good illustration of a programme that was too simplistic to deal with a complex series of problems, while the re-engineering phase is an illustration of the problems associated with the introduction of a programme that runs counter to existing goals.

Despite the numerous failures associated with culture change, TQM, and BPR, in each case the stories are told in a way that does not undermine the basic premise. Most stories of failure manage to maintain the myth that change is imperative and one or other change programme can save the day; the problem is with how it is carried out, not in its essential theory. Perhaps that is why companies continue to adopt and implement such programmes in the face of known problems.

Problems with traditional models of change

Over time the management of change has developed as a discourse that focuses on several key stages or elements of change. There is, of course, some disagreement on how to approach the study of the management of change but the dominant model focuses on issues of adoption, implementation and outcomes.

For example, the starting point of the traditional model of change is a functionalist 'real' approach, while the management of change discourse is normally broken into three distinct areas; action research, group dynamics and attitude change (Cooke, 1999). Each addresses a different element of the change process. Action research focuses on the relationship between the change agent and organizational members, group dynamics considers the socio-psychological processes of organizational members, and attitude change is, as Cooke (1999) says, 'synonymous with organizational culture'.

The notion of the inevitability of change promotes the idea of change for change's sake. Employees are reeling from all the new fads in management techniques and it is so confusing that, according to Howes (1994), the fads are actually slowing down change because employees are getting tired of quick fixes. (One employee at Nova Scotia Power said, following the introduction of culture change, that there had been a different change about every five years, so why should he believe this was going to be the right one.) Despite this, new change programmes continue to be introduced and heralded as the 'ultimate solution'. And organizational culture, which targets employees' value systems, becomes either a direct or indirect focus of all change techniques.

Examination of traditional theories of change indicate that their ability to influence practice lies in their ultimate simplicity and the fact that they fit within perceived knowledge.[23] Lewin's model offers a classic example of a simple idea whereby change involves 'unfreezing' employee attitudes to performance, changing those ideas and then fixing (or 'refreezing') them. The assumption is that attitudes can be uniformly held, changed and reformulated: change is an entity that can be understood and thereby managed.

One of the most common means of studying the management of change and assessing its success is to measure how well employees have adapted change policies and procedures. Usually, at this stage it is too late to correct errors that have occurred in the implementation or lack of success. Selecting a change programme does not guarantee it will be consistently understood and enacted by all managers, or that employees will interpret and act upon the rules set by the managers.

While current models offer a piecemeal explanation for 'successfully' implementing change, these ideas do not adequately account for psycho-sociological forces which impact on the decision-maker's desire to 'fad surf' (i.e., an organization's willingness to adopt the latest in managerial trends, Jackson, 2001). Clark and Salaman (1998) state that satisfying the psychological need to predict and control makes managers more receptive to gurus' ideas, but this does not explain why some change techniques are more appealing than others, despite evidence that they are, for the most part, not successful. Nor does it explain how some organizations are more or less successful with change.

By the mid-1980s, because of the different focuses of the change literature, organizations had became divided over the issue of who the change processes were serving. Management often appeared unaware that changing one part of the organization (e.g., focusing on customer service or quality control) was ultimately changing the underlying philosophy of the entire organization and downplaying the importance of the employee. The very simplicity of change theories made it not only easier for management to grasp and apply but gave the appearance of a relatively easy solution to a complex problem.

Ultimately, a major drawback of the traditional models of change is a failure to address the lack of longitudinal research on change. Little has been written about organizations that have 'failed' and why. While Keidel's (1994) 'organizational cognition' approach appears to come close to an understanding of organizational change that takes into account the way people think and communicate in the development of organizational design, it still assumes that individuals share similar values and understandings and does not recognize that problems can occur with people's understanding. The solution is seen in managers learning how to understand and manage the employees' meaning of change. Through this management of meaning, therefore, employees will come to the same understanding. However, Keidel's (1994) approach, on closer examination, despite the use of 'familiar' terms (i.e., 'framing') – fails to contextualize 'thinking' and 'communication', focusing more on a rationalized framework (i.e., an assumed ideal, and shared framework) that fails to get beneath the surface of thinking and communicating in context. (This was problematized by events at Nova Scotia Power, which demonstrated that despite attempts to give the same meaning to four corporate values, even those who agreed with them in principle understood them differently.)

Some thoughts on change

To begin with, the notion that organizational change is a real and pressing issue can blind managers to their own primary role in the decision-making process. Some organizations have survived by resisting the urge to change, or by arguing that change will unacceptably alter its fundamental character (e.g., the Catholic Church). In the case of Nova Scotia Power, it is arguable whether the introduction of re-engineering actually helped or hindered organizational effectiveness.

Second, giving in to an imperative to change can lead to a 'garbage can' approach to managing (Cohen *et al.*, 1972), where change is adopted as a solution to a non-existent problem. The classic example is the 1985 decision by Coca-Cola executives to launch 'New Coke' on the mistaken assumption that consumers were tired of the old Coke (Oliver, 1986). Arguably, Nova Scotia Power's adoption of re-engineering was a solution to an over-exaggerated concern with competition. Seven years after privatization and six years after the introduction of re-engineering Nova Scotia Power still retains a monopoly over electricity supply in the province of Nova Scotia.

Third, the belief that organizational change is in any event desirable can discourage examination of important consequences. Certainly a change in the mandate of NATO helped that organization to survive beyond its original and now defunct purpose. But it is questionable whether that is ultimately something that benefits humanity. At Nova Scotia Power the introduction of re-engineering following a culture change programme can be linked to improvements such as the ability of employees to handle greater numbers of customers but similarly it can be linked to downsizing and a decreasing number of employees.

Fourth, despite a well-reasoned rationale for change, a change programme can be selected because of its popularity rather than its mesh with the identified problem. Arguably, the adoption of TQM and BPR by a number of North American hospitals has led to a mismatch between the philosophies and concerns of health care and the underlying philosophies and concerns of production-oriented change programmes (Armstrong *et al.*, 1997; Hospitals, 1992). The same can be argued about Nova Scotia Power's adoption of re-engineering. A perceived need to improve efficiency within a developing 'humanistic' culture was met with the adoption of a programme that in fundamental ways clashed with the established values.

Fifth, an assumed or desired unity of organizational beliefs can ignore the role of divergent perceptions in the process of change, or the fact that human cognition and competing notions are at the heart of change process. Nova Scotia Power's problems with its Cape Breton employees during the period of culture change training, for example, suggests that the common experience of training, rather than acceptance of the values may have gone some way to avoiding conflict.

In the next two chapters I will explore some of these issues in detail, through a strategic application of Weick's (1995) model of organizational sensemaking.

5 Sensemaking and identity construction

Since organizational activity is lived in nine-minute bursts . . . people seldom have time to reflect on what the bursts mean. When culture and strategy are intact, they don't have to. But when cultures rupture, and bursts lose their meaning, that is when we realize that 'good managers make meanings for people, as well as money'. . . . There is no shortage of attention to money. Unfortunately, the same cannot be said for meaning. That is why the concept of culture is significant.

(Weick, 1985b: 388)

Introduction

In the previous chapter a number of problems were identified with the process of change management, and some key observations were made. In particular it was contended that managers need to understand that organizational change is socially constructed, that actors make sense of change in different ways, and that this has consequences for the adoption and application of specific change programmes. In other words, whether the culture of an organization 'ruptures', or organizational 'bursts' lose their meaning may depend on the ability of managers to 'make meanings for people'.

In the next chapter, Karl Weick's (1995) properties of organizational sensemaking are applied to the process of change at Nova Scotia Power to reveal what we would expect to see in the change process, to uncover some of the problems of organizational change, in order to understand the management of change, and to show the strengths and limitations of Weick's approach itself.

Although it was generally felt throughout the company that the impetus for change was synonymous with Louis Comeau, and that his leadership style was responsible for Nova Scotia Power's journey into change, not all employees viewed the changes in the same way as Comeau. For example, while employees in mainland Nova Scotia agreed with the direction that Comeau was taking, most of the resistance to change came from the Cape Breton employees. Yet during the re-engineering phase resistance was mainly covert and seemed to resonate from those employees not actively involved in the decision-making processes, yet directly affected by them.

This suggests that identity construction, in combination with other factors such as time and levels of involvement, affected how employees perceived Nova Scotia Power's change processes. Therefore, an in-depth analysis of the identity construction of these various actors provides a useful way to analyse the different responses, in order to try and understand how different meaning is attached to the same experiences and how particular events are more important for some than others. For these reasons, it is useful to take a chronological approach to the property of identity construction, rather than focus only on one actor or one key event. Different influences on identity construction, over time, show how this differentiation occurs and what role it plays in sensemaking. Once the origins of identity are understood, the use of the other sensemaking properties falls into place.

In this chapter, therefore, the relationship between identity construction, leadership style, the management of change and the interpretation of its meaning, will be explored by focusing on three sets of sensemakers at Nova Scotia Power – senior management, in particular Louis Comeau, and employees, from both Cape Breton and mainland locations. It is the influence of identity construction on the sensemaking of Louis Comeau and his employees that had the greatest impact on Nova Scotia Power's change programme.

Identity construction and the management of change

According to Weick (1995), an important aspect of sensemaking is the individual actor's need for affirmation, that a person will be influenced in a 'reading' of events by what light this shines on his or her sense of being. In simple terms we can say that people see what they want to see. As Weick (1995) argues, this is not as facile as it seems. It is a mundane aspect of the process of making sense that needs to be foregrounded to understand the problems of organizational change.

Weick's discussion of sensemaking and identity construction bridges (modernist) theories of cognitive psychology, with references to real psychological 'needs', and post-modernist accounts of subjectivity, with references to discursive practices. In the former case, Weick grounds his approach in a process account of identity construction that relies on three main areas of 'need'. Drawing on the work of Erez and Earley, Weick (ibid.: 20) contends that a 'person's changing sense of self' is rooted in (a) the need for self-enhancement, (b) the self-efficacy motive to perceive oneself as competent and efficacious, and (c) the need for self-consistency. We may note here that Weick acknowledges the existence of a somewhat established self, i.e., something that serves as a reference point for 'self-consistency'. Nonetheless, his main focus is on a 'changing sense of self' which references the post-modernist notion that a person's sense of self, or subjectivity, develops and thus changes through involvement in discursive practices. Here Weick (ibid.: 18, 20) quotes Knorr-Cetina's notion of the individual as 'a typified discursive construction', and Mead's contention that an individual is 'a parliament of selves'. Putting this in an organizational context, Weick is interested in the influence of the process of identity construction on decision-making.

This is interesting for the management of change in that individual sense-makers have the potential to arrive at very different senses of a situation and to develop, support or reject decisions based on their own identity needs. It provides an important clue to organizational conflict and resistance to change, but also to the potential for the development of inter-subjective meaning, i.e., where 'individual thoughts, feelings, and interactions are merged or synthesized into conversations during which the self gets transformed from "I" into "we"' (Weick, ibid.: 71). Here in a nutshell we have the dichotomy between the notion of the individual self and that of the social self discussed in Chapter 3.

But what does this tell us about meaning and the management of organizational change? On the surface it suggests that an organization may be in trouble when different senses of a situation come into conflict. For example, where managers see differentiated training (i.e., one-day versus four-day training sessions) as a legitimate way to achieve value change, while employees view it as a new form of inequity. The result is a breakdown in the change process. On the other hand, there is a strong argument within the management literature to suggest that an absence of conflicting notions can, as in the phenomenon of 'groupthink' (Janis, 1971) for example, also be problematic for organizational decision-making. This suggests that the real problem may lie with making sensemakers conscious of the process of sensemaking rather than the direction the sensemaking takes. For example, had the consulting firm encouraged managers to be aware of their own sense-making and the sensemaking of others they may have been able to predict – and thus avoid – conflict over training. Some employees may have continued to feel that culture change was a new form of management manipulation but the absence of certain cues (e.g., differentiated training schedules) may have undermined the emotional content of resistance.

Weick's (1995) discussion of identity construction also suggests that the 'successful' transformation of an organization's culture may depend upon the extent to which each individual's sense of self can be positively experienced through a sense of organization. In terms of organizational change this is open to different interpretations. There are those who may interpret this to mean that unified organizational cultures depend on shared values and beliefs (cf. Schein, 1985). Certainly, Weick's (1995) notion of inter-subjectivity seems to lend itself to the idea of shared beliefs, if not values. He seems almost to suggest that 'inter-subjective meaning' depends on a transformation of self through adoption or negotiation of a collective sense of meaning. This idea of a collective sense of organization is central to a number of theories of organizational culture (e.g., Deal and Kennedy, 1982; Ouchi, 1981; Peters and Waterman, 1983).

Yet, elsewhere in his discussion of identity, Weick (1995) appears to resist the notion of shared beliefs, substituting instead shared experiences as the dynamic for a shared sense of organization. For example, a group of people may disagree on what it is they are trying to achieve but their involvement in a common set of activities may result in a particular outcome. The problem here is that the term 'experience' implies meaning, implying some shared or agreed sense of a situation. Thus, I would argue, the significance of identity construction for organizational change depends on the ability of the actors involved to achieve a shared sense of experience that, at the very least, does not threaten the individuals' sense of self. To return to the example of differentiated training, the provision of training sessions that were uniform in duration may not have led to a unified belief in the new culture programme but could have provided the cues for a sense of shared experience and a related sense of training equity.

Another area where the property of identity construction may help to identify potential problems in the management of change revolves around the adoption and assessment of change programmes. The objectification of the change process may discourage self-awareness and discussion of self-interest. This can be psychologically problematic for individual managers and employees alike, and financially problematic for organizations (see Chiaramonte and Mills, 1993; Kets de Vries, 1980, 1989a, 1989b, 1991; Kets de Vries and Miller, 1986). For example, a process of change management may be embarked upon unnecessarily (e.g., the change from 'classic' to 'New Coke'; see Oliver, 1986). Did Louis Comeau have to adopt a culture change programme?

A change programme may be adopted more because it is suited to the sensemaking of the leader than the demands of the organization (e.g., the curious twists and turns of TWA (Trans World Airways) under the leadership of Howard Hughes – see Dietrich, 1972; Rummel, 1991; Serling, 1983). Was the consultant's model of culture change appropriate for Nova Scotia Power's needs?

The success or failure of a change programme may depend more on the identity needs of senior managers than actual results (e.g., ten years after the fact, there is still controversy about the outcome of the Gulf War). When Louis Comeau claimed that culture change (and re-engineering) had been successful, how much was based on actual outcomes and how much on his need to identify with a successful career?

Identity construction and Louis Comeau

Therefore, why and how was change introduced at Nova Scotia Power? To answer these questions, sensemaking theory, in large part, directs us to the actions of senior managers who 'construct, rearrange, single out and demolish many "objective" features of their surroundings' (Weick, 1979: 243). The perceptions of top managers plays an important role in identifying a need for change, and specific change programmes (Child, 1972; Choi and Behling, 1997). The chief executive in particular often plays a significant role in the creation of an organization's culture (cf. Schein, 1985; Trice and Beyer, 1984, 1993), or 'level of social reality' (Weick, 1995: 71), and yet is not always aware of the role of identity construction in the process.

To the extent that this is true, we may be able to gauge the outcomes of change through an understanding of the sensemaking of Louis Comeau. As Kets de Vries argues (Kets de Vries, 1989; Kets de Vries and Miller, 1986), an important starting point for management is recognition of self in the process. As I have argued above, Louis Comeau's identity construction is threaded throughout the change strategies adopted in the name of Nova Scotia Power. As we review how Comeau dealt with the shocks we gain more insights into the strengths and limitations of Weick's (1995) sensemaking model.

Factors influencing Comeau's identity construction

In addition to the influence of current management trends and practices, Louis Comeau's sensemaking was grounded in an identity premised on several different formative roles, including residency in a small Acadian village, former Federal Member of Parliament, former university president, being a political appointee and CEO of a major Canadian corporation, and, eventually, assuming the role of charismatic leader. Over time these positions shaped his understanding and interpretation of Nova Scotia Power's journey into change and the management of the process.

When he took over as President of Nova Scotia Power, Comeau had little experience in running a large-scale organization. In many ways he was forced to rely on previous experiences (cf. Weick, 1996), a sense of the political requirements of the job, and an understanding of how other large corporations were being run. To that extent his leadership style was influenced by experiences (i.e. university president; MP, etc.) which required him to establish a rapport with his constituency by gaining trust and an understanding of people's expectations. At Nova Scotia Power, Comeau was, from the beginning, interested in the pulse of the organization. He actively sought out the opinion of employees. Early on Comeau sought to resolve the uncertainty and ambiguity created by Nova Scotia Power's recent mergers by becoming familiar with the issues that would face him as head of the company.

From the beginning, in the process of travelling throughout the province to meet with employees and hear their concerns, Comeau established a reputation as a charismatic leader: 'He sought input and opinions of his employees through questionnaires and the values came from this' (supervisor, Lingan, Cape Breton). It was during these meetings that he came to the realization that a major attitude problem existed, which was reflected in low morale throughout most of the company. While there were various ways that solutions to this perceived problem could have been interpreted, Comeau's sensemaking was framed by his prior experience in the public sector, his desire to get along with people, and the knowledge that he had been appointed by the Conservative Government in the hope of straightening out the troubled public utility. As such, his values were centred round creating a 'family-like' environment which would stress the 'humanization' of the organization while, at the same time, meeting the needs of his government employers, and allowing him to be seen as on the cutting edge of the latest management trends.

In the first instance, it would appear that Comeau was faced with a situation of low morale that he needed to solve, that he then looked around for solutions to his 'problem' and discovered 'culture change' as an answer. Using the sensemaking approach a different story is uncovered. It is clear that, from the beginning, Comeau was appointed to turn the company into one that would overcome certain political perceptions about its operation. When Comeau took over the company in 1983 the Conservative Government of the day was concerned that Nova Scotia Power was not only a drain on the financial resources of the province but that it was also unpopular with the public, and that both could result in votes against the Party (Bruce, 1991; Jobb, 1994). Thus, arguably, Comeau started his appointment as President with a particular view of the company he needed to achieve: he had, in Weick's (1995) terms, 'invented' a particular reality – an ideal view of the company and of its problems:

> I told the government right off the bat that my objective was to make this self-sufficient. We had to run this as a business – as a business with some public purpose. A Crown corporation has to have a public purpose.
>
> (Comeau, quoted in Bruce, 1991)

Comeau's vision involved a notion of a hybrid organization that combined elements of the private (i.e., a self-sufficient business) and the public (i.e., public purpose) sector. It was an image of a company that should somehow balance those two elements and, in the process, appeal to the public.

Part of this invention was a developing notion that the existing 'unpopularity' of the company had internal consequences in the form of 'low morale'. This 'shock' to expectations encouraged Comeau to commission an attitude survey, which eventually revealed a situation of low morale that was widespread throughout the company. This further shock was in fact a perfect example of what Weick (1995) means by 'discovering your own invention'; Louis Comeau had developed (i.e., constructed, invented) the idea of low morale, and commissioned a survey that consequently 'discovered' low morale. Simply put, people make sense of things by seeing a world on which they have already imposed what they believe (Weick, 1995: 15).

As Comeau sought to make sense of the 'evidence' of low morale, he saw it as a threat to his vision of the financially self-sufficient, but politically popular Crown Corporation. In attempting to deal with the problem he 'discovered' culture change as a solution. This solution was again informed by Comeau's own invented sense of the organization, which, in turn, owed much to the formative context in which he operated – including political pressures, a broad discourse of management change, and organizational rules shaped by the nature of Crown Corporations.

The 'discovery' of poor morale was grounded in an identity which satisfied his need to play up the humanization aspects of change and choose a change programme that was both timely and people oriented. With the adoption of the Culture Change programme, it was clear to a number of people that Comeau was very much identified with it. To some extent culture change and Louis Comeau became synonymous:

> It all started with Louis Comeau. There's no doubt in my mind about that whatsoever.
>
> (Jim Woods, Nova Scotia Power, 1990/1991)

> The idea (for culture change) came from open meetings with Louis Comeau.
>
> (Customer service representative, Halifax)

> [In regard to culture change] Louis Comeau has his finger on the pulse of the company.
>
> (supervisor, Milton Zone Office)

However, with a growing emphasis being placed on the notion of competition, and with the advent of privatization, Comeau experienced cognitive dissonance as the decisions he made as President were being influenced by new ways of understanding. In a 1994 interview, Comeau admitted 'a decade ago a monopoly power utility paid scant attention to the idea of competition' (Nova Scotia Power, 1994a). Prior to Nova Scotia Power's privatization, the identity that guided his decision making (as President of a Crown Corporation) was grounded in an understanding of competition as a non-threatening factor to Nova Scotia Power's survival. At the time, the government had placed little restriction on how he chose to run the company. Comeau was, therefore, able to place competition secondary to the social well-being of his employees and implement change that was activity rather than results oriented.

Despite this, five years after the culture change, Comeau, in keeping with the times, was claiming success of a new kind, anticipating improvements from the introduction of re-engineering. Although the introduction of a programme of downsizing in a former Crown Corporation raised questions about the viability of a culture change programme focused on 'commitment to employees', the switch from culture change to re-engineering entailed a switch in Comeau's sense of self, in order to sustain a coherent reading of events.

Here Comeau linked self and programme in a number of ways. He called the programme 'innovative' which, by implication, shed light on his own 'cutting edge' leadership style. In several places he referenced the cultural climate as the basis of future success and, in so doing, indexed his own role in the Culture Change programme:

> In November of the past year, we introduced our Strategic Business Plan entitled 'To Be The Best'. The Plan is the result of considerable hard work and innovative thinking. Its objectives are challenging but not complex. . . . The climate at Nova Scotia Power is right for such an initiative. In 1995 we shall see concrete examples of our ability to produce results in the short term, as well as the long term. . . . There is a great new sense of mission that binds all areas of the company and all who work at Nova Scotia Power into one determined and energetic team. Our common goal is this: *'To be the most effective energy company in Canada, providing the best possible level of customer satisfaction and shareholder value'*.
>
> (President's Message, Nova Scotia Power,
> 1996a: emphasis in the original)

The result was that his earlier desire to humanize the face of Nova Scotia Power clashed with the perceived need to make it more cost effective, as a means of addressing competition. In order to reduce this dissonance, he made sense of these issues by placing himself in the role of politician, taking on the provincial government viewpoint. In this way, Comeau started to reframe his understanding of competition, and in this context he viewed it as a key element of the company's future viability and success. Once Comeau became committed to the plausibility of using competition as an engine of change, he sought cues to support this understanding and disregarded or re-interpreted those which posed a threat to his sensemaking.

With the introduction of re-engineering, Comeau found himself trying to rationalize differences between old and new change techniques and his values. His objective as President of a newly privatized company, was to find a change technique that would satisfy the needs of Nova Scotia Power's stakeholders and meet the demands placed on his company by increased competition. Yet at the same time, his understanding of BPI was also influenced by multiple identities that were constructed around his roles in government, in business, in academe and by his personal values. Often these different influences worked against each other to affect his interpretation of how re-engineering would be implemented.

In 1993, when asked why Nova Scotia Power had chosen re-engineering, Comeau's response indicated his awareness of the importance of competition in framing the way they did business:

> Companies cannot survive by simply doing what they have always been doing in the past. It's just too competitive. We've got to consider the

90's customer. . . . [If] we want to meet the needs of our customers, we've got to do it together. That means eliminating bureaucracy and developing skills that will ensure that Nova Scotia Power operations are efficient and effective. BPI is an essential part of Nova Scotia Power's continued success.

(Nova Scotia Power, 1993d)

Still, the principles of re-engineering contravened the identity which Comeau had tried to establish as a concerned leader. The possibility of massive lay-offs created a dissonance for Comeau that he found difficult to accept. Early on, he revealed this uncertainty at a meeting of BPI team members and the consultants, where he expressed concern about the effects restructuring procedures would have on worker isolation, productivity and performance. Although he was able to rationalize this by stating that he believed employees would feel that the changing job content still fit in with the original values (Core Team Meeting notes, 25 January 1994), he remained relatively detached from the BPI processes. His participation was limited, mainly to attendance at Core Team Meetings and membership of the 'Effectiveness Steering Committee', where his role was more nominal than active.[1] By the time the first of the major lay-offs was announced, Comeau, who was visibly upset by the outcome, still made sense of the lay-offs as being a necessary part of successful re-engineering (Conversation with Louis Comeau, July 1994).

The influence of Comeau's sense of self and evaluation of change programmes is evident throughout corporate pronouncements on the company's 'successful' progress over the years. For example, in 1990 Comeau informed shareholders that he was,

particularly grateful for, and proud of, the efforts made by our employees in maintaining our corporate values – our customers, our environment, our employees and our province. This annual report highlights just some of the examples of the contributions made by Nova Scotia Power employees to the overall benefit of Nova Scotia.

(President's Report, Nova Scotia Power, 1990a)

During the changes, examination of Comeau's cited examples, suggest that organizational outcomes were (a) selectively read; (b) potentially the result of factors beyond the control of management, and (c) nonetheless, framed in a way that reflected favourably on company management, in particular, Louis Comeau, the man most associated with culture change. Comparing the company's performance in 1990 with 1989, there was a 2.06 per cent increase in the number of customers, the ratio of employees to customer increased from 1:155 to 1:156.8 (see Figure 5.1), net income improved $32 million over the previous year (see Figure 5.2) and revenue increased $52 million.

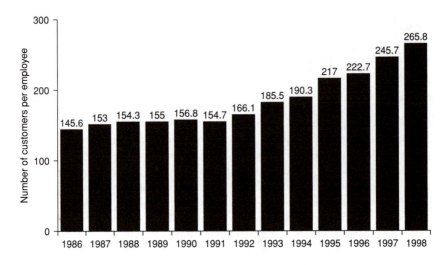

Figure 5.1 'Efficiency' as measured in improved customer–employee ratio

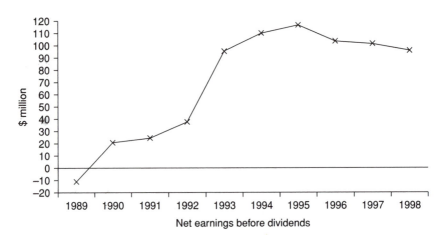

Figure 5.2 Net earnings before dividends at Nova Scotia Power, 1989–98

On the other hand, the company's cash position fell from a $51,763,000 in 1989 to a deficiency of $22,182,000 in 1990, and the long-term debt increased from $1,196,998,000 to $1,479,136,000 (Nova Scotia Power, 1990a).

It would be difficult to say what, if any, contribution the culture change made to the financial gains. According to the company's own financial review

(Nova Scotia Power, 1990a), the 'positive operating income' was the result of several factors, including an approved rate increase of 6.3 per cent which accounted for $28 million of increased revenue, 'the impact of favourable market factors', and productivity improvements. Even in the latter case it is difficult to unravel the impact of the culture change from other changes within the company. Indeed, on some indicators the company recorded greater improvements prior to culture change. Prior to 1991 the greatest improvement in customer–employee ratio, for example, was between 1986 and 1987, and the only decrease occurred in 1991. These discrepancies draw attention to the problem of 'success' claims.

During the re-engineering phase, financial success tended to be measured in terms of 'value-added' or 'non value-added'. By the time re-engineering was completed, three major rounds of lay-offs had occurred. Over 400 jobs had been cut, a linesman apprentice programme had been cancelled (leaving approximately 45 linesmen without work), and employee numbers had decreased by over 1,000.

In his final report as CEO, Comeau framed the culture change, privatization, BPI and strategic planning under the single umbrella of innovative leadership:

> Our efforts and accomplishments in 1995 have been diverse. We have introduced extensive changes in our corporate structure. We have successfully reduced our cost of operations. We have transformed the means by which we provide service to our customers. We have introduced a number of exciting new programs and services. And all these initiatives have one thing in common: the potential to add significantly to the value of the electricity we generate, transmit, and distribute . . .
>
> This message is my last as the president and CEO of Nova Scotia Power. Serving in this capacity for the past 13 years has been one of the greatest privileges and biggest challenges of my life. My time here has been rich in associations and satisfaction. Among the noteworthy events of the period were our successful transition from a crown corporation to an investor-owned company listed on the TSE 100 index, the observance of our 75th Anniversary as Nova Scotia's electric utility and the undertaking of our corporate restructuring. The energy market itself has undergone exciting changes as well, and I am convinced that Nova Scotia Power has the ability to make the most of each new opportunity that arises. I thank the Board of Directors, employees, investors and customers alike for their confidence in me. My successor inherits the executive responsibility for a splendid organization with a promising future.
>
> (Louis Comeau, 1995 – Nova
> Scotia Power, 1996a)[2]

Employee identity construction

Comeau's ability to impose his sensemaking on others raises several issues about sensemaking and the process of organizational change, in particular issues of power, formative contexts, organizational rules and the differing perceptions of other actors. As I will argue later, Weick's notion of sensemaking is somewhat confusing in regard to power. At times he references the significance of the sensemaking of selected actors (i.e., managers), and he makes reference to the influence of social sensemaking on individuals, but he falls short of drawing implications of structural power for sensemaking in organizations.

Other actors (e.g., employees) can and, in this case, did approach the changes with very different frameworks. From the series of interviews that I conducted at Nova Scotia Power, and a number of first-hand observations, it was clear that employees were divided on how they viewed the implementation of the change programmes. Indeed, many of the employees at Nova Scotia Power had 'invented' their own notions of the organization; some of which were positively confirmed and some of which were negatively confirmed by the various change programmes. For example, many employees, particularly within a Crown Corporation, had a notion of the ideal organization as one that offered job security and fair treatment. For some this was allied to the notion that job security and fairness were attainable through enlightened management practices, but for others, particularly many Cape Breton employees, these things could only be achieved through labour–management conflict and negotiation.

Thus, for some employees the changes seemed not only to reveal a number of deep-seated inequities but a willingness to address them, while for others it confirmed a continuous process of inequity and managerial manipulation. An instrument technician from one of the company's plants illustrates the former and an electrical technician at a zone office the latter sensemaking approach. Asked about the objective of the culture change (see Appendix B, Question 7), the plant employee answered that it was to make the company 'less technically oriented' and more 'people oriented'; that it 'appears to benefit employees'. The zone employee, on the other hand, thought that the company 'recognized a need for change in how management and labour communicate' because that 'seems to be what big companies are doing'. When asked whether his or her values had changed (see Appendix B, Question 8), the zone employee gave an emphatic 'no', while the plant worker went on at length about being 'more conscious of the other guy and his job', talking 'to people a lot more', 'mutual respect, communication and understanding' of and with others.

Likewise, with re-engineering, a range of responses could be found when talking to employees about its impact. One Halifax Engineering employee described the BPI programme as, 'the beginning of the descent into hell'. Another MIS employee felt that 're-engineering "success" was too focused on technology and less on the human aspect'. This was reiterated by a senior Halifax manager, who felt BPI was an excuse to get rid of long-serving employees, 'Nova Scotia Power sees experience as a negative. They look at experienced employees as excess baggage but it's a bad move to get rid of them'.

In the great majority of cases, understanding of the changes was coached in terms of how a person viewed his or herself in the process. Many employees, mainly those who had taken an active role in the process teams or were directly affected by the initiatives, were convinced re-engineering was in the best interests of the company. In contrast to the opinion of her boss, an MIS clerk saw BPI 'as a way to get rid of the dead wood and move away from the Crown Corporation mentality'. One could argue that, if there is a 'trick' to managing change, senior managers needed to reinforce some attitudes while undermining others. During the Culture Change programme, the resistance of Cape Breton employees can be attributed to their identity construction.

Identity construction and Cape Breton employees

Geographic differences Anyone who has grown up in Nova Scotia has some awareness that there are both perceived and real differences between those from 'the mainland' and those from 'the island' of Cape Breton. Cape Bretoners have a firm identity, which is based on a set of values that unites them in their view that anyone from 'across the causeway' (i.e., mainland Nova Scotia) is a foreigner whose ideas should be regarded with suspicion.

During the culture change, the most notable divide between employees, in their reaction to the programme, was between those based on the 'mainland' of Nova Scotia, who supported Comeau's culture change initiatives as a positive step towards improving employee relations, and those on the island of Cape Breton, who saw this as a threat to their well-being.[3] The following comment from an employee sums up the perceptions that Cape Bretoners had about differences between themselves and other employees throughout the province. 'The change was definitely needed, although it is tailored to specific groups [for example Scotia Square] and not suitable for others. There's inequality and [the change] could have been more applicable for all' (engineer, Sydney). Yet geography alone can't wholly explain the animosity employees from this region had about any ideas that originated outside the island.

In addition to difficulties in merging Eastern Light & Power with Nova Scotia Power, the company experienced most of the resistance to culture change in Cape Breton. Indeed, some of the workers in the region had openly defied the culture change by walking out on the one-day training seminars. This strong resistance suggested to me that factors influencing the identity construction of these employees were sending powerful cues that caused employees to assign different meaning to the same experiences. In addition to expectations attached to their nominal roles within the organization something was powerful enough to cause these employees to mistrust any ideas put forth by head office.

In fact, a number of the local managers, as well as lower-ranking employees, had trouble accepting these ideas and many chose to ignore mandates set forth by the company. It was evident to me throughout the time I spent in Cape Breton that many employees were cynical about managerial ideas and were biding their time until management moved to a new change technique. The following quote verbalized what many were thinking: 'Lots of people in customer service think it's a joke. Things will revert to old ways after the values are over' (collector, Sydney).

It appeared to me that individual identity was being shaped by the broader influences that resulted from geographic location, and it was these ideological differences that set Cape Bretoners apart from other employees. These included class identity, unionization and local leadership, all of which can be attributed to the mistrust of head office management.

Impact of geography on the construction of class identity   While Cape Bretoners' identity was framed by a number of factors, which cued their reaction to any ideas put forth by management, at the root of their values system was a class identity which set their responses apart and created a division, not only from the rest of the province, but between union and management, and also between head office and local management. This class identity goes back about 200 years and is grounded in a set of beliefs, shaped by events which occurred long before Nova Scotia Power existed.

Essentially, Cape Breton shares a number of similarities to the Walloon region of Belgium, northern England and Scotland, in that it was the site of industrial development built around coal mining, steel production and the railway, that brought with it class consciousness, unionization, union militancy,[4] and, later, economic depression and high levels of unemployment.

For example, in the first quarter of the twentieth century (1900–25) Nova Scotia contained less than 6 per cent of Canada's population but accounted for more than 17.3 per cent of all 'working days lost' due to strikes in the whole of the country. The strike figures, however, 'reflect the well documented disputes in the Cape Breton coalfields and the adjacent steel industry' (Gilson, 1987: 12–13). In the thirty-year period 1956–86 Nova Scotia had a 'high proportion of wildcat strikes, averaging 58% of all recorded strikes in the 30 year period under review', however, 'as a caution to generalising from these figures, it should be noted that the majority of these wildcats can be attributed to Dominion Coal and the construction industry' (Gilson, 1987: 13) both of which are associated with Cape Breton.

Like the Scots, northern English and the Walloons, the Cape Bretoners came to establish an identity that was distinct from other regional groups of workers. While this was exacerbated by language in the case of Walloon, national identity in the case of Scotland, and regional identity in the case of northern England, geography played a large part in the creation of a Cape Breton identity, as Cape Breton is an island that until the 1950s was only accessible by ferry.

In recent years a consistently high unemployment rate has added to the sense of class hatred and mistrust that dominates the island.[5] In order to protect the workers from being taken advantage of, the unions have become a way of life. The result is that management has been, and is still, held responsible for the 'oppression of the working class'. So by the time that Nova Scotia Power had become a major employer in the region, a strong union presence, which was enacted through a mistrust of management, had, regardless of working conditions, become a key force in the strategic planning of any organization operating in the region.

Impact of the union on identity construction   The geographic isolation that limited the workers' capacity for overcoming a sense of class oppression contributed to a rise in union activity. In the past, employees, needing ways of overcoming poor working conditions that existed in the coal mines and steel plants, turned to the unions for protection. Subsequently, their children learned by example that the union held more power than management and that management couldn't be trusted.

Over the course of the three weeks I spent in Cape Breton, it became clear that the identity of 'the employee' was still constructed around these beliefs. The most concentrated areas of unrest appeared to be in the unionized thermal plants, 'The union has washed its hands of the culture change due to previous union problems and management's attitude' (supervisor, Lingan). This was followed by unionized employees in the trades (i.e., linesmen, meter readers and installers). Although I was told that within the T&D offices I would not see the same level of union resistance from the other employees in Cape Breton as I had in the thermal plants, that: 'the farther away from Cape Breton you get, the less influence the union will have' (interview with senior manager, 1990), I saw that Cape Breton employees' attitude to management was generally less flexible than unionized employees elsewhere. In fact, members of the union led the overt defiance of the culture change shown by those walking out of the culture training sessions. But in other areas, union members had been co-opted to support the culture change. One linesman seemed to sum up the Cape Breton attitude when he said: 'It might be a good idea but I don't think it will work. You have to change the structure first.'

Because of Cape Breton's turbulent industrial history, it is easy for an outsider to attribute the opposition to change to fear. Long-standing unemployment problems, the closure of much of Cape Breton's steel and coal industry, labour unrest, and specialized skills all contributed to feelings of panic when Nova Scotia Power's President started talking about bad attitudes, poor morale and creating a humanized company. In a culture where plant managers were treated as gods, employees had little reason to believe that these new ideas would create better working conditions. The nature of the work and the workforce had bred an atmosphere that encouraged a division between managers and rank and file. This was not helped by an autocratic management style which I witnessed in all but one of the thermal plants.[6] Based on the historical background, little had changed in the employment relationship where an authoritarian style of management is still common in this region. Indeed, when asked about how well he thought the culture change had been accepted a 'utilityman' (sic) in Cape Breton told me: 'There are too many hard feelings between management and staff'.

Structural differences and identity construction

> Local management and head office have two different views.
>   (Instrumentation technician, Glace Bay)

When Louis Comeau first toured the province, many of the problems with attitudes and morale seemed to be occurring in the Cape Breton thermal plants. Indeed, stories I was told during my visit to the Cape Breton plants exemplified a culture quite different from the one head office was promoting. In the Cape Breton plants the so-called humanist, employee-centred culture change was enacted in the context of a rigid class-structured system.

Local management attributed the problems to labour unrest, but much of it was also the result of local management's inflexibility and unwillingness to negotiate. Specifically the managerial styles of the respective managers of two of the Cape Breton plants contributed to the reaffirmation by employees that management oppressed them.

One plant manager, who was a self-confessed autocratic manager, was feared by many of the employees, but employees fell into line with the style of management because this was their role and their livelihood depended on their behaviour. Similarly, one employee felt that his manager was not concerned with their well-being: 'He should pay more attention to what's going on . . . find out the sore spots. Maybe walk through the plant and talk to the guys. Be more accessible . . . approachable . . . flexible' (utilityman). A hierarchical situation existed at the plants. This is exemplified by a comment, made by one of the managers that it would be difficult for 'the lowest guy on the totem pole to take part in practising the values'.

Factors like these, contributed to an atmosphere that strengthened employees' beliefs about management and inevitably reinforced management's beliefs that employees were inherently confrontational. In turn, this reinforced employees' sensemaking that the culture change was something to be mistrusted: 'The Union has washed its hands of the culture change due to previous union problems and management's attitude' (plant supervisor).

Despite the rules of how to manage being changed by the Culture Change programme, the two managers continued to manage their meaning and enforce the rules in a way that appeared to contradict the corporate ideology of a more participatory style of leadership. For example, when the employees in one plant attended a staff meeting to discuss culture change, the plant manager's parking space was still reserved nearest the building and the employees were restricted to parking in a more distant lot. Within the plant, separate lunch rooms existed for management, while non-management personnel and other employees were not allowed on the floor where the executive offices were located, unless summoned to a meeting with a manager.

Indeed, the comment 'I don't believe everybody has to be happy to be at work', which I heard during one of my Cape Breton interviews seemed to indicate that some people had trouble with Nova Scotia Power's new philosophy. As well, it appeared that some felt that because there had 'been no complaints prior' to the culture change, thus, 'there was no vast change' needed. With regard to communication (see Appendix B, Question 3), I was told 'Communication. Nobody knows what it means. You hear what you want to hear. . . . You can find out anything you want to know.' The culture change also appeared to clash with the sense of what it took to be a good manager. When asked about progress within the organization (see Appendix B, Question 14), one manager responded that 'it was slow' and that this was 'because [managers] are called on to respect others and that should not/doesn't deal with incompetence. [We need to get] back to discipline. [Employees] should be told if they are doing a good or a bad job'.

Yet another manager gave a similar impression of events. The only difference was that he was more confrontational in his approach. At a meeting, he made it clear to me that he was opposed to the culture change, did not see a role in it for employees, and was only agreeing to the interview because he felt Louis Comeau had forced him to do so. From his perspective I got the impression he thought that employees were inherently lazy and the culture change promoted this behaviour at the cost of efficiency: 'Louis Comeau talked to a bunch of people and the attitude survey picked out the morale problem. He expects a happy and homogeneous perfect workforce and I'm not sure if he's interested in the efficiency of the company.' In regard to improvements in the treatment of employees, the manager stated that it 'was evident that they were trying to apply the values' yet, he added, this was 'not necessarily more visible'. When asked about the advantages of the culture change (see Appendix B, Question 11), the manager stated that he didn't 'know advantages. [There] is a need to measure. I would like to see a new attitude survey of the entire corporation [using] the same yardstick'. He was clearer on disadvantages (see Appendix B, Question 12), stating that it had a 'bad effect on supervisors who are now scared to discipline', and that the introduction of new values was 'easier said than done'. Yet, despite numerous grievances and industrial disputes, none of these managers considered that management styles could have been the cause of poor morale.

All of this led to a working atmosphere where ideas put forward by head office of the Nova Scotia Power Corporation were doomed before they were given a chance, which helped solidify the chasm between Cape Bretoners and mainlanders. It also strengthened the division between management and staff because employees could sense that the managers were manipulating the values to suit their purposes.

The strength of a 'class identity' outweighed a loyalty to organizational values. While there was a strong mistrust of management on one level, local managers in the Cape Breton region were also strongly influenced by a set of regional cultural values, which influenced their work ethic. The result was that in some locations each layer of the organizational hierarchy mistrusted the one above or below it.

In Cape Breton this layering effect of mistrust of management, combined with previously held values arising from the companies that had existed prior to the mergers, created cognitive dissonance (Festinger, 1957) for the local managers who felt that their loyalties were being divided between the organization and the region. In order to resolve the dissonance most managers chose to interpret the change as something they were not wholly committed to: 'Lots of information comes out from upper management and a certain amount filters down, but it's pretty diluted when we receive it' (shift supervisor, Glace Bay).

Reconstructing identity

After privatization, the concerns of Nova Scotia Power's Cape Breton employees became blurred as they blended with the bigger concerns from all employees, following the implementation of re-engineering. One of the biggest differences between the implementation of the culture change and re-engineering, as it relates to identity construction, was the focus on measurable gains, effectiveness and productivity. The management of BPI had moved from being a human resources issue to an auditing function. As such, factors, which had previously divided employees, and increased the gap between them and management were forgotten. Employee identity was constructed around inclusion and involvement in the BPI initiatives. Values had become a thing of the past. As one employee said, 'introducing the values when they did was a big mistake'.

Re-engineering employees' roles and workplace identities

As Nova Scotia Power moved ahead with re-engineering it was sending mixed signals to employees. No longer were employees complacent with their jobs. Although Louis Comeau had publicly stated: 'The transition of our company to a more customer sensitive work place is an exciting and challenging time for all of us and there will be opportunities for employees to get involved' (Nova Scotia Power, 1993f), and there were references to the continuance of

the culture change, with its emphasis on the employee and employee participation, the emphasis on efficiency and customer focus did not read like
activities involving any 'valuing' of the employee.

Unlike the Culture Change programme, which assumed that the success
of organizational change depended to a large extent on employee commitment, Nova Scotia Power's application of BPI had at its core the notion of
engaging an elite of approved workers. At the heart of the re-engineering
process was an 'Assessment Team', which decided not only which employees
would be allowed an active part in the re-engineering process, but whether
an employee was designated a 'good' or 'bad' worker. This suggested that
some employees were to be favoured over others, which led employees to
question their roles and identity within the company. By this act the
company helped to solidify opposition to BPI and may have created ill feeling
among some employees where none existed. This can be contrasted with the
previous era where notions of 'commitment to the culture change' and 'living
the values' were broader and more vague notions of the ideal employee
(Townley, 1994). By imposing identities on employees, based on their past
performance, the Assessment Team restricted their involvement in and their
sensemaking of re-engineering. Those who were accepted had to meet a set
of criteria, which imposed a particular identity on them: 'their knowledge
of the process, their interest in change, previous accomplishments, communications skills, and their ability to think creatively, work with large groups
of people in a team environment, and implement new work methods' (Nova
Scotia Power, 1993c).

In the final analysis, inclusion on the BPI teams appeared to be limited
to anyone who had actively supported the previous initiative and to those
whose jobs added value to the corporation.[7] At one level, this suggests
that inclusion is linked to an identity, which is constructed by the company
for the employee, but at another level, the influence of the broader societal
factors, which affect individuals' identity, cannot be discounted. This
helps to explain why fewer Cape Breton employees were involved in the
initiatives.

Strengths and limitations of identity construction

Identity construction raises several issues in connection with the management of change, including the role of individual versus collective
sensemaking, power, changing senses of self, and the contextualization of
sensemaking events.

That sensemaking is grounded in identity construction sheds light on
perceptions of a need for change, the identity of specific programmes and
change agents, the social construction of organizational success, and overcoming resistance to change. As we have seen, Comeau's sense of what he
needed to achieve in terms of Nova Scotia Power and his own sense of self
influenced his perception of a need for change and his adoption of the

two change programmes. It also influenced the presentation of the outcomes of the change programmes to appear as a series of successes, whereas other actors have a different sense of a situation that this can derail, or at least cause problems for, the change process. This suggests that the management of change needs to involve a careful management of the sense of a process. It is clear from the case, that senior managers can and do influence the sense of events.

On the other hand, an application of the link between identity construction and sensemaking points to some limitations. To begin with, there is the issue of individual versus collective sensemaking. In Weick's view of sensemaking, there is ambivalence about the weighting of different voices. In some places he appears to suggest that managers play crucial roles, over and above other organizational actors, in enacting a sense of a situation, yet implicit throughout his work is the notion that all voices hold more or less equal weight. The study of Nova Scotia Power suggests that while individuals do make different sense of a given situation it is broader collectives (e.g., trade unions, geographical groupings, senior managers, consultants) that make a greater impact on the public sense of activities. Where individual sensemaking did have any impact was where the actor was in a key organizational position, i.e., senior management and local trade union leadership, external consultant.

That brings us to the issue of power. Weick's notion of sensemaking is somewhat confusing in regard to power. At times he references the significance of the sensemaking of selected actors (i.e., managers), and he makes reference to the influence of social sensemaking on individuals, but he falls short of drawing implications of structural power for sensemaking in organizations. In certain contexts, particularly involving hierarchical structures, individual enactments of sense are clearly unequal. While it was clear that employees responded in many different ways to culture change it was also clear that the notion of change was a framework enacted by senior management, in particular Louis Comeau. In other words, some voices are more powerful than others.

Senior managers played a key role in defining the sensemaking context within which employees made sense. Nonetheless, the power of management was limited to the extent that they were able to create a plausible sensemaking framework. This limitation concurs with Foucault's (1980b) notion of power and knowledge, and how people draw a sense of power from how they are positioned within, and are able to interpret, a particular discourse. Senior managers were well positioned within an on-going discourse of culture change but, at least in Cape Breton, were unable to keep control of the interpretation of events. The managers of change would do well to take a leaf out of the Marxist philosopher, Antonio Gramsci's (1978) book in regard to the notion of 'organic leadership'. Gramsci argues that effective organizational leaders are those who are attuned to the cultural nuances of a situation, and are capable of translating those nuances to their own ends.

Nor does Weick adequately account for what might be termed the sense-making structures (i.e., the on-going outcomes of sensemaking that influence the generation of new sensemaking), or the possibility of contradictory sense-making within a given situation. In the latter case, activity theory appears to offer a way forward (Blackler, 1992a, 1992b, 1993; Blackler *et al.*, 1997, Blackler *et al.*, 2000). In the former case, a way forward is offered through a contextualization of sensemaking within formative contexts (Unger, 1987a, 1987b), and organizational rules (Hatfield and Mills, 2000; Mills, 1988; Mills and Murgatroyd, 1991).

A third limitation is the issue of context. Weick (1995) says little about the contexts in which sensemaking occurs beyond discussions of responses to on-going events. Yet in order to understand the identity construction of those involved we need a sense of the formative contexts, the framework of expectations or rules, and the combination of activities in which the actors are operating. To understand Comeau, for instance, we need to know some-thing of the changing frameworks in which Crown Corporations existed in the late 1980s, the meta-rules of management that were extant at the time, and something of the actors that Comeau had to convince.

A fourth limitation is the changing of selves. Weick (1995) contends that our sensemaking is constantly adapting to match individual identity with organizational image,[8] that we have many 'selves' according to the situation. And while identity construction explains Comeau's need to seek out different changes as part of an on-going process, it does not address the reasons for the different presentations of self. The implication is that different restric-tions are being placed on the individual and the organization, which serve as boundaries for certain behaviours. In other words, to understand why it is that people fine-tune the congruence between identity and context we need to understand something of the dynamics of those contexts. As we saw, top-down initiatives requiring dramatic changes of self (i.e., from humanist to efficiency focused) are highly problematic and need either to be avoided or handled with great skill.

Conclusion

Sackman's (1991, cited in Weick, 1995) definition of sensemaking – 'mech-anisms that include the standards and rules for perceiving, interpreting, believing, and acting that are typically used in a given cultural setting' – captures well the value of a sensemaking approach to the study of Nova Scotia Power.

Sensemaking provides a useful framework for understanding different pers-pectives of change and the management of these disparate understandings. If we want to understand something about the changes at Nova Scotia Power we need to make sense of the sensemakers. This starts with an understanding of how different identities of the key players are constructed. For example, identity construction clarifies why certain cues were extracted by some but not others, how they came to be interpreted differently, why some events seemed plausible to some and not to others, and how the change was retrospectively made sense of by those involved. In short, the establishment of different identity constructions is important because it draws attention to the sensemaker.

6 Application of the sensemaking model to the Nova Scotia Power case

Introduction

As the events at Nova Scotia Power unfolded, it became evident that throughout the organization disparate understandings and expectations of the change process, and of specific change techniques, existed. In the previous chapter, it was evident that many of the employees and senior management held conflicting views of the success of each of the change programmes. The idea that sensemaking reflects different psychological frameworks helped me to analyse and explain these different responses to change. In this chapter, the utilization of the remaining sensemaking properties takes into account the relationship between pre-packaged change solutions and local realities.

Throughout my study at Nova Scotia Power, I noticed key issues which reflected several recurring themes: (a) employees had different perceptions about the implementation of the handling of both programmes and there were differences in interpretation of the symbolism used to represent each; (b) geographical differences had a major impact on the acceptance or rejection of change; (c) Cape Breton employees, in particular, were resistant to change and the values; (d) there was a great deal of animosity between union and management in Cape Breton; (e) the switch from one change programme to another was viewed as contradictory; and (f) a culture of fear had evolved as a result of the changes.

Usefulness of the properties

The properties of sensemaking are particularly useful in analysing and explaining how events at Nova Scotia Power came to be understood in certain ways. Identity construction started the process of the unravelling of psychological frameworks, which influence different interpretations in the social construction of change. In this chapter, I will draw upon certain events in the recent history of Nova Scotia Power to highlight how the remaining properties help our understanding of the process of change, and where they are limited in that understanding.[1] Stories and events will be extracted from these observations, interviews and secondary sources, which occasioned my retrospective sensemaking and are important in understanding the process of change at Nova Scotia Power.

Social sensemaking

Each of the sensemaking properties offers a partial explanation for what led to different outcomes in the sensemaking processes, among the different explanations for how these outcomes come to be negotiated from an individual activity into a collectively shared meaning of the same experience. The notion of social sensemaking gets us to the heart of organizational sensemaking in that, more than most other sensemaking situations, organizations are collectives of people bound together, however loosely, by a common set of objectives, structure and practices. Whereas social sensemaking suggests that individual sensemaking is 'contingent on the conduct of others' (Weick, 1995: 39), it gives us insights into why it is that, despite employees disagreeing with management's ideas, Nova Scotia Power was able to achieve some level of consensus for its plans. In short, it explains how 'inventions' are mediated.

When Louis Comeau took over as President of Nova Scotia Power the basis of social sensemaking was fragmented due to class differences in Cape Breton and regional differences between different units. But this fragmentation was also partially the result of previous mergers, which brought together employees from different companies under one banner but not necessarily one social entity. Although Comeau set out to address the problem of fragmentation through his leadership style, and in many ways he achieved his desire of creating a unified company, it was perhaps not quite in the way he expected or would have wished. The following two events illustrate how social sensemaking was used as a means to make sense of change during the two different processes of change at Nova Scotia Power.

The legend of the company showers

As we saw in the previous chapter, Cape Breton employees had been socialized to resist managerial ideas, and many of the senior local management reinforced this belief by using an authoritarian style of management. Employees, therefore, conducted themselves in a way that anticipated their audience's reaction. Knowing that management expected them to be resistant, and mindful of their mistrust of management, employees often refused to even consider that change could have positive benefits for them.

The following story, told to me by both management and employees, had taken on legend-like proportions, and both unions and management, respectively, used it to demonstrate both the oppression by management and the inherent laziness of workers. For the researcher, it is an important story because it shows how social sensemaking can be used to arrive at different understandings of the same situation.

The managers' story   The managers at one of the Cape Breton plants, in an effort to enact the new commitment to valuing employees, decided to allow unionized employees fifteen minutes before the end of shift to shower, so that they could leave the plant, clean from the coal dust, at the end of their shifts. However, it soon became evident that employees were not bothering to make use of the time to clean up. Instead they were leaving the plant fifteen minutes early. Rather than ignoring this, management responded by saying that employees were free to use the time to shower, but if they chose not to, they must stay on the floor until the end of shift. In the end, the employees defied management's orders and continued to leave early. When management retaliated by suspending these employees, the union filed a grievance and the employees walked, en masse, off the job, at the request of the union.

Needless to say, the plant manager viewed this act as another example of union disobedience and defiance. Not only did this reinforce his perception that these employees were troublemakers, but his original ambivalence towards the culture change became overtly hostile since he blamed the employees' actions on the values, which originated from head office. His frustration with the culture change and the implementation of a values-driven workplace are best expressed in the following quote, taken from an interview with one of the managers shortly after this incident:

> These values are terrible . . . anything can be a values issue. They only think of values to employee. They have become a negotiating tool. People don't remember values to the customer, they only think of the employee. They don't believe in discipline and they forget that values are a two way street. In this plant the union wants nothing to do with it. One loudmouth can express his own values on the majority.

The union's story   Not surprisingly, the union shop steward had attached a different meaning to management's actions. Instead of seeing this as a gesture of goodwill, he claimed that the company was violating the value of employee-centredness by not offering them the choice of showering or leaving for the remaining fifteen minutes of their shift. Rather than focusing on the positive aspects of this action, the showers served as a sensemaking device to reinforce their long-standing belief that management was treating them badly and that the culture change was a vehicle to validate this behaviour: 'We've rejected the values because of this shower thing . . . not NSPC but this plant. Management must change their attitude' (journeyman, 28 years).

The value of this story, for an outsider, is in the way it captures the animosity which existed between management and labour, and local and head office management. As a form of social sensemaking, the story of the showers sheds lights on how the same experience can be given different interpretations, because of the meaning attached to it and the values of those involved.

As well, it demonstrates how sensemaking is tested out, or imposed on individuals, and when it deviates from the routinized scripts, it is questioned or resisted. However, what social sensemaking doesn't account for, in this instance, is how the issue was mediated and negotiated into a collective 'sensibility'.

The CSFR pilot project

The following is a description of the creation of the CSFR position, done during the re-engineering phase of Nova Scotia Power's change history. This story also demonstrates social sensemaking, showing how employees worked within a given framework by assigning their own meaning to the task. 'The customer receives first class service, employees enjoy more variety, wider responsibility and greater job satisfaction, and the company reduces cost' (Comeau, cited in McShane, 1998).

The customer service field representative (CSFR) position, which was introduced as one of several re-engineering pilot projects, incorporated the previously distinct tasks of meter reading, meter installing and bill collecting, and involved employees who were located in outlying regions. The purpose of the CSFR position was to address different customer service issues and eliminate some of the waste that resulted from 'down time' in each of these separate positions. (Prior to re-engineering, meter readers, installers and bill collectors would have a specific number of customers to service in a specific territory, but once they completed the assignments they were free for the remainder of the day.)

Specifically, in evaluating multi-functional processes and the multi-skilling of employees, the BPI team analysing work processes suggested that 'non value added' activities were occurring within all three categories of jobs because employees were too specialized in their knowledge and skills. As well, there was a great deal of time wasted and redundancy, as the request for service usually involved three or four different phone calls back and forth from the customer to the call centre to the meter reader or installer, and then back to the customer. The combination of several tasks, it was assumed, would benefit the customer, the organization, and the employee.

Under the new system, the CSFRs would operate out of offices set up in their own homes. These were to be equipped with computers and set up with modems, which allowed them to receive instructions from call centre employees, who would relay requests for installations, etc. In addition, CSFR employees would be given a hand-held computer while on the job. This system would tell them their assignments for the next day, track their work, and eliminate the need to report back to an office location each day. Instead the CSFRs would report results back in the evening from their home computers. In their new capacity, CSFRs were trained in all functions. The following excerpt, from a 24 June 1994 newspaper article, describes the essence of the position:

Mr Farcey used to just read meters. If a meter was broken, he'd report it to the regional office. Eventually an installer would get around to changing the meter. Today he is a CSFR and he's been trained to replace broken meters himself. One part of his job is truly unpleasant. He cuts off power to customers of Nova Scotia Power. But he has found a way to cope with this tricky assignment in his rural district Southwest of Halifax. Twenty minutes before he is supposed to cut off the power, he phones the customer and offers one last chance. Mr Farcey saves a trip out and another one to reconnect. The bill payer is relieved not to be cut off; and it's a good deal for Nova Scotia Power, who gets paid and saves on its employee's travel expenses.

This little initiative by Mr Farcey is one sign of Nova Scotia Power's determination to turn itself into a 'customer driven corporation'. Mr Farcey likes the variety. 'Everyday is different.' And he can use more personal discretion as in his approach to late payment.

(LeBlanc, 1994)

However, the skills required to read meters are quite elementary, whereas the skills required to install meters are more complicated, and, even with training, involve some risk for those previously unfamiliar with working with live electricity. Although the meter readers and bill collectors received special training to do installations, there were reported cases showing that these employees were working unsafely with live electricity. This lack of technical skills caused concern for many senior managers, too. One senior manager said he was surprised there hadn't already been a serious accident. This was confirmed by a retired meter installer, whom I spoke with, who told me of several instances of meters exploding because they had been improperly installed by new CSFRs.

As well, the collection of late payments called upon another entirely different set of skills unrelated to technical competence. One minute the CSFR was required to treat the customer 'as the lifeblood of the company', and the next minute, the CSFR could be threatening to cut off the electricity for non-payment of the bill. Needless to say, many employees were having problems coping with the different strategies required of the new job. To make matters worse, the BPI project team had overestimated the number of customers each CSFR could service. It was assumed that each employee would be responsible for approximately 5,000 customers, yet they could barely provide adequate service to 4,000 customers. The appearance of successful implementation was made plausible by borrowing staff from other positions to help with the overflow of work (e.g., getting linesmen to read meters), juggling data and, on management's part, tacitly accepting the informal restructuring of the job by employees. In the same way, the expenses arising from lost debts, the ratio of cost to savings from re-engineering, and savings on paper, which actually translated into bigger costs for the company because of overtime, were not made part of the equation. Yet fearing that this would signal failure on their part, managers continued to present information to the senior managers and consultants so that the programme would be socially constructed as 'successful'.

The whole implementation of the pilot projects during the re-engineering phase reflects the nature of social sensemaking. Employees acted in a way that made it appear as if they were enacting the new job descriptions. Rather than disobey the BPI guidelines, which clearly spelled out the details of the job, they anticipated their expected behaviour and collectively recreated its meaning by reverting to their previous tasks. While this is clearly not what had been intended by the consultants when they introduced re-engineering, it appeared sensible to employees to do what they did best. In this way, managers were able to rationalize the juggling of employees so that it appeared they had sufficiently trained staff to carry out the re-engineering process. On the other hand, it saved face for the consultants who wanted to appear successful, no matter what that meant. At one level, this exemplifies socially negotiated meaning, but at another this sensemaking was certainly not representative of the understanding of the employees in these positions.

Limitations of 'social sensemaking'

Social sensemaking means that to be part of an organization an individual makes sense within a given framework of ideas. In the case of the Nova Scotia Power employee, he or she was operating within institutional ideas of electricity supply and, until 1991, the role of Crown Corporations. The implications of social sensemaking, for the management of change, are that managers need to pay attention to those social factors that influence individual sensemaking. This may involve identifying and addressing social factors that have an undue influence on employee action.[2] It may involve efforts to establish some form of cultural leadership so that corporate expectations are rooted in established forms of social sensemaking. It may also involve attempts to take into account existing understandings when introducing change. Gramsci (1978) describes this as 'organic leadership' whereby the leader is followed by dint of his or her ability to draw on extant ideas of the sense of things.

The importance of social sensemaking is to remind us that individual sensemaking occurs within social contexts and, importantly, that individuals are potentially open to the influences of various social collectives (e.g., trade unions, the informal group, immediate supervisors, senior management, etc.). For the management of change this suggests that a sense of direction and change that engages the activity of employees is more likely to succeed where the changes are (a) clearly spelled out in words and in practices, (b) translated into routines; and (c) sufficiently rooted in the thinking and behaviour of individual employees to be the primary sensemaking guide for workplace developments.[3]

While social sensemaking appears to provide an adequate explanation for the problems which beset Nova Scotia Power in their attempt to use a universalist approach in managing the culture of the company, it raises questions about the issue of power, the social-psychological dynamics of control, and the implications of shared meaning versus shared experiences.

Weick maintains that social sensemaking is mediated through discourse and conversation, but he does not adequately take into account the underlying formative contexts (Unger, 1987), discursive practices (Foucault, 1979), and the activity systems in which people engage (Blackler, 1992a), which influence what will be social influences for some people and not others. Weick (1995) also underdevelops the role of power in social sensemaking, be it through the powerful influence of class discourse in Cape Breton, the role of senior management in introducing a discourse of culture change, or the changing design of the job. Instead of taking into account the differences which existed among Cape Bretoners, and trying to manage change by selling the idea of culture change and values to them, Comeau used his legitimate power to impose his sensemaking on all employees. Again, this failure to discuss the relevance of power in relation to sensemaking makes one question the validity of the social sensemaking argument. Or is what Weick calls 'social sensemaking' merely power is disguise?

Extracted cues of sensemaking

> If people are not getting the four-day course they don't think management is living up to their expectations.
>
> (administrative department head, Halifax)

It is obvious that in the process of decision-making people extract certain cues from the environment to help them to make sense of events. According to Weick (1995) cues are linked to a series of ideas and actions and as such influence not only what is extracted but also how something is interpreted. Thus, cues can serve to 'tie elements together cognitively' (Weick, 1995: 54). This has implications for change management as follows. First, a set of decisions will influence which cues are extracted from several in the environment. In certain circumstances the extraction of selected cues can help to solidify decisions and provide a framework for selling and maintaining a particular decision-making process. By the same token, certain decision-making processes may be hindered where participants are blinded to alternative cues. And the referencing of inappropriate cues can undermine a process of change where those cues are out of sync with the professed decision.

Perhaps the best-known cues during both stages of Nova Scotia Power's change were the four corporate values (see Table 6.1). The term culture change served as a prominent label to cue certain expectations and outcomes, but just how far something involving a one-off, one- to four-day training session for all employees, the introduction of a few selected symbols, and repeated reference to the 'four values' (see Table 6.1) can be characterized as a 'culture' change is questionable. As for the outcomes, it would be hard to judge given the limited nature of the Culture Change programme and its development alongside a number of other organizational initiatives and traditions (cf. O'Mahoney and Newell, 1998).

Some effort was made to provide cues that would reinforce and enhance a specific set of changes. In that regard, the four values were developed and highlighted in a number of corporate documents, used as a company logo, and as the basis for a series of slogans, themes (see Figure 6.1) and statements (see Table 6.2).

To begin with, the values were themselves cues for a culture framework: think the four values, think organizational culture. As we see from some of the statements (see Chapter 5), much of this had an impact on the thinking of employees. Indeed, 'Living the values' was a phrase often used by employees, until, eventually, the values became synonymous with culture.

On the surface each of the four values was equal, yet interdependent. However, people were free to bracket or select one or the other cues. Thus many employees chose to focus on valuing employees, while managers saw the values as a much more complex package. Generally speaking, employees' reactions to the four values introduced with the culture change, depended on what cues were extracted to give them meaning.

To begin with, the consulting company's pre-packaged culture change, with its corresponding four values, did not allow employees input into the process. Even though a company document stated that the 'new values we are trying to create represent *our* "vision" of the way things should be' (Nova Scotia Power, 1990a, my emphasis), many employees felt a detachment from the process and sensed that culture change did not involve them. Then there were the training sessions. In the first place, they were mandatory. Management did not seem to pick up the irony that employees were to be forced to 'be valued'. If employees were beginning to get a sense that things were not really changing, that only the content not the substance of management actions was different, the provision of a differentiated training programme probably convinced them. One-day training for employees versus four-day training sessions for managers was a powerful cue to those employees who felt that management remained paternalistic and aloof.

As one manager expressed it: 'If people are not getting the four-day course they don't think we (management) are living up to their expectations, so they won't live up to ours' (administrative manager, Halifax). Or as Comeau, himself, expressed it, 'The variance in training clearly sent a signal to most employees that they were not as valued as managers' (Nova Scotia Power, 1990a). Extracting the two-tiered training system as a cue, one of the district managers said, 'The ordinary people were left out of this process'.

Senior management's ambivalence to some aspects of the new values was not lost on the employees: 'Values should go both ways but the programme

Table 6.1 Comparing company attitudes with company values

Attitudes	Cultural values
1 In many ways, customers were not being treated as the lifeblood of the business. Keeping the lights on was the priority, but little attention was being paid to the interrelationships between the Corporation and its customers.	*Our Customers –* Service is our priority. Our goal is customer satisfaction. We provide our customers with quality, responsive and reliable service in an efficient, courteous and cost-effective manner.
2 As the largest employer of engineers in the Province, the Corporation was often referred to as a construction company, rather than an electric utility. Certainly, there was a tremendous focus of resources on building things, as opposed to the provision of electricity and associated services.	*Our Environment –* We respect and recognize our responsibility for the quality of the environment we share. We will continue to develop cost effective ways to fulfil this responsibility. We will continue to broaden our understanding of the environment and be considerate of potential impacts resulting from our activities.
3 Little attention was being paid to the human element; i.e., employees. Paternalistic, at best, task accomplishment was the objective. Inanimate resources were given much more consideration than human resources.	*Our Employees –* We work together safely with mutual trust and respect. We make effective use of modern technology and innovation to produce quality results. We recognize employee contributions through timely feedback, fair and equitable rewards, opportunities, and compensation.
4 Although government-owned, management seemed to be trying to operate in isolation from the government, resenting direction being given to them based on political directives, rather than good business practices. There was a failure to recognize the Corporation as an instrument of public purpose for the overall socio-economic benefit of the Province.	*Our Province –* We are proud to belong to the Nova Scotia community, and to be a major contributor to its economic and technological development. We strive to be a leader in the energy sector in providing a resource vital to the people of Nova Scotia. As a good corporate citizen we conduct ourselves in a manner that is responsive to and respectful of community needs.
(NS Power, 1990b: 1)	(Ibid.: 2–3)

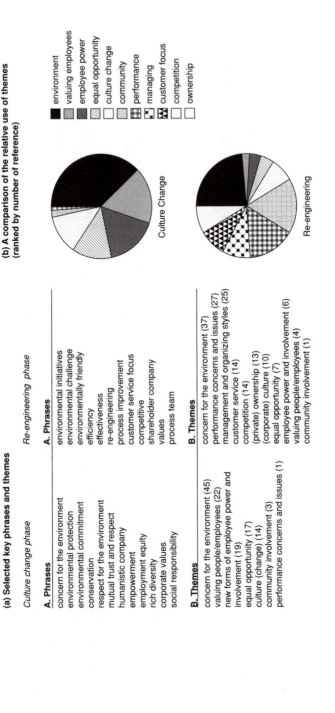

(a) Selected key phrases and themes

Culture change phase

A. Phrases

concern for the environment
environmental protection
environmental commitment
conservation
respect for the environment
mutual trust and respect
humanistic company
empowerment
employment equity
rich diversity
corporate values
social responsibility

B. Themes

concern for the environment (45)
valuing people/employees (22)
new forms of employee power and
involvement (19)
equal opportunity (17)
culture (change) (14)
community involvement (3)
performance concerns and issues (1)

Re-engineering phase

A. Phrases

environmental initiatives
environmental challenge
environmentally friendly
efficiency
effectiveness
re-engineering
process improvement
customer service focus
competitive
shareholder company
values
process team

B. Themes

concern for the environment (37)
performance concerns and issues (27)
management and organizing styles (25)
customer service (14)
competition (14)
(private) ownership (13)
(corporate) culture (10)
equal opportunity (7)
employee power and involvement (6)
valuing people/employees (4)
community involvement (1)

**(b) A comparison of the relative use of themes
(ranked by number of reference)**

- environment
- valuing employees
- employee power
- equal opportunity
- culture change
- community
- performance
- managing
- customer focus
- competition
- ownership

Culture Change

Re-engineering

Figure 6.1 Content analysis of changing themes at Nova Scotia Power, 1989–96*

Note: Content analysis involved the counting of words and phrases from Nova Scotia Power Annual Reports for 1989/90 and 1990/91 and the Draft Corporate Plan of 1991 – for the culture change phase, and the Annual Reports for 1992 (published in February 1993), 1993, 1994, 1995, and 1996, and the Employee Attitude Survey of 1993 – for the re-engineering phase.

is concentrated on management's side' (supervisor, Halifax). Ultimately, the use of a two-tier system of training was focused on as a cue by a large majority of the rank and file employees who felt that a lack of information excused them from taking part in the change process: 'People in the lower ranks were not given enough information to understand how the values work' (administrative services employee, Halifax).

During the culture change, cues such as different levels of training reinforced the belief for many employees that nothing had changed and that the value of the employee had been discounted. Many of the lower-level employees felt that the amount of time and money invested by the company in training the managers for four days versus a one-day information session for the majority of employees was directly related to the employees' worth to the organization.

Changing cues

> Since the province sold its debt ridden power utility to private share-
> holders last August, concern has been raised that the public's interest
> may have gotten bumped down the priority list.
>
> (Myrden, 1993)

Without purposely setting out to radically change the culture again, through the introduction of re-engineering, the company was creating a new culture, which reflected a concern for the customer and profitability. New ways of doing business, or of enacting a sense of business, changed not only the structure of the organization, but contributed to a culture which now regarded employees as a commodity in terms of 'value added' and 'non value added' worth to the organization. It was this focus on benefits to the company, and not the individual, that was at odds with a culture that had worked towards integrating corporate values into daily work routines. What success the company had in creating a sense of an integrative culture, built around the four values, now dissolved into a situation of fear as employees feared job loss or a restructuring of the way they did their jobs.[4]

For many employees, privatization supported the belief that Comeau had shifted his interest away from creating a 'humanistic' organization, to emphasizing an 'efficient' organization at their expense. Most of the long-service employees, whose identities were forged by their roles in a Crown Corporation, and further enhanced by the culture change's emphasis on valuing the employee, viewed privatization as a threat to the 'job for life' culture that Nova Scotia Power had fostered.

Despite this fear being initially allayed by Premier Cameron who, early on, reassured employees 'that there would be no lay-offs' (Myrden, 1994), other cues, such as the language (e.g., 'investor owned'), the focus (e.g., market driven) and the actions (e.g., the effectiveness programme), surrounding the privatization, cued many insiders to believe that privatization was more

Table 6.2 Most commonly used words and phrases in corporate materials during the culture (1989–92) and the re-engineering (1993–6) phases of change

Culture change (1989–92)*

concern for the environment	accomplishment through people	cooperation
high standard of environmental behaviour	help employees	employment equity
environmental plan	the value of employees	systemic discrimination
environmental commitment	interpersonal skills	visible minorities
environmental benefits	human potential	the right thing to do
quality of the environment	imagination	more women in management
environmental protection	creativity	appropriate representation of females
environmentally sound	accomplishment	(employ more) disabled people
Environmental Assessment Act	mutual trust and respect	rich diversity
respectful of the environment	recognize employee contribution	(employ more) aboriginal people
environmentally acceptable	feedback	equal emphasis in relationships
environmental impact	enhancing employees' work environment	culture change program
environmental enhancement	employee development	improve the culture
environmental groups	more humanistic company	corporate values
positive environment	empowerment	values training
preservation	individual control	values awareness
conservation	employee involvement	values opinion
recycle	employee participation	vision
global warming	employee freedom to act	cultural awareness training
protect endangered species	employee innovation	corporate culture
new energy ethic	team work	volunteerism
people centered approach	task forces	public participation
bring out the best in people	delegation	social responsibility
people are the most important resource	job sharing	efficiency ethic
belief in people	flex time	

Table 6.2 (continued)

Re-engineering (1993–6)**

responsibility for the environment	effectiveness	better value to customers
task force on the environment	effectiveness plan	customer service focus
cleaner environment	effectiveness program	competition
environmentally acceptable	quality	competitive marketplace
environmentally responsible	financial flexibility	competitive
environmentally sound	cost control	competitive demands
environmental action project	comprehensive strategy	global competition
environmental costs	market development	global challenge
environmental week	growth	competitive product
environmental care	market-driven company	cost competitive
environmental regulations	promoting the company	privatization
environmental initiatives	participative management	shareholder company
environmental studies	flat organization structure	corporate culture
environmental benefits	effective management	values
environmental challenge	managing for change	cultural change
environmental impact	aggressive business approach	culture change program
environmental protection	BPI	vision
environmental principles	revolutionary change	employment equity
environmental friendly	process	discrimination
department of environment	process change	employee equity program
respectful and protective of the environment	process improvement	empowerment
greening the workplace	process improvement ideas	employee participation
recycle	business process	process team
best performing utility	corporate restructuring	trust
productivity	customer service	respect employees
cost control	customers as co-drivers	people skills
cost effectiveness	customer driven organization	employees as greatest resource
corporate success	customer program	community involvement
company-wide (efficiency)	developing new customer options	
effective	customer consultation	

Notes: * Content analysis of Nova Scotia Power Annual Reports for 1989/90 and 1990–91, and the Draft Corporate Plan, 1991. ** Content analysis of Nova Scotia Power Annual Reports for 1992 (published in February 1993), 1993, 1994, 1995, 1996 and the Employee Attitude Survey, May 1993.

focused on the shareholder and customer than the employee. At this point, the culture change itself was reconstructed so that it no longer reminded anyone of this contradiction. Instead, the focus was redirected towards 'a new lean and effective style' (Myrden, 1994) that Comeau now felt was necessary to achieve effectiveness.

The central factors cueing BPI were mixed in their potential. Even allowing for the fact that these cues were weakened by the on-going sense of culture change, their value, in a plausible account of BPI, was limited to some extent by confusing messages (BPI as a continuation or move away from culture change), a failure to take account of employees preconceived notions linking BPI with lay-offs, the advent of lay-offs which reinforced fears, and a focus on efficiency and customer focus that was not linked to positive outcomes for the employee. In contrast with the culture change, where employees were offered a vision of an involving, self-rewarding workplace, the best that employees could hope for under BPI was that they would keep their jobs, and that perhaps economic rewards would improve, if the company was efficient.

The company's attempt to use cues from one change to promote another change failed. Far from dealing with a sharp turn from the employee, to a focus on efficiency, the changes that the company introduced were experienced by employees as confirmation of the abandonment of the culture change. These experiences had various effects. For some employees it signalled the end of something they had believed in. For some, it confirmed their working-class view that management adopts whatever is the latest fad to achieve profitability. For others, fear compelled acceptance of the new reality.

Limitations of extracted cues

This property is important at several different levels of analysis. First it helps to explain reasons for management's choices and second, it explains employees' responses to some of the ideas put forth by management. By studying some of the central cues at work in Nova Scotia Power's corporate accounts over the years, we can track how managers are able to create plausible accounts (e.g., the ability to use cues to strengthen belief in a certain framework), and some of the causes of organizational breakdown (e.g., disjunctures between old cues and new frameworks).

Through a focus on extracted cues, the manager of change is alerted to a number of potential problems, including the need to develop a coherent strategy of identifying and matching appropriate cues with the intended programme of change. This is not a simple process. On the one hand, managers need to avoid a commitment to a particular course of action that blinds them to alternatives. On the other hand, they need to avoid the appearance of ambivalence and confusion in the pursuance of an adopted course of action. It may be that management training needs to make managers aware of the influences on courses of action (e.g., through consciousness of the cues emanating from discursive practices), alongside encouragement to be coherent in chosen courses of action. There is also the problem of the need to adopt a series of coherent cues that solidifies a programme of change while avoiding strengthening existing problems through the inadvertent employment of inappropriate or problematic cues. This suggests that the management of organizational change should be anything but simple, but should identify and address key problems as part of the strategy of a change programme.

Looking to some of the limitations of extracted cues, Weick (1995) states that they are familiar structures which people draw upon to make sense of issues. While he acknowledges that this extraction depends on context, and that context affects interpretation of the cues, Weick again downplays the notion of power and politics as an element of context and leaves us wondering why certain cues are given credence over others. Instead, Weick suggests that the value of an extracted cue lies in its ability to act as a point of reference, which ties elements together cognitively and ensures action. In other words, action, not outcomes, is the central issue.

This raises questions about the validity of the cues that were extracted to make sense of the situation. At one level it can be asked, whose cues are extracted? At another level, we can question how these extracted cues are transmitted and imposed on organizational members with less power? For example, Louis Comeau, Wayne Crawley and the consultants chose to selectively ignore the reinterpretation of the work processes after privatization and instead focused on the 'success' of the re-engineered positions. Yet, employees who interpreted these same cues as signs of 'failure' failed to have their cues recognized.

Although he acknowledges 'the politics of interpretation' Weick (1995: 53) suggests that any discrepancies in the interpretation or selection of the cues will be overcome once people begin to act. Weick (1995: 55) likens cues to 'acts of faith which set sensemaking in motion'. But this does not appear to take into account the consequences of different interpretations. The following quote illustrates the problems involved with different interpretations of action: '[The culture change] is the biggest waste of money Nova Scotia Power has ever been involved in. One of the problems with the values is that they assume equality and that just isn't so' (customer adviser, Sydney). Whether it is naivety or ignorance, Weick's assumption that the greatest strength of cues is their ability to animate people to generate cues ignores the reality of conflictual sensemaking and how to deal with it.

On-going sensemaking

It's time to take a look at where we are in this never ending journey.
(Louis Comeau, 1991)

Making sense of continual change

Two major questions which concerned me with this case study were, trying to understand why change was introduced into a company that had remained relatively untouched throughout its history; and why the culture change, which seemed to personify the President's values, was suddenly dropped in favour of the more radical and non-complementary re-engineering?

A study of the on-going sensemaking (both within and external to the company) at Nova Scotia Power can shed light on how organizational change can be effectively (i.e., plausibly) dealt with, and where the potential for breakdown exists. In 1992, a turning point had been reached at Nova Scotia Power when the focus seemed to shift from a concern for the employee to a concern for the bottom line: 'The customer service focus is a vital part of the evolving corporate culture but our goals for effectiveness as an organization are equally important. At the heart is a new style of work place, lean and effective; (Nova Scotia Power, 1993f).

Yet, despite major discrepancies among Nova Scotia Power's objectives, and the means to achieve them, Louis Comeau had managed to make the switch in strategies appear as a seamless process of change and to convince employees that BPR was a natural extension of the culture change and the most viable means of achieving effectiveness and addressing competition: 'For us, Privatization represented a logical step in our company's history . . . as a Crown Corporation, Nova Scotia Power's borrowing power and flexibility to determine its own future would always be limited' (Nova Scotia Power, 1993f). Indeed, by the end of the first year of privatization, Comeau was able to reassure shareholders that the company had been re-invented as a successful company, which focused on the bottom lines of productivity and competition:

> I am happy to report that Nova Scotia Power's first year as a shareholder-owned company was a success from both a financial and operative perspective. We are well on our way to creating a company performing at its competitive best.
>
> (Nova Scotia Power, 1993f)

According to Louis Comeau, by the early 1990s 'competition' had taken on a new level of importance previously unheard of in a public utility company. Once Thatcherism and Reaganism took hold and spread, the notion of competition at Nova Scotia Power went from being a fairly innocuous concept, loosely related to notions of effectiveness,[5] to being assigned new meaning and taking on more importance as a cue for change.

The influence of 'organizational shocks' – such as low morale, increased competition, and the privatization of the company – can be explained as triggers, which led to sensemaking events and were part of the on-going process of making sense of issues as they arise. In each instance, Comeau and his team had to make sense of the issues and decide on a course of action. In so doing, a focus on a solution to a problem had long-term consequences for future changes, but this was not evident at the time:

> It is no exaggeration to say that the past 12 month period has been the most significant in Nova Scotia Power's history. To evolve from a Crown Corporation to a fully functional, free-standing public company with 30,000 shareholders, in less than a year, was a singular achievement.
>
> (Louis Comeau, Nova Scotia Power, 1994a)

These events, and their interpretation, reinforced the on-going nature of sensemaking, as Nova Scotia Power tried to make the switch from culture change to re-engineering seem plausible, despite what appeared to be a contradiction of the original values that the culture change promoted.

But why was privatization such a pivotal moment in Nova Scotia Power's history and how did it influence the sensemaking of the decision-makers? On-going sensemaking suggests that a shift in focus away from 'standard operating procedures' (Weick, 1995: 48), in this case, those that revolved around the four values, was forced by the greater emphasis that was being placed on competition. Instead of realizing organizational goals by practising what he had earlier preached,[6] on-going sensemaking allowed Comeau to adjust his thinking so that dissonance between old and new methodologies was resolved, and he believed that, 'Privatization made eminent good sense at this stage in our history' (Nova Scotia Power, 1993f).

Comeau's notion of change was punctuated by the need to change the company's strategies so that they were more in line with the enactment of competition:

> Competitive success demands determination, hard work and some special inner qualities. Six of Nova Scotia's successful young athletes shared their ideas on what it takes to succeed. We discovered they have a lot in common, with each other, and with us. Nova Scotia Power, like a competitive athlete, is preparing to be the best.
>
> (Nova Scotia Power, 1994a)

In the past, Comeau may have ignored 'competition' but now he was receptive to cues, which offered him a way to address his problems. A turning point in his sensemaking occurred in 1993, following privatization and immediately preceding the introduction of BPR, when Comeau stated that: 'Companies today cannot survive by simply doing what they have always been doing in the past. It's just too competitive' (Nova Scotia Power, 1993c).

In spite of these conflicting views, Comeau made sense of the notion of competition by understanding it to be a seamless part of the culture change 'project' rather than an 'interruption'. In other words, he attempted to enact a sense of current events by which the company was no longer a Crown

Corporation, had to answer to a powerful group of shareholders, needed to become profitable to stay in business, and faced deregulation whereby other utilities could eventually sell their product in Nova Scotia. Competition was, in many ways, an ideal term that served to summarize changes within the company.

Nonetheless, the idea of aggressive competitiveness did not sit well with the existing enacted reality of the culture change, and Comeau had to work particularly hard to suggest that one was a continuation of the other. Part of the problem was that events were dictating and shaping Comeau's sense, as it had not done previously. This time Comeau appeared to be more a product of this new environment than its creator. The dominance of the free-market notion of competition had taken on the force of a meta-discourse among managers and politicians alike.

The impact of broader, 'external', on-going sensemaking is interesting in this case because senior management adopted widespread change programmes, viz. culture change in 1988 and re-engineering in 1993. Yet, failure to adequately address on-going sensemaking can, and in this case did, encounter negative emotive responses. There is a sense that sensemaking needs to be at one and the same time internally consistent (e.g., not saying one thing and doing another), apparently in tune with aspects of on-going sensemaking, and yet able to move beyond existing understandings.

Limitations of ongoing sensemaking

As a property, on-going sensemaking lays out the conditions for sensemaking to occur, showing how each of the other properties fit in the model. For example, sensemaking only appears active when interruptions, cued by past events, bear on current 'projects' (Weick, 1995). When and how these interruptions occur influences the emotions of the sensemaker, or, as Weick (1979: 49) puts it, 'these emotions affect sensemaking because recall and retrospect tend to be mood congruent'. Whereas emotions are engaged in identity construction, the on-going property of sensemaking requires a commitment to a course of action, which is the result of emotional responses shaped by identity construction. While on-going sensemaking offers an explanation for Comeau's reconciliation of events into a seamless process of change, it fails to explain why most employees saw them as discrete and contradictory processes. This emphasizes the ambiguities of on-going sensemaking.

The primary value of the on-going property is to draw attention to the way that on-going sensemaking stabilizes a situation and how change acts as a shock, generating emotional response and new acts of sensemaking. This alerts the managers of change to the problem of causing shocks in ways that attempt to predict and address emotional responses, whether that be the inducement of deliberate feelings of shock (e.g., the philosophy behind the radical intent of re-engineering), or actions that prepare the way for the acceptance of change.

Although sensemaking is an on-going process, a critical element of sense-making is that the outcome develops a prior definition, instead of fulfilling the definition. That is, the outcome is determined by experiences that are familiar, that we view the outcome by making prior experiences fit the outcome by seeing only those actions that will support it. This questions the on-going nature of sensemaking. For if we discover what we have already invented, are we not in some way also fulfilling that definition by constantly recreating the original definition? Part of the answer lies in how Weick differentiates between sensemaking and interpretation, but it does not wholly explain the subtleties of the property.

The on-going property explains the 'stocktaking', which takes place when key events act as shocks and cue the sensemaking process. Anything that appears non-routine (i.e., low morale, having to make selections, methods of implementation) can trigger a process, whereby individuals formulate a retrospection of extracted cues to help them attach 'feeling' to the event. In this way, they can decide if the event is 'good' or 'bad'. In terms of change management, we might expect that Nova Scotia Power's culture change programme represented a 'shock' to existing routines, suggesting that management need to take care to prepare for the emotional response of those involved.

Retrospection

> The concept of sensemaking is helpful because it highlights the invention that precedes the interpretation.
>
> (Weick, 195: 14)

> We want to measure our success so far.
>
> (Jim Woods, explaining why an evaluation of culture change was necessary, Nova Scotia Power, 1991a)

Weick (1995) argues that sensemaking is always retrospective because people act first and then make sense of their actions. In so far as making sense is an ever-recurring process that takes place within a specific context, the notion of retrospection has implications for change management. Situations of organizational change present various actors with new, some-times unique, sometimes stressful, situations. Thus, following Weick (1995), it might be expected that when actors are unprepared for changes, they resort to cues other than the logic of the change itself to make sense of events.

To begin with, there is the potential for a multitude of interpretations of any given situation. That potential is constrained somewhat by the context in which action occurs, by the reactions of others, and by the actor's own history and personality. Where a situation is either new, confusing, and/or dangerous the actors involved will have a heightened need to make sense and will look to others for clues, or will fall back on contextual or individual routines (Weick, 1993; 1996). At Nova Scotia Power the introduction of the Culture Change programme was both facilitated and hindered by the extent to which management was able to impose their version of sense on events.

Retrospection is connected to the extracted cue property whereby the influence of past accounts guides the extraction of specific cues to support current sensemaking activity. This offers some explanation for the selection of both change programmes at Nova Scotia Power. Based on their popularity, the selection of consultants was also influenced by their success with other companies and the belief that each programme achieved the goals that were set (i.e., what worked for them should do the same for us).

In the first case, senior management at Nova Scotia Power were, arguably, drawn to culture change, and then to re-engineering, because they were made sense of as widespread (and thus successful) programmes. In the second case consultants (at the first firm and then Ernst & Young) were selected based on the contention that they were experienced and successful in introducing, respectively, culture change and re-engineering into other companies.

Using retrospective sensemaking, Nova Scotia Power's senior management first understood culture change as a way to humanize the organization. In the second instance, they understood the re-engineering initiatives as the medium that 'transformed the existing culture into one which shifted the corporate focus to the customer where it belongs' (Crawley, 1995). Here re-engineering was presented as a development within, rather than away from, the existing culture change. What happened in the process was that some existing sensemaking cues – efficiency and customer – were highlighted, while others, such as the employee, were downgraded or ignored (i.e., valuing the province). Despite all efforts, it was clear to most employees that the sense made of 'efficiency', 'customer' and 'employee' were very different from past understandings, and that the humanization spirit of the culture change was gone.

Managerial retrospection

At Nova Scotia Power, retrospective sensemaking of events appears to have influenced managers and employees in different ways. For example, when Louis Comeau was first appointed President in 1983, there were several steps which occurred before the culture change was implemented. Each can be attributed to a retrospective sensemaking of the previous activity. In the first instance, Comeau initiated a number of visits throughout the province in order to meet his employees. Using retrospection, he soon interpreted the complaints he was hearing as indicative of a low morale problem. The next step was to uncover the reasons for poor morale. In order to do this, Comeau commissioned the employee attitude survey, which concurred with his diagnosis. Here low morale was officially identified as a problem. In attempting to deal with the problem he 'discovered' culture change as a solution. Comeau's own invented sense of the organization again informed this solution, which centred on creating a financially self-sufficient, but politically popular Crown Corporation.

All this changed following privatization, when competition shocked the retrospective sensemaking of Louis Comeau. Events which had not previously provoked action had suddenly taken on new meaning, while previously important issues, such as the culture change, were being set aside. Whereas previously employee satisfaction occupied centre stage, it was now being treated as potentially threatening to Nova Scotia Power's competitive edge. By 1992 the Nova Scotia Power annual report was stating that 'for competitive and corporate success we must now evolve into a customer driven organization' (Nova Scotia Power, 1993f) and the company was again shocked into seeking out a change technique that addressed that issue.

For management, particularly senior managers, it was relatively easy to adjust to current trends and demands. Once they had accepted the need for efficiency and profitability as prime concerns it was not difficult to translate re-engineering into activities that made sense for the organization. The focus on competition had become a way of doing business and the mantra of remaining competitive to avoid 'losing out' replaced a previous concern for the values. Re-engineering had forced Nova Scotia Power to take stock, and this stocktaking resulted in the most widespread structural changes to date. As one employee, who was a twelve-year veteran, described it, 'the new way of management has become a new way of working'.

Employee retrospective sensemaking

While senior management were relatively successful in constructing the notion of change as an explanation of developments within the company, they were not always able to get employees to commit to the company's new vision. In part this had to do with established traditions within the company, who people looked to for cues (i.e., managers or union leaders, head office or local management), and senior management's ability to address existing routines.

On the one hand, the context of on-going change provided a number of cues for employees as they retrospectively made sense of different events. On the other hand, management's own interpretation of events through corporate documents and activities also served to shape employees' retrospective sensemaking: 'It was a great year for enhancing employees' work environment. . . . The main focus of employee development this year was the intensive education program for the change in corporate culture' (Nova Scotia Power, 1990a).

As employees of a Crown Corporation, many had developed a 'job-for-life mentality' and expectations of fair and humane treatment by their employer. The culture change had reinforced those notions. But privatization and BPI challenged their sensemaking and provided various points of contrast with previous enactments that sometimes made it difficult for managers to sell the new versions of reality to employees. Indeed, the consultants acknowledged that employee retrospective accounts had caused serious morale problems when BPR was first introduced.

It is hard to say what impact this ultimately had, but in the short term it added to feelings of cynicism about change that other researchers have noted in the literature (Duck, 1998; Reichers *et al.*, 1997). Some employees saw the various changes as beneficial: 'Change is a way of life. If it makes sense to change, we will do so. Right now we are too entrenched with the old systems' (head of network services, Halifax). While others described it as 'another flavour of the month': 'Like anything new it starts out great and then peters off. People are more concerned with other interests . . . don't want to get involved with this stuff' (technical assistant, New Glasgow).

This period has been described as 'the beginning of the descent into hell' (head office manager). Because retrospective sensemaking focuses on the present to make sense of the past (Weick, 1995: 26), Louis Comeau's attempt to integrate privatization as part of the evolution of the culture change only emphasized the differences between the two periods and strengthened employees' beliefs that the original culture change was not suited for the challenges of privatization. What is clear is that retrospective sensemaking is a constant process. People act and then make sense of the action but, at a later stage, new actions may lead to further retrospection of the earlier sensemaking.

Limitations of retrospection

By drawing our attention to the role of retrospection in sensemaking, Weick (1995) provides a useful explanation of the underlying causes of organizational misunderstandings that have led some to seek redress through the management of meaning (Smircich and Morgan, 1982), or the manipulation of cultural beliefs (Peters and Waterman, 1982). This contributes to our knowledge of change management by helping us understand something about the origins of equivocality and the need for clear guidelines and adequate preparation.

In the earlier stages, retrospection explains the lack of an integrated culture, the suspicion and mistrust of management, and the strength of the union during the culture change. Based on their long history of 'oppression' by management and because of previous unpleasant experiences, these employees believed that any plans implemented by management would have a negative impact on them. Relying on retrospection, their habitual response was to reject all ideas that originated from head office.

Nonetheless, retrospection is one of the most difficult and controversial concepts in the sensemaking model to grasp because it is unclear what constitutes retrospection and what role contextual factors play. According to Weick (1995), action has to have taken place before retrospection can occur. Yet Weick (1979) maintains that retrospection can be applied to future events by treating them as if they were already finished. What he refers to as 'future perfect thinking' relies on assigning a meaning to an event as if it had occurred, based on past experience. Not only does this seem contradictory, but it also changes the meaning of retrospection.

The events which occurred at Nova Scotia Power during this time frame present another major problem for which both on-going and retrospective properties offering conflicting explanations. How did the co-ordination of past activities, such as the culture change, which arose from a different understanding of competition, develop into the current understanding of competition, and how did re-engineering come to be selected as a solution to this problem?

While retrospective sensemaking offers a partial explanation for Comeau's reconciliation of events into a seamless process of change, it fails to explain why most employees saw them as discrete processes, which contradicted each other. Not only does this challenge the meaning of social sensemaking as a negotiated social and collective process, and raise issues about the validity of social sensemaking, but it also emphasizes the ambiguities of both on-going and retrospective sensemaking.

Perhaps the answer points to one of the biggest weaknesses of the sensemaking model. That is that the sensemaker, because he or she relies on routine scripts, does know what he or she is thinking before acting. In other words, people *do* make sense of their actions *before* they act.

Plausibility

One of the keys, if not *the* key, to understanding how managers achieve some semblance of unity of purpose relates to the issue of plausibility. For managers introducing change programmes, it does not matter whether the programme is said to be 'widespread' and 'successful' so much as whether this can be translated into a real sense for employees. Can employees be made to see the same sense as the managers who are introducing the ideas? It depends, in large part, on how plausible the management's argument is. The study of Nova Scotia Power suggests that the plausibility of a story succeeds when it (a) taps into an ongoing sense (e.g., low morale, competition); (b) is consistent (e.g., the employee attitude survey both identified and provided an outlet for low morale); (c) facilitates, rather than disrupts, on-going projects (e.g., the presentation of culture change as a solution to low morale); (d) reduces equivocality (e.g., the reduction of a number of disparate problems to low morale, and the reduction of multiple solutions and to four values); (e) references a sense of 'accuracy' (e.g., the widespread application of culture change; the 'successful' track record of the consultant); and (f) offers a potentially exciting way forward (e.g., the introduction of a culture change programme that promises to reward employee enthusiasm).

Weick (1995) maintains, and Nova Scotia Power's case demonstrates, that accuracy plays a secondary role in the sensemaking process. At Nova Scotia Power, Comeau's reliance on plausibility over accuracy was evident right from the beginning, influencing every step in the process of culture change, from identification of the problem to later claims of successful implementation. The ultimate success of the Culture Change programme was heralded through a number of stories that drew on appropriate cues to build plausibility. For example, Comeau focused on cues which would make his decisions seem plausible, and developed plausible stories around the hiring of the consultants.

The roots of the culture change lay in two sources that were mediated by Louis Comeau's sense of the situation. First, there were the needs of the government for a more politically sensitive organization: if Nova Scotia Power was perceived as a good and fair organization it might have positive repercussions for the government. Comeau was able to read into this a need to improve employee–management relations, and company–customer relations. This led to the second source, the attitudes survey, which identified low morale stemming from a series of problems.

Whether the survey accurately described the extent or depth of certain feelings was never an issue. There was some level of dissatisfaction within the company and the attitudes survey, cloaked in the appearance of a 'scientific' process, provided a plausible account of that dissatisfaction:

> [The culture change] followed the attitudes survey, which showed that people were unhappy. To get the best productivity you must start with employees and make them want to come to work.
>
> (payment processing clerk, Halifax)

> [The culture change] was based on the attitudes survey. There was a bit of a morale problem.
>
> (supervisor of customer service and meter reading, New Glasgow)

> [The culture change] was the result of surveys. People at Nova Scotia Power were unhappy in their jobs. People didn't come to work.
>
> (electrical maintenance supervisor, Milton)

The survey results provided important cues for the construction of an argument for a culture change. The problems identified in the survey lent themselves to various solutions. But senior management at Nova Scotia Power focused on one simplistic version of organizational culture, centred on values, and sold it to employees by developing a story that was plausible in its referencing of the attitudes survey. In a document titled 'Cultural Change at Nova Scotia Power', which was distributed company-wide, senior managers clearly placed 'the impetus for the change' at the feet of the 'employee attitude survey'. By a careful use of balancing statements the document manages to match issues from the attitudes survey with the new values of the Culture Change programme (see Table 6.2).

The building of a plausible link between culture change and business success was helped, on the one hand, by the absence of a clear definition of what a successful outcome would look like, and, on the other hand, by reference to the widespread adoption of culture change throughout industry. Throughout the period there was nothing to indicate that other solutions wouldn't have worked just as well, or that the morale problem, in part a result of the mergers, would not resolve itself over time. So the senior management team, in numerous corporate bulletins (Nova Scotia Power, 1991a, 1991b, 1992a), continued to present their plausible account of why the change was necessary.

Over the next year or so stories of organizational success were linked to the culture change using a variety of plausibility-building devices. One device involved a simple reproduction of key words in conjunction with expressions of success. In the following example, saying is believing, especially when the words are those of the Lieutenant Governor of Nova Scotia:

> Through the care and dedication of Nova Scotia Power employees, Nova Scotians have continued to enjoy safe, cost-effective, and reliable electric service. Of particular note this year is our ever-increasing emphasis on the protection and enhancement of the environment.
>
> Nova Scotia Power and its employees strive to meet the needs of Nova Scotians for electrical energy in an environmentally sensitive manner and to contribute to the growth and development of our province.
>
> (Nova Scotia Power, 1990a)

Once all the cues of plausibility had been established, competition began gaining momentum as a driver of change, and its influence on the key organizational decision-makers was also being felt. The actions of the Thatcher and Reagan governments, respectively, in the UK and the US,[7] helped convince Canadian governments of the plausibility of their decision to privatize Crown Corporations in their region. But while this may have seemed a plausible solution, in reality companies like Nova Scotia Power were unprepared and poorly equipped to become competitive in their current state.

Indeed, the values that Nova Scotia Power tried to instil during the culture change supported their primary mandate, which was centred on providing a service to the customer and maintaining a satisfied workforce. But what had seemed plausible at one time, appeared to contradict the notion of competition, which developed from Thatcherism. With an increased emphasis being placed on cost effectiveness, Louis Comeau began to equate Nova Scotia Power's survival to the plausibility of privatizing the company. As Comeau became more entrenched in the Thatcherite notion of competition, the plausibility of privatization as a tool for addressing the competitive environment influenced his sensemaking. As part of the on-going nature of sensemaking, the cycle was repeated (i.e., choice of solution, choice of consultant), with the implementation of re-engineering.

In adopting a strategy of BPI, senior managers at Nova Scotia Power had been convinced by a number of cues that made it plausible. Cues included the aftermath of privatization and the existence of a powerful shareholding group, the language of private enterprise and profitability, a discourse of globalization (Mills and Hatfield, 1999), the widespread application of re-engineering, and the track record of the consultants, Ernst & Young, that included 'successful' implementation of BPI at the Calgary and Quebec Hydro companies.

But the introduction of re-engineering emphasized the differences between the two change programmes and forced the rethinking of cues to make the latest change both plausible and non-contradictory. The problem for senior management was how to enact a new strategy that appeared plausible to different constituencies, specifically employees and shareholders. In the latter case it was relatively easy to link privatization, efficiency and the introduction of BPI. There had never been any pretence that re-engineering was anything other than a system to revolutionize late capitalism through radically altered work processes. If anything, BPI spoke to private enterprise and efficiency.

It was a harder sell to employees. The problem is that senior management was introducing ideas that were not only new but also contradictory to on-going sensemaking. The central factors cueing BPI were mixed in their potential. Privatization certainly helped to convince employees that new ownership encouraged new strategies. BPI was portrayed as a widespread and successful strategy for profitability and the consultants were sold as BPI experts. In the words of one senior analyst, 'We needed the consultants, . . . They legitimated change . . . gave it credibility' (interview, 21 July 1994).

Yet efficiency stressed work processes at the expense of employee concerns, and a focus on efficiency and customer-focus was not linked to positive outcomes for the employee. Constant references to globalization encouraged both fear (e.g., lay-offs) and optimism (e.g., growth). Even allowing for the fact that these cues were weakened by the on-going sense of culture change, their value in a plausible account of BPI was limited to some extent by confusing messages. In contrast with the culture change, where employees were offered a vision of an involving, self-rewarding workplace, the best that employees could hope for under BPI was that they would keep their jobs, and that perhaps economic rewards would improve, if the company was efficient.

Limitations of plausibility

What is interesting about plausibility is the light that it casts on success and the management of change. The selection of pre-packaged and popular solutions raised questions for me about the uniqueness of this culture to Nova Scotia Power. In the first instance, I questioned the accuracy of choosing a set of common values that could be interchanged from organization to organization. How embedded could these values be to employees throughout the organization? Nova Scotia Power appeared to ignore the differences that exist among employees and between different organizations. The same could be said for re-engineering. Was it selected because it really was in the best interests of the company, or was it chosen because its popularity and promise of dealing with competition made it plausible?

What Nova Scotia Power thought they bought, came with an implicit promise to deliver the same success to them as it was claimed to have done for other companies. This made me think more closely about the distinction between accuracy and plausibility. By contrasting plausibility with accuracy, Weick (1995) appears to suggest that there is a difference in quality between the two. But I would argue that they are both, in fact, forms of plausibility; that a reliance on accuracy is in fact a form of plausibility building. Thus, when I point to the fact that Louis Comeau and his senior managers used plausibility rather than accuracy to develop change, I am not suggesting that they avoided 'factual evidence', but rather forms of evidence that did not rely on accuracy for its plausibility.

This means that the issue of change management is not whether a company reverts to plausibility rather than accuracy, but whether they are able to develop a sufficiently convincing level of plausibility. To that end, it could be argued that Nova Scotia Power became quite adept at selling the idea of successful culture change in so far as a number of employees attributed positive feelings of change to the values programme. The real problem, therefore, was not so much in building a plausible link between positive attitudes and culture change, so much as explaining the need to depart radically from existing ideas by adopting a programme of re-engineering.

This case also raises questions about another limitation of plausibility. That is, how do we explain something has been made plausible (e.g., the change programmes) and then shift focus to a different set of cues that conflict with what has previously been stated? This suggests that an understanding of plausibility depends on the context and the activity systems in which stories are developed. Would the changeover to re-engineering, for example, have been as plausible if it had not been raised in the context of privatization? What is the role of power and organizational coalitions? As studies of culture change and corporate mergers indicate, ideas are less acceptable when they come up against a number of powerful people who are acculturated in different ways of thinking to the dominant coalition (see Mills and Murgatroyd, 1991).

Enactive of the environment

> There's no question that the fact that we are now an investor owned utility means we must focus on a market driven economy.
>
> (Comeau, quoted in Myrden, 1994)

The concept of enactment brings us to the core of sensemaking. If the other six properties are about influences on sensemaking, enactment is about imposing that sense on action. This is of particular interest to the study of the management of change. Through a study of the articulated activities of senior management at Nova Scotia Power, we can gain a sense of what influences those articulations and how they influence not only the way others (e.g., employees) make sense but of future sensemaking possibilities.

Enactment directs our attention to the ways that people impose sense on a situation. It tells us that in the management of change we should not be interested in whether, in fact, a programme of change is successful so much as whether a strong sense of successful change is imposed on on-going events. One of the more interesting questions that the re-engineering of the pilot projects raised relates to how notions of success and failure were socially constructed. To answer this, sensemaking demonstrates how Nova Scotia Power used the property of enactment to benchmark itself against other organizations' success or failure with re-engineering, and to the goals established by the consultants, to determine their achievements. Examining events at Nova Scotia Power, what we are interested in, therefore, is the extent to which senior management were able to enact the idea of change and the impact that this enactment had on subsequent events.

In fact, the property of enactment serves several purposes in the analysis of Nova Scotia Power. At one level, more so than the other properties, it describes the 'mechanical' process of how people sort data so that it can be given meaning. Weick (1979) describes enactment as a 'bracketing activity', whereby raw information is presented to individuals, who then 'punctuate' it so that it makes sense. This aspect of enactment is useful in helping to explain Comeau's understanding of the need for change, i.e., his individual enactment of events.

Another important aspect of enactment is the notion that it is about the social construction of reality that goes beyond the individual sensemaker, imposing a sense on events for a number of people (Weick, 1995). Louis Comeau used this type of enactment several different ways as he developed different 'enacted truths' through various communications techniques, in order to give the changes credibility. The third level of analysis where enactment is useful focuses on the impact of enacted environments on those caught up in its sense.

The impact of enactment

Weick (1995) contends that the enactment of a sensible environment influences those who created it. For Comeau, once committed to a sense of change, he became to some extent trapped into believing that Nova Scotia Power's problems were only fixable by changing the culture. Anything that appeared to contradict the rules imposed by the changes, as well as previously enacted management styles, was now viewed as counter-productive to the organization. And what had previously made sense was now viewed as unacceptable because it didn't fit with the new construction of reality. During these times, symbolic artefacts were used by Nova Scotia Power to enact both the culture change and re-engineering.

Reacting to the environment

While the social characteristic of sensemaking is supposed to ensure a nego-tiated process, where outcomes are contingent on the conduct of others, at Nova Scotia Power the enactment of change seems to have its origins at the top, specifically the sensemaking of Louis Comeau. At first glance, employees' enactment of events appears to be a reaction to the rules and regulations of an environment that has been created for them. But enactment is more complicated than this linear view. Environments are not fixed. Members of an organization will enact the part of an organization that exists for them. Enactive sensemaking, therefore, is a valuable tool that can be used to explain employee response to an imposed environment.

Through employee enactment, we are able to see the different faces of enactment more clearly, both how it creates and restrains behaviour. For example, nowhere was employee enactment more problematic than in Cape Breton. Here sensemaking was both constrained by, and enactive of, an envir-onment, which had long been resistant to managerial ideas. Employee action supported Weick's (1995) contention that 'people create their environments as their environments create them'.

Enactment and the pilot projects

The restructuring of the call centre and the creation of the CSFR roles, based on a re-engineering template provided by Harrington (1991), whereby existing jobs were made to fit into pre-existing moulds, provides an example of employee enactment. Goals were set and targets established so that any variances from the expected outcomes were construed as failure because they weren't enactive of the principles of re-engineering. Likewise, Nova Scotia Power compared itself to the 'successes' of companies such as MT&T, Quebec Hydro, Ontario Hydro, and Florida Power and Light because they were companies that had enacted similar change programmes.

Yet discrepancies between desired outcomes occurred because the E&Y consultants were enacting a reproduction of Harrington's (1991) interpreta-tion of other re-engineering models. This continual recreation of the concept of re-engineering meant not only that different interpretations were being brought to bear on the re-engineering concept, but also that the E&Y consul-tants were trying to fit existing operations into a template for change, with little knowledge of the intricacies of the skills required for the job.

The CSFR position was created with expectations of what the job would accomplish. This, as we have seen, wasn't always the same as what could realistically be accomplished. While the consolidation of three diverse skills and aptitudes seemed a sensible and plausible method to reduce employee downtime and maximize cost effectiveness, the accurate assessment of the skills and aptitudes of the employees involved was not a factor in designing either the CSFR or call centre positions. Still, managers were led to believe that results, which differed from the expectations of the project teams, would be blamed on their poor management skills, so they changed the outcomes in a way that made them appear to fit with the solution. Having committed to the programme, the re-engineering teams and the consultants were unwilling to admit that their estimations were inappropriate for the task at hand. Instead, they sought a way to transform this unexpected outcome into a prior definition of a solution (Weick, 1995: 11). By ignoring the juggling by employees to revert to their previous jobs, or their attempt to make the data fit expectations, the inaccuracies disappeared.

Limitations of enactive sensemaking

One of my on-going criticisms of sensemaking has been Weick's failure to explain the relationship between power and the sensemaking voice. For instance, in this case how can we explain the extraordinary influence that one man, Louis Comeau, can have in the enactment of a sensible environment? How is it that a number of people (i.e., employees) appear to be the passive receivers of enactment? Why is it that alternative forms of enactment (e.g., a union's sense of a situation) may not be enough to resist let alone replace management enactments of reality?

When sensemaking is described as enactive of the environment, one is left wondering *whose* environment? The re-engineered CSFR position was not representative of the understanding of employees in those positions. But instead of negotiating a shared meaning, the most powerful actors' voices took precedence. Participation by invitation during the planning stages had been replaced by participation by coercive and normative power (Etzioni, 1975).

In the first case, Weick (1995: 38) explains that 'power privileges some meanings over others'. While his notions of cues and plausibility go some way in explaining how that privileging takes hold, it falls short of explanation. I suggest that part of the explanation needs to be sought in the relationship between knowledge and discursive practice (Foucault, 1979), imagination and formative contexts (Unger, 1987), and meta-rules and organizational rules (Mills and Murgatroyd, 1991).

In relation to the second point, Weick (1979) agrees that there is a correlation between enactment and organizational hierarchy, but he warns us not to get lulled into believing that the relationship is simply linear. Instead, Weick (1979: 16) claims that lower members of the organization can affect enactment because of 'majority rule', yet often they don't realize the amount of control they actually have, so they remain passive. As he (1995: 31) further explains, it is the 'active people' in the organization, whose environments are placed in front of 'passive people', who get their voices heard. While this may well be the case, and offers a limited explanation for events, such as the union resistance in Cape Breton, it still doesn't explain how some individuals become active, why their activity becomes more acceptable than others, and why it may be limited to pockets of resistance. Here Blackler's (1992a, 1993a) activity theory offers an understanding of the processes by which different enacted viewpoints can co-exist, conflict and encourage change.

The third question raises issues of cultural leadership in organizations, which has been the subject of some debate throughout various literatures (cf. Bryman, 1986; Gramsci, 1978; Kanter, 1979; Kotter, 1990; Schein, 1985; Smircich and Morgan, 1982). Weick (1979: 16) suggests that the failure of cultural leadership is in part due to the fact that 'vulnerability of those at the top' contributes to enactment from those below them, whereas critical management theory suggests that cultural leadership arises out of an ability to relate new and novel solutions to important aspects of existing discourse (Gramsci, 1978). Here there is considerable promise in an exploration of Weick's (1995) notions of cues and plausibility, Foucault's (1979) notions of discourse and knowledge, and Gramsci's (1978) notion of organic leadership.

However, a closer look at the way that the various properties can be said to describe the influences on enactment reveals some limitations by raising questions about contexts (Unger, 1987b), activities (Blackler, 1992a) and rules (Mills and Murgatroyd, 1991). A prime example is the contrast between the adoption of culture change and the adoption of re-engineering. In tracking issues of retrospection, cues, on-going sensemaking, identity construction, social sensemaking, and plausibility we need to understand the influences on framing in the first place. We need to explore the relationship between the actions of individual managers and the broad discourse of change within which those actions are framed.

Nova Scotia Power management introduced culture change and re-engineering at the points when both were at the height of their popularity. This raises questions about the context of ownership and its influence on how sense is made of change. When Nova Scotia Power introduced culture change, the four values meshed well with the perceived needs of a Crown Corporation. Yet, when the company introduced re-engineering and effectiveness teams, they meshed well with its new status as a privatized, 'investor-owned' company. What role did context play in the sensemaking of those who enacted these fashion fads?

Enactive sensemaking draws attention to the relationship between action and the sense that is made of it. In regard to the management of change, we are drawn to the idea that action, and the sense of that action, are both important, and that effective enactment relies to a great extent on the bracketing of felt experience. In other words, for a change programme to be sensed as such it should speak to ongoing experiences (e.g., a felt need for a change in job design that is followed by an improved job description). Thus we could surmise that the more removed a desired enactment is from experience and on-going action, the less likely will it be to succeed.

Projective sensemaking

Finally, the notion of projective sensemaking, and the discovery of our own inventions, can be compared to interpretation because its narrow focus partially accounts for a bias against understanding others' points of view. Although not as encompassing as Weick's sensemaking properties, it is an important concept because it recognizes the role of power in the sensemaking voice. As such, it is useful because it helps to clarify some of the 'misunderstandings' Nova Scotia Power experienced in having less than universal acceptance of change.

Whereas Weick's (1995) sensemaking focuses on an individual level of analysis that is mediated through social interaction, projected sensemaking explains what happens when a more powerful actor's interpretation tries to shape the sensemaking of others. For example, with the introduction of culture change Louis Comeau expected to create shared meaning. This was based on an understanding that all employees would co-operate with the consultant, that change could be handled with what I call a 'franchised culture', and a downplaying of the strength of the union and its feelings against management in Cape Breton. It can be argued that Comeau and his senior managers, convinced of the importance of culture change and the successful track record of the consultant, projected their sense of occasion on to employees. At best, senior management assumed that a short period of training could instil a sense of commitment to values that they had more readily sensed.

Unlike Weick's sensemaking properties, which provide a way of understanding what informs the sensemaking process, projective sensemaking is useful in describing the process whereby some organizational actors have a stronger voice than others. However, projective sensemaking is limited by its inability to do much more than signpost the undervalued role of power in the sensemaking processes.

Conclusion

Throughout this chapter, sensemaking properties supply answers to some of the questions posed in Chapter 1. At the broadest level, the sensemaking properties improve our understanding of the process and management of change at the implementation level. Certainly the social construction of change is evident in the way ideas of change were devised and enacted. Sensemaking also demonstrates how different managers make plausible different opinions on change and the process. As well, it explains how these views are grounded in a certain construction of identity.

Working with the complex definition proposed by Weick (1995), I have suggested that sensemaking provides us with a framework to begin to put together the pieces of the puzzle in understanding the change process. At one level, the properties of sensemaking provide reasons for different understandings of the same event. Sensemaking offers an explanation for the adoption of different change programmes over time by the same organization and it shows how plausibility can take precedence over accuracy in the assessment of these programmes. Most importantly, sensemaking offers an explanation for outcomes that differ from what is anticipated. Simply put, sensemaking makes sense of the process of change.

Yet there are some issues that sensemaking ignores and where I feel it can be strengthened by the addition of other organizational approaches. For example, sensemaking fails to deal with the power of some actors over others. At the same time, it doesn't adequately explain the importance of structural influences on the sensemaking process, nor does it provide clear links that connects these influences to social-psychological outcomes. How is it, for example, that the actor, Louis Comeau, came to 'invent' the notion of organizational change as an important tool to achieve efficiency and profitability? Sensemaking could be enhanced to include motives for the interpretation into certain change programmes, and to offer sufficient explanation for the outcomes.

Some of the inadequacies of sensemaking became evident in the application of the properties to the case study material. In the case of identity construction, for example, we saw how an identity was imposed on employees. But what happens when the employees' viewpoint isn't considered? Although we see that the rules are reinvented and circumvented, sensemaking doesn't adequately account for this. The same can be said to be true for the other properties. Whose plausibility is being considered? For example, while combining the tasks in the CSFR positions might have seemed plausible for the consultants, because it was enactive of an environment that was familiar to them, it didn't take into consideration the opinions of others who were opposed to such action.

Again, it appears as if the sensemaking of a few was imposed on the many. This raises questions about the validity of the cues that were extracted to make sense of the situation. At one level it can be asked, whose cues are extracted? At another level, we can question how these extracted cues are transmitted and imposed on organizational members with less power? For example, Louis Comeau, Wayne Crawley and the consultants chose to ignore the sunk costs of buying the re-engineering solution, and instead focused on the amount of money BPI would save them. They also selectively ignored the reinterpretation of the work processes (including the loss of revenue from uncollected bills and the hiring of laid-off management in newly created positions) and instead focused on the 'success' of the re-engineered positions. Yet, employees who interpreted these same cues as signs of 'failure' did not succeed in having their cues recognized. Ultimately, the limitations of the sensemaking model lie in their inability to represent fairly the sensemaking of all the participants of the same experience.

Sensemaking makes sense in context, but one of the limitations of contexts is that they have, in this case, represented only the dominant ideology and

Weick underestimates their influence on the sensemaking process. Certainly sensemaking fills in the gaps that we are left with using traditional models of change, but there are still many events where sensemaking offers only a partial explanation, or where events could be better analysed by taking into account other complementary management theories.

To summarize, sensemaking's biggest weaknesses are: (a) its inability to explain adequately pre-existing influences on the process of sensemaking (i.e., what influenced social and enactive sensemaking so that it was negotiated to fit Comeau's understanding of change? How did employees react to this?); (b) a disregard for the role of power play in the sensemaking process (i.e., how did Comeau's dominant sensemaking affect the social-psychological dynamics at Nova Scotia Power?); and (c) a failure to develop an explanation for the rules of behaviour which mediate organizational activity (i.e., why didn't the selling of culture change to Cape Breton employees take into account the need to manage?).

Taken on their own, the properties of sensemaking can be used to demonstrate what happened at Nova Scotia Power and to make sense of the change process. But there needs to be something that links together the different types of sensemaking. In making sense of the culture change phase, sensemaking only takes us so far. The concluding chapter will take up the relationship between sensemaking and other theories of organization.

7 Making sense of sensemaking

Suggestions for sensible modifications of the sensemaking model

Introduction

The intention of this concluding chapter is to make sense of the sensemaking model in the analysis of the Nova Scotia Power case. In doing so, I will discuss how, taking into account my late arrival to sensemaking, I retrospectively discovered limitations of the sensemaking model as an analytic tool. I will suggest that the possibility exists for a modification of Weick's sensemaking model to include the rules perspective of change (Mills and Murgtroyd 1991) and activity theory (Blackler, 1992a; Engestrom, 1987; Unger, 1987a). This offers a means of enriching and complementing sensemaking, and answers some of the questions that the sensemaking approach fails to take into account. In conclusion, the validity and usefulness of these modifications for future research will be discussed, as well as the limitations of this particular application of sensemaking to this case.

Usefulness of sensemaking as a model of change

As I have argued earlier, the need exists for a way to understand change that looks at the process from a holistic perspective, as well as having a solid theoretical grounding for the academic audience and a practical application for the non-academic audience. Despite the symbiotic relationship between management education and change programmes there are still deep levels of suspicion between the two different worlds.

I feel that the events that occurred at Nova Scotia Power help to illustrate some of the issues that become evident in many organizations after expensive and 'revolutionary' programmes have been implemented, and these are relevant for these two audiences. Many times management and employees ask, 'was the change necessary and who did it benefit?' The use of sensemaking, as a means of uncovering why individuals think the way they do, alerts managers to the problems they could encounter in trying to introduce a change programme.

For the academic, this study and analysis suggests an alternative way to explore the process of change and culture that takes into account the many influences on the process. But I feel that there are also some lessons to be drawn from this case study that are useful for practitioners. If, as Mills and Murgatroyd (1991) argue, organizations are composed of specific configurations of rules, what are the implications for applying a generic change programme (e.g., Business Process Re-engineering) across a number of different organizations?

This is not to say that Weick's sensemaking model is not a valid tool to unravel the intricacies of change. It is, however, fair to say that sensemaking can only take us so far in the quest for a holistic change model, and while it is good at understanding the sensemaking processes of individuals it fails to connect the sometimes disparate points of view.

I am suggesting that activity theory (Blackler, 1992a), utilizing formative contexts, explains the motives, or origins of the sensemaking process, and rules theory (Mills and Murgatroyd, 1991) offers an explanation for the consequences interpretation has on the behaviour and enactment of sensemaking, and subsequently the culture of the organization. Although I came late to this realization, I will use *my* sensemaking to weave together elements of activity theory and rules theory with the sensemaking properties, in order to enhance and develop sensemaking. This is not meant to diminish the importance of sensemaking; rather, it can heighten and secure its role as a sensemaking device.

Limitations of the sensemaking model: a retrospective

As I have stated, a key part of the process of identifying, adopting and implementing change programmes involves sensemaking by the actors involved. As a 'sensemaker' Weick's (1995) concept of sensemaking provided me with a useful starting point for exploration of sensemaking and organizational change. However, after an analysis of the data, I realized that there were certain limitations with the sensemaking model because of what it failed to do in helping to understand change.

Motives

First, I recognized that, on its own, sensemaking is not comprehensive enough to include the motives for the selection of certain change programmes, or to offer sufficient explanation for the outcomes when they differ from what is expected. Sensemaking frames our understanding of the change literature and its limitations, but in understanding the decisions that led to key events at Nova Scotia Power, the background for motives of individual enactment are sketchy and the limitations of its structural analysis become apparent. Thus, while frames and cognitive mapping offer a preliminary explanation for enactment, they do not adequately account for the origins of the differences in subtleties that underlie individual and societal ideologies. In order to provide a foundation for sensemaking, I suggest Mills and Murgatroyd's (1991) rules perspective uncovers these ideologies.

Individual versus organizational sensemaking

This brings us to the issue of the levels of sensemaking and how they can lead to inconsistent behaviour or dissonance. Jackson's (1996) 'fad surfing' seems, at first glance, to be a good example of how individual sensemaking takes a back seat to organizational sensemaking in the creation of a myth and shows how frames provide varying cues and scripts at these different levels. But it still doesn't explain why some programmes are more popular than others and how they gain or lose popularity over time. Indeed the making of a successful fad depends on both individual and organizational sensemaking and many other factors. While the problems may be clear to see, coming up with a solution that will be acceptable to all is more difficult. In order to articulate these issues more clearly, I suggest drawing instead upon Unger's (1987) notion of formative contexts in activity theory.

Contextual limitations

Even though sensemaking makes sense in context, it has been shown that one of the limitations of the concept of 'context' is that there is an unequal distribution of power within given contexts, which, as I have argued in the previous chapters, is unexplained. As well, another important contextual limitation, and one which I had not grasped until well after the data collection stage of the thesis, is that contexts are gendered (and racio-ethnic – see Cox, 1990). As I turned to Weick (1995) for insights it was clear that organizational sensemaking does not confront the issue of gender (Hatfield and Mills, 2000) nor race. Yet, as I reflect on events at Nova Scotia Power I realize that gender (and race) are important influences on the sensemaking process that need to be taken into account. For example, I have referred at different points to the gendered descriptions of various jobs (e.g., linesmen). Content analysis of the Annual Reports of Nova Scotia Power indicates a

Table 7.1 Images of women and people of colour in the Annual Reports of Nova Scotia Power, 1989–96

Annual Report	Number of male images	Number of female images (% of all images*)	Number of white images	Number of images of people of colour (% of all images*)
1989–90	62	13 (18%)	61	1 (1.5%)
1990–1	25	3 (11%)	28	0 (0%)
1992	31	9 (22.5%)	37	3 (7.5%)
1993	19	2 (9.5%)	21	0 (0%)
1994	29	9 (24%)	37	1 (2.5%)
1995	22	18 (45%)	34	6 (15%)
1996	14	6 (30%)	18	2 (10%)

Note: * Percentage adjusted to the nearest 0.5.

gendered and racio-ethnic understanding of sensemaking within corporate statements (see Table 7.1).[1] But beyond these indications there is a need for further research on how gendered (and racio-ethnic) realities influenced the sensemaking activities around adoption and implementation of change programmes. What, for instance, is the role of masculinity (Collinson and Hearn, 1994) and of femininity (Fondas, 1997) in the role of organizational change (Itzen and Newman, 1995). How does the racio-ethnic background of the actors influence how they make sense of the world (Prasad, 1997; Said, 1993)?

Intersubjectivity

While Weick's model is a valuable heuristic for understanding organizational life, it gets caught up in the literal notion of 'face value' as a social-psychological activity. Sensemaking in Weick's model is a cognitive process that is influenced by intersubjectivity but we get little understanding of how intersubjectivity is structured (e.g., systems of organizational co-ordination and control) and what impact it has on the sensemaking process. Why, for example, did some employees have different understanding of what the changes were supposed to mean? This ambiguity was demonstrated by the different meaning assigned by employees and management to 'the showers incident' and the creation of the CSFR position (see Chapter 6). If shared experiences are the root of shared meaning, sensemaking still does not adequately explain the origins of different interpretations of shared experiences, nor does it explain what occurs when there are no similar starting points.

Culture

Sensemaking offers a useful understanding of organizational culture as a framework of sensemaking activity, but it fails to explain how the factors that shape the culture are the result of sensemaking and, at the same time, inform the sensemaking process. Why, for example, did Comeau pick the four values and why were they acceptable for some and not for others? What is needed is something that places culture into the process of management of change and sensemaking. What is missing is an understanding of the broader sociological influences on individual and group sensemaking.

Specifically, I only realized retrospectively that Weick's (1995) model lacks the ability to explain why/how some 'inventions' come to be developed in the first place, or how/why 'inventions' are mediated through a series of on-going interactions that are guided by rules of behaviour. For example, how is it that Louis Comeau came to 'invent' the notion of cultural change as an important tool to achieve efficiency and profitability? How did the rules of interaction influence which elements of an 'invention' were able to emerge, how was meaning assigned to a situation, and how did 'inventions' come to be enacted?

Taylor and Lerner's (1996) attempt to 'make sense of sensemaking' by grounding it in narrative manages to suggest broader influences without ultimately dealing with those influences. The questions that confronted me were, how are 'deep structural links' developed' and 'how do they play out in ongoing situations'?

Solutions: strengths and weaknesses

While Blackler's (1992a) notions of formative contexts and activity systems seek to explain the relationship between broad social factors and specific social-psychological processes in action, I was still struck by the absence of influences at the organizational level. For example, Comeau chooses these programmes. What happens next? To that end, Mills and Murgatroyd's (1991) notion of organizational rules, which seeks to explain the relationship between established rules of behaviour and the mediation of rules (including enactment, ignorance and resistance) by individual actors, provide a way forward.

Blackler's activity theory

As a model of change, Blackler incorporates Unger's (1987a, 1987b) notion of formative contexts, and the work of Vygotsky (1978) and Engestrom (1987) on activity systems, as a way of understanding disjunctive change by viewing organizations as activity systems and exploring 'the tentative nature of knowledge' (Blackler, 1992b: 1). Combined with sensemaking, activity theory's strengths add another dimension to the change perspective. Whereas sensemaking offered a linear view of change, the added dimension of activity theory helps not only to explain the key background factors that shape sensemaking but the impact that those factors have on on-going activity.

The work of Blackler and his colleagues (1992a, 1992b, 1993, 2000) offers a way of understanding not only the micro and macro contexts within which sensemaking occurs but the possibilities of change (Hatfield, 1994, 1996). Blackler's work on activity systems provides a more comprehensive explanation of the 'social' element in Weick's notion of sensemaking while providing a way of conceptualizing a link between socio-cultural factors, discourse and organizational rules.

Central to Blackler's work are the related notions of activity and activity systems. Drawing on the work of Vygotsky, Blackler (1992a: 289) defines activity as 'a sociocultural interpretation imposed on the context by the participants themselves', that is, that activity is not merely 'action' but the inter-relationship between the processes of acting and making sense of the action. Thus, for example, Nova Scotia Power managers and their Cape Breton employees responded to culture change activities through reference to broader socio-cultural understandings imposed on the situation (see Figure 7.1).

In other words, sensemaking occurred in a context that influenced how sense was made of events. To take another example, the activities of a Nova Scotia Power engineer should be seen not simply as engagement in the physical act of engineering (e.g., machine tooling) but in a process that is framed by a particular understanding of what engineering is (e.g., an undertaking involving the exercise of certain skills, etc.). 'Activity' alone does not tell us anything about the roots of the sense that people impose on an action and this is where Blackler (this time drawing on the work of Engestrom) develops the notion of activity systems.

Activity systems refers to 'the context of actions' that is constructed, by social actors, through a series of influences

> which mediate the interactions between the individual and his or her context; by the appearance of traditions, rituals and rules which mediate the relationship between the individual and his or her community; and by a simultaneous emergence of a division of labour that mediates the relationship between the community and the actions of its members.
>
> (Blackler, 1993b: 868)

Thus, a social actor draws upon broad understandings to make sense of a particular activity. In the examples above the engineer does not simply make sense of his activity from a peculiar personal understanding of the situation (although this is always a possibility) but, rather, draws on established notions of the character of engineering tools, skills and knowledge;[2] and the Cape Breton employee may have put a personal spin on culture change, but that spin was influenced by the lens of class conflict and labour–management relations.

The strengths of activity theory lie in its ability to explain on-going action as a relationship between past assumptions rooted in 'formative contexts' and interpretive situations embedded in 'activity systems' (Blackler, 1992a). In simple terms, 'formative contexts' are broad normative contexts that are established over time and influence how actors develop behavioural routines (Blackler, 1992a: 284), whereas 'activity systems' refer to the fact that while formative contexts shape behavioural routines they can never do so in a standardized fashion.

Behavioural routines, developed in a different time frame from the formative contexts that influenced them, are more directly influenced in social processes, which mediate formative contexts, and their interpretations that are brought to bear on a given situation. As we can see from Figure 7.1, the actor as manager (e.g., Louis Comeau), and the actor as employee (e.g., Cape Breton workers) share a social process, or activity system (e.g., change programmes), that are framed not only by their on-going interactions but by the formative contexts that shaped those processes.

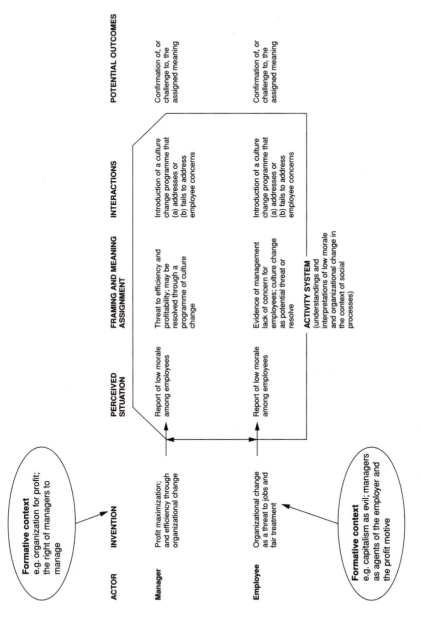

Figure 7.1 Organizational change, formative contexts and activity systems

Through exploration of key aspects of social life that contribute to the construction of an activity system, Blackler reveals the potential for organizational change. Here, while consistently focusing on contradictions and ambiguities, within and between activity systems, Blackler's understanding of the 'essentials of such contexts' shifts from an emphasis on Unger's notion of formative contexts to an emphasis on Engestrom's model, which includes 'culture, division of roles, and physical artefacts' (Blackler, 1993: 868–9). In brief, Unger (1987a) contends that

> the origins of social arrangements lie in past social conflicts and the institutional and imaginative arrangements that followed their resolution. [That such] 'formative contexts' are deep seated and pragmatic in their effects on everyday life [and] provide an implicit model of how social life should be led.
>
> (Blackler, 1992a: 283)

Unger's notion of formative contexts links activity at the local level with dominant social assumptions about the character of social life and helps to explain how people come to reproduce existing practices.

For example, when Nova Scotia Power privatized it did so in a context where privatization was seen by many as an essential aspect of organizational development and profitability.[3] In Canada the privatization of Nova Scotia Power was part of a process that began with the election of the Conservative Government of Brian Mulroney in 1984, 'the first federal government in the post-war era committed to reducing the state-owned sector' (Tupper, quoted in Lawson, 1992: 10). Compare this with the period prior to 1929 when Canadian governments placed an emphasis on creating national unity by, among other things, direct involvement in the transportation, communications and energy sectors to provide a necessary infrastructure for development (Snair, 1993: 18). In a similar vein, the context in which Nova Scotia Power adopted BPI included the recent collapse of Soviet communism and the popularization of 'globalization' and 'free enterprise capitalism'.

While Unger recognizes 'the privileged hold that certain groups and traditions have upon the mass culture [exerting] a unifying influence over expectations and ideals' (Blackler, 1992a: 280) he nonetheless provides 'a somewhat restricted account of human agency', having little to say about how 'the distinctive characteristics of a formative context may be learned and internalized by those affected by them' (Ibid.: 287–8). To this end, Blackler turns to Engestrom for answers, sadly, in the process, losing sight of the role of dominant actors. Engestrom's focus on processes of mediation – 'of *tools between* subject and object, of *rules* between community and subject, and of the *division of labour* between community and object' (Blackler, 1993: 869, emphasis in the original) – appears no less vague in its specifics than Unger's concept of formative context but is important in focusing attention on

(a) the idea that different elements, or essentials, contribute to the construction of an activity system; (b) that each essential may contain conflicting and ambiguous elements; (c) that an activity system can be composed of actors who are more or less influenced by different essentials or reflect a different aspect of an essential; and (d) that an activity system may contain conflicting and ambiguous ideas. From this perspective change can occur when actors confront or are confronted by conflict and ambiguities in their activities. For Blackler (1993: 881) this can help managers and others to effect change by making participants aware of the social constructionist nature of their activities and 'encourag[ing] people to stand back from their everyday routines and to perceive the overall pattern that such routines fall into'.

Thus, the notion of organizations as activity systems encourages a focus on different areas of dominant social, institutional and local practices in the maintenance of a particular set of rules and the role of conflict and ambiguities in how those rules change or might be changed. For example, in order to explain why Cape Breton employees, more than those on the mainland, rejected the culture change, we would need to examine the contribution of such things as local practices (e.g., militant trade unionism), institutional practices (e.g., the existence of segregated workplace amenities, including parking, washroom and canteen area), broad social understandings and practices (e.g., the role of class conflict in Cape Breton), and the potential for contradiction within and between levels (e.g., conflict between local management and head office; corporate concern with employees in a hierarchical workplace, etc.).

Blackler's work complements that of Weick in that it explains the broad historical framework of sensemaking, but is less detailed on the social-psychological factors that constitute 'activity systems'. While Weick (1995) explores the micro behavioural processes of sensemaking, he is less detailed on the macro ('formative contexts') and the meso ('activity systems) aspects. For example, Weick discusses the notion of 'invention' as a solution that is already familiar. How does that familiarity occur? Activity systems based on expertise would suggest that our solutions be based on collective activity that reflects a mediated and familiar pattern of behaviour. This would explain Comeau's choice of change programmes, which were made because other corporate and utility company CEOs were using these change programmes at the time.

There are, however, several areas where I feel that Blackler's work on activity theory falls short of a complete explanation for understanding the management of meaning, and where rules theory (Mills and Murgatroyd, 1991) and sensemaking can compensate for these blank spots. For one thing, its limitations are in its inability to adequately explain constraints on members' behaviour (i.e., rules). For another thing, it downplays the role of power, a fact that is particularly evident in his individual-centred notion of 'emancipation' as a process of making people aware of the social constructionist 'dynamics of their situation' (1993: 872).

First, Blackler's approach to understanding disjunctive organizational change by linking social, institutional, cognitive and emotional theories appears to be managerialist (Mills and Simmons, 1998) in its focus and concerns:

> managers may find an emerging alternative sketched out at the start of this paper to be both unfamiliar and perplexing. The approach ... is intended ... to facilitate an orientation to management that is based on contemporary theories of knowing and doing.
>
> (Blackler, 1992b: 1)

His comments that activity theory 'reframes matters of central concern to management' and has 'implications for the management of knowledge work', while making reference to 'the relationship between knowledge and economic success' (Blackler, 1992b; 1) implicitly suggests that the focus of activity theory is on managers' understanding of the well-being of the company. Understanding (disjunctive) change through the social interactions of organizational actors (activity systems) and the formative contexts which influence their actions provides a means to manage change more effectively but leaves little room for the role of the employee. This omission is similar to Weick's failure to deal with issues of power but also undermines the notion of activity by only focusing on some of the actors in the activity system.

Second, Blackler, following Unger, argues that the conventional rational approach to understanding is breaking down, and that alternative solutions must be sought. Activity theory, he contends, provides such an alternative, that 'social theory can serve an emancipatory function by demonstrating the arbitrary origins of social systems and by helping people to rethink and rework their behavioural routines and normative attributions' (Blackler, 1992b: 4). While this may explain the possibility of change, it underplays the fact that people continue to act in rational–cognitive ways (Reed, 1992). Indeed, as Blackler (1992b: 3) recognizes, 'the rhetoric of traditional rationalism has retained its attractions. Objectivist images of professional knowledge retain a powerful mystique'. Blackler does not say what the implications of this are on studying culture from a cognitive and emotional perspective, and what happens once people have acted out the possibilities of change. I would again argue that people still need to return to rules for a sense of order or guidance, and that an understanding of organizational rules is a necessary aspect of the change process.

Unger's formative contexts

In his model of activity theory as a change model, Blackler incorporates the work of Unger (1987a, 1987b) who views society as an artefact. Unger (1987a) argues that unless underlying institutional and imaginative structures of societies are made explicit and disturbed, we will mistake the regularities and routines that persist for general laws of social organization. Unger's (1987a) approach is to repudiate traditional assumptions that, (a) there are a limited number of stages of social organization, whose parts combine to form an invisible package; and (b) general explanations of the origins, workings and reinventions of these frameworks must 'take the form of appeals to deep-seated economic, organizational and psychological constraints or to irresistible developmental forces supposedly underlying the chaos of historical life' (see Blackler, 1992a). In terms of organizational change this suggests, according to Blackler (1992a, 1993b), that the managers of change need to be encouraged to focus on the social constructionist aspects of organizational life. This is a valuable point and one worth noting. However, it is but one side of the story and does not take into account conservative psychological processes and the desire for order (i.e., avoiding constant change). There is no explanation for how rules that constrain our activities at one level become accepted because of the routines (guidance?) they provide at another level. For example, Unger (1987a), in a statement akin to sensemaking, states that:

> Our thoughts and desires and our relations to one another never fit, completely or definitely, within the structures we impose upon belief and action [but] . . . often we treat the plain lustreless world in which we actually find ourselves. . . . as if *its* structures of belief and action were here for keeps, as if *it* were the lost paradise where we could think all the thoughts and satisfy all the desires worth having. What we think in this way. . . . [as] a basis for understanding, it is worse than a sin. It is a mistake.
>
> (Unger, 1987a: 18)

But where does our sense of self come from? To what extent are we, or can we be, divorced from the structures of thought and action that we inhabit?

Unger is primarily concerned with the radical intent of 'disturbing' our notion of structure as standing over and above human action. Blackler adopts that approach as a method of disturbing existing organizational realities to bring about change. Again the point is well made that structures are the outcomes of human activity but that their power lies in the fact that people rarely recognize that fact. This is a useful lesson for change agents who are, on the one hand, attempting to evaluate new structures (e.g., BPI) and, on the other hand, finding ways to change existing structures. Nonetheless, we still need to be reminded that the structuring of human activity cannot be avoided; those forms of resistance can be built in (cf. Wicks, 1997), but we cannot rid ourselves of structures. Thus, it would be also interesting to understand the role of, as well as departures from, structures in the process of sensemaking. How does it occur that, as Unger states, people's social arrangements are 'deeply entrenched in their imaginations, so that bases of authority, legal dogmas, role systems, technologies and styles of organising become accepted as normal and acceptable' (Unger, cited in Blackler, 1992b: 4)?

Again, I suggest that the rules perspective (Mills and Murgatroyd, 1991) offers another level of explanation. While formative contexts appear to be similar to what Mills and Murgatroyd (1991: 129) call meta rules, these (e.g., modes of production, competition, privatization) are broader, vaguer, and more flexible, and actually transcend and influence a number of formative contexts. From a coherence of specific meta rules, certain rules, according to Mills and Murgatroyd (1991), come together particular to that formative context. Therefore formative contexts can be explained as a configuration or class of meta rules. This would explain how the meta rules of privatization and competition influenced Nova Scotia Power's formative contexts of 'organization for profit' or 'management as agents of the employer' (see Figure 7.2).

Finally, Unger refers to terms of access people have for practical activity. He calls these terms 'powers and rights'. As such, they draw an outline within which people can make claims upon one another's help. He states that 'a stable system of powers and rights must work as a practical expression of a certain way of imagining society, of conceiving what the relations among people can and should be like in different areas of existence'. I would call these 'rules'.

Engestrom's activity systems

The work of Engestrom (1987), which defines activity systems as the context of actions, rounds off Blackler's model. With mediation central to Engestrom's theory, Blackler states:

> Human activity systems are distinguished by the emergence of tools and concepts which mediate the interactions between the individual and his or her contexts; by the appearance of traditions, rituals and rules which mediate the relationship between the individual and her community; and by a simultaneous emergence of a division of labour that mediates the relationship between the community and the actions of its members. The goals or objective, which provides the system with its coherence, is partly redefined for those involved (through culture, division of roles, and physical artefacts); in part it is recreated and modified by the actions of those involved.
>
> (Blackler, 1992b: 7)

Again I would argue that this provides a useful way of understanding the mediation of sensemaking, but that the somewhat vague notions of 'tools and concepts' are enhanced when understood as organizational rules and when the 'recreation and modification' of actions is understood as a form of rule enactment.

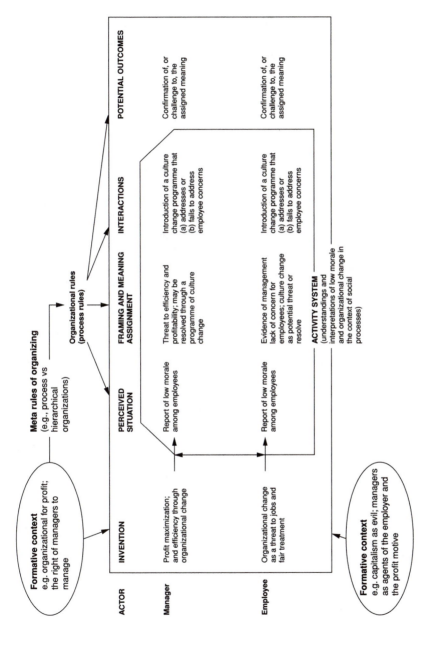

Figure 7.2 Organizational change, formative contexts, activity systems and organizational rules

The rules perspective

Despite the addition of activity theory to delve deeper into the socio-psychological aspects of sensemaking, what is still missing from the process is an understanding of the influence of organizational rules on the process of sensemaking. This is where the work of Mills and Murgatroyd (1991) is useful. There are two elements to the rules approach, (a) the rules themselves; and (b) the actors who engage in the process of establishing, enacting, enforcing, misunderstanding and/or resisting rules.

By 'organizational rules' Mills and Murgatroyd (1991: 3–4) refer to the configuration of written/unwritten, moralistic/legalistic/normative, and formal/informal 'phenomena whose basic characteristic is that of generally controlling, constraining, guiding and defining social action'. At the macro level, Mills and Murgatroyd (1991) refer to 'meta rules' as broad ways of organizing. These rules are often beyond the control of organizations (e.g., competition, privatization), but impact on how the organization structures itself (i.e., creates new technical or strategic rules). At the micro level, the rules perspective uses Clegg's (1981) six strategic areas of control to categorize rules pertaining to organizational action.

The rules are then categorized according to how they are officially or 'informally' enacted. Formal rules are described as the official rules used by management to specify how 'things are supposed to be'. But in the process of formal organizational development a series of informal rules reflecting 'how things are done', develops alongside, and sometimes in contradiction to, formal rules. For example, people develop various forms of association at work (e.g., social groups, friendship groups, unofficial pressure groups) beyond those that are officially defined (e.g., a specific unit, division or department). In the process of forming informal groups or relationships (i.e., those activities not specifically designed to conform to the formal requirements of the organization) people typically develop norms that govern aspects of their behaviour. This is the link between the culture the organization hopes to create, and the one that actually exists.

Mills and Murgatroyd (1991) also describe rules as sensemaking phenomena. But enactment is the response to measures of control (rules), which have resulted from an earlier sensemaking event, leading to the creation of the rules again being made sense of. Like Weick (1995), Mills and Murgatroyd (1991) cite individuals' sensemaking as an influence on the enactment of these rules, but this is restrained by individual rules (i.e., notions of morality, legitimacy, conformity, etc.).

Reed (1992) termed this approach 'managerial realist', arguing that

> the development of the rule concept is itself theoretically grounded in a model of the organization as an interrelated network of social practices, through which a wide multiplicity of activities are assembled to

form institutionalised frameworks or patterns of collective action, which are sustained over time and place by a matrix of rules.

(Reed, 1992: 133)

According to this model, the outcome of a series of processes and events determines the enactment of organizational rules and, thus, culture (Mills, 1988a). Simply put, organizational members make sense of the rules and then enact them.

The theory of organizational rules (Mills 1988a, 1988b; Mills and Murgatroyd, 1991) as a sensemaking 'activity' incorporates these different views of enactment to include social forces, institutional theory and socialization and demonstrates how the management of change is enacted through the creation, resistance or acceptance of organizational rules, which in turn serve as a device to maintain or change organizational culture. The strengths of the rules perspective is its ability to show how sensemaking, based on activity theory, is translated into behaviour.

While the rules approach fails to explain the processes through which actors come to develop and make sense of organizational rules, it nonetheless provides a missing element of the sensemaking puzzle – drawing attention to the fact that organizations are localized aspects of formative contexts and, as such, shape not only the next generation of formative contexts but help to bridge the divide between formative contexts and activity systems. Organizational rules mediate between formative contexts and activity systems – forming a localized framework in which sensemaking occurs and, in turn, influencing the development of future formative contexts.

The primary strength of the rules perspective is that it fills in a missing piece of the puzzle for making sense of the change process and it provides the link between that behaviour and the (re)creation of organizational culture. If formative contexts and activity systems explain the motives for patterns of behaviour, how are these motives made sense of and how does this translate into that behaviour? Whereas Weick's (1979, 1995) notion of enactment focuses on people creating their own environment and having their actions constrained by these environments (sensemaking), rules theory is more holistic. Mills and Murgatroyd (1991) suggest that while organizational rules may be an outcome of the sensemaking process, at another level rules serve as pre-existing sensemaking devices (i.e., organizational rules inform a person's sensemaking process).

The notion of formative contexts helps to explain organizational rules by rooting them in broader institutional and imaginative assumptions and, in combination, provides an understanding of the pre-existing influences on the processes of sensemaking. Activity theory provides a link between sensemaking activity, organizational rules and the broader 'formative contexts' which inform rule formation and sensemaking.

Sensemaking revisited: future implications?

Retrospectively, I realized that a composition of all three perspectives provides an opportunity whereby the limitations of sensemaking could be overcome by the strengths of activity theory, whose limitations in turn would be strengthened by rules theory. For example, it is implicitly understood that organizational shocks provide the impetus for change (Weick, 1995). Yet what causes these shocks? Meta rules and formative contexts can both explain how a shock occurs (i.e., the discourse on privatization forced Nova Scotia Power to re-evaluate their business strategy, while the formative context created by the meta rule of privatization brought with it organizational rules to control routines within this context). Yet organizational rules alone can't explain how rules are interpreted and enacted.

By emphasizing the role of power, while downplaying the universalizing assumptions in sensemaking, Weick's theory provides important directions for a rules approach. To begin with, through an examination of the role of founders and senior managers in the enactment of rules we could usefully explore the particular ways that sense was made of specific events, especially challenges to the existing order and the extent to which there was a felt need to impose 'order, clarity and rationality' on events (Weick, 1995: 29).

The following discussion is not meant to downplay the importance of sensemaking. Instead, the purpose is to demonstrate the ability of sense-making to analyse the change process, and to show how activity theory, formative contexts, and rules theory can be used to complement and strengthen the sensemaking of each of the properties, as they relate to the Nova Scotia Power case. As well, the value of this analysis is that it pro-vides an impetus for future research and refinement of the sensemaking model.

Grounded in identity construction

The notion that sensemaking is 'grounded in identity construction' meshes well with the idea of Mills and Murgatroyd's (1991) organizational rules as a set of experiences that have consequences for how people view them-selves and others as particular men and women. Louis Comeau's shift from a commitment to culture change to support for BPI, for example, is only partially explained by his attempt to promote a sense of self-enhancement, efficacy and consistency. Our understanding of his sensemaking is furthered when we understand the changing contexts of organizational rules that he seeks to align with his sense of self. In this case culture change meshed well with the organizational rules of a Crown Corporation that placed serving the community above profitability. In this context, a positive sense of self could be achieved where the CEO could be seen as promoting the interests of various constituents, including employees, the wider community and customer. Once the company was privatized BPI meshed well with the expectations of a for-profit organization, and in this case a positive leadership image centred on the ability to appear competitive, efficient and profit oriented.

Nonetheless, while Weick (1995: 23) contends that, 'people learn about their identities by projecting them into an environment and observing the consequences', he does so in a way that downplays the role of more powerful actors, in action and in relationship to organizational rules. Although focused on 'action', much of Weick's theory centres on the imposition of ideas on situations that have consequences for those beyond the primary sensemakers. This is at its clearest where Weick references managers as sensemakers who 'construct, rearrange, single out and demolish many "objective" features of their surroundings' (Weick, 1979: 164). Thus, while it may be true that everyone can be said to engage in sensemaking, it is far from clear that everyone is more or less equal in the process, nor is equally interested in enacting realities that come to dominate others' sensemaking, nor equally interested in the creation of ordered understandings of reality. The decision to privatize Nova Scotia Power, for example, was an imaginative action (Unger, 1987a) that originated with actors outside of the company. Comeau may have been party to the decision but as someone responding to a sensemaking event that originated elsewhere (i.e., in the Nova Scotia government). Employees of the company were clearly out of the loop and had little option but reaction to enacted decisions.

Weick states that sensemaking is grounded in basic values and beliefs, but what is not addressed is the reason for the different presentations of self. To adapt to the changing needs of the organization implies that there are different restrictions being placed on both the individual and the organization, which serve as boundaries for the change. So while values and beliefs are an ingredient in sensemaking, they do not wholly explain why people make sense of things in a particular way, or why there is a constant need for change and adaptation in organizations.

This perceived need to adjust our presentation of self is better understood when we take into account the way sensemaking can be guided and limited by formative contexts and activity systems. While based on values, these contexts and systems are much more intricate and complex because they offer an explanation for how the values and social interaction come to shape the sensemaking process. Therefore, this 'grounding' complements and serves as a starting point for the notion of formative contexts (Engestrom, 1987).

For example, by using Weick's definition of grounding, it could be said that the mistrust of management by employees in the Cape Breton region of Nova Scotia Power was made sense of based on values and beliefs that supported trade unionism in this area. But this offers only a partial explanation for the sensemaking. The values and beliefs created and sustained contexts that guided sensemaking and these contexts in turn limited the sensemaking options. Mistrust created a formative context whereby employees made sense of change programmes initiated by management as something bad, and the response to this was to defy any ideas put forth by management.

On-going sensemaking

According to Weick, sensemaking does not have a starting point but it does have a series of 'interruptions' which occasion the sensemaking process and precipitate the extraction of cues. While Weick's concept of on-going sense-making is useful in explaining how Nova Scotia Power moved from one change programme to another, it fails to explore the issue of compliance or resistance during these periods. Nova Scotia Power's continual recreation of change suggests that as the scripts change they act as 'reference points' for making sense of new events and dealing with interruptions to existing plans and actions. This is invaluable in directing us to explore how particular rule activities at any one time serve to maintain order, and how challenges to certain rules are dealt with through reference to 'rule activities'. This also offers new insights to the rules approach (Mills and Murgatroyd, 1991). For example, as Nova Scotia Power moved from culture change to privatization to re-engineering the problem for the managers of change was not whether the rules would change but how to manage rule changes. According to Mills and Murgatroyd (1991), rules are sets of expectations in action but they don't explain how explanations change. Weick (1995) deals with that issue through the notion of plausibility. Thus, management dealt with the change by developing a set of ideas, or a script that drew on several cues that constructed a plausible account. Sometimes plausibility resided in a reinterpretation of existing rules (e.g., a customer focus, efficiency, environmental protection), and sometimes through reference to a set of imperatives (e.g., global threat) or a powerful discourse (e.g., privatization, re-engineering) that challenged existing expectations and led to new rules (e.g., the ending of the no lay-off policy, the introduction of the CSFR and call centre positions). Thus, the notion of 'enacted cues' suggests that it may be possible to identify significant elements in the development of rules that have served to define particular situations.

Enactment

Simply put, enactment, as a property of sensemaking, means that we create an activity that reflects our making sense of the experience within our environment. However, Weick's enactment is broad in its focus and doesn't fully explain how the constraints come to be selected in the first place. Although his concept of enactment shares similarities with Mills and Murgatroyd's (1991) organizational rules, Weick suggests that enactment can be a subjective interpretation of one's environment, which can be constrained by external forces such as rules and regulations, whereas Mills and Murgatroyd focus on activities of socialization, whereby employees enact organizational rules and maintain organizational culture.

Weick (1979) explains enactment as the rediscovery of knowledge, or a self-fulfilling prophecy, but, in the process, he downplays the issue of the extent to which organizational actors are bound by individual limitations and biases, and he does not explain where such limitations originate. Implicitly there is an assumption that everyone works from a common set of organizational reference points based on patterns of behaviour. The concept of frames, defined as ways to categorize these cues or references, and cognitive maps as patterns of knowledge (Weick, 1995) places an emphasis on the ability of the organizational actor to draw upon sets of scripts to make sense of situations, but it doesn't explain how these scripts came to be. Enactment can, however, involve the institutionalization of social constructs into the way things get done so that we have predetermined roles and scripts to follow (DiMaggio and Powell, 1991). For example, Nova Scotia Power introduced change programmes to overcome low morale. By so doing, they created an environment that could constrain actions within the guidelines of those programmes. Employees were free to set limits on their behaviours, and some did.

In this way, rules theory offers an explanation for why enactment doesn't always reflect the wishes of those creating the constraints and opportunities. And in this case, it helps to explain why the change process wasn't universally accepted at Nova Scotia Power. According to Mills and Murgatroyd (1991), rules that govern our individual actions, such as non-conformity to the culture change in Cape Breton, impact on how we enact the organizational rules.

Social sensemaking

In a similar vein, one of the questions that emerged from the study of Nova Scotia Power was, 'how do different meanings come to be attached to the same experience?' The 'social' character of sensemaking (as a 'social process' whereby 'conduct is contingent on the conduct of others, whether imagined or physically present', Weick, 1995: 39) strengthens our view that the enactment of rules has consequences for all involved, by shaping the sensemaking contexts in which new rules are developed and in which identities become known. This raises questions about the influence of both shared meanings and shared experiences (Weick, 1995: 42) on collective action.

Instead, another way of understanding the divergent meanings and overcoming the issue of shared meaning versus shared experience is to consider how Mills and Murgatroyd's (1991) rules of action are understood (and experienced) in different ways by those involved. Whereas formative contexts provide a way to interpret ideas (e.g., the interpretation of change may be seen as 'good' if one is in head office management and 'bad' if one is not), rules theory, in turn, demonstrates how the different meanings are enacted through various activity systems, resulting in different consequences. Thus, for example, on the surface, mainland and Cape Breton employees all went through a similar culture change training experience, but the experience was mediated by different formative contexts (i.e., strong versus weak class values) and activity systems (i.e., established authoritarian versus participative management styles). The result was different understandings of the experience.

Extracted cues

The importance of extracted cues, according to Smircich and Morgan (1982) is to serve as a reference point for those in control. While Weick doesn't argue this point, he also doesn't make explicit this assumption of power. Instead he leads us to believe that some voices will be heard more clearly than others, but without saying why. By placing the notion of 'extracted cues' within the framework of 'formative contexts' (defined as 'assumptions that guide the ways in which interests are defined and problems approached', Blackler, 1992a: 280), we have a clearer understanding of the way that some cues become prioritized. In the introduction of privatization, for example, Louis Comeau's choice of cues were in great part provided by the formative socio-political context of conservative ideology and the drive to privatize Crown Corporations.

Plausibility

The influence of formative contexts on extracted cues also helps to explain elements of plausibility, in that it can be argued that certain cues carry a degree of plausibility by their link to powerful discourses. In Unger's (1987a) argument that the imaginative aspects of a formative context become powerful as they are institutionalized, we have a direct link to Mills and Murgatroyd's (1991) notion of organizational rules as, in large part, reflections of meta rules. This strengthens the idea of enacted cues as rooted in broader discourses that, as a result, lend plausibility. Of course, it is not simply a matter of selecting something because it is plausible. One must question how this decision has been reached (i.e., what assumptions have shaped this approach?). The example of Nova Scotia Power choosing first culture change and then re-engineering was enacted through plausible accounts, but it was still guided by contexts of being first a Crown Corporation and then a privatized company. In the first instance, elements of the rules of a Crown Corporation (e.g., the need to 'serve' the public) were used to justify the advent of culture change (e.g., values focused on serving customers). In turn those very rules lent plausibility to the culture change. This may appear circular logic but it is like a gestalt (Kohler, 1961) where figure and ground are understandable in relationship, or a jigsaw puzzle where each piece cues the overall puzzle but it is the puzzle itself that makes sense of any individual piece.

Retrospective

The 'retrospective' character of sensemaking (i.e., that 'people know what they are doing only after they have done it') can be traced through such things as corporate materials, with the view to revealing how enacted rules influenced specific notions at a subsequent point in time. Using a change programme as the invention, we see that the need for change is understood based on prior knowledge of similar change programmes, resulting from current discursive practices, but that its meaning is managed in a way that is individualized by both prior experience and restrictions imposed by the institutional norms. Once the change is interpreted into rules governing behaviour and woven into the sensemaking process through the management of meaning it becomes the fabric of discursive practices and continues to shape future sensemaking of other changes in the same manner.

Using the rules perspective (Mills and Murgatroyd, 1991), we are left wondering how the existence of specific rule-sets will influence how or when a change programme is introduced and implemented? If, as Blackler (1992a) contends, specific actions within an organization are framed by peculiar 'formative contexts' (or established ways of thinking and being rooted in particular historical developments) how will the implementation of a specific change programme be influenced by the existence of widely differing formative contexts across a number of companies? How will individuals' ways of thinking and being influence when and how a particular change programme is introduced and implemented? And if, as Weick (1995) suggests, making decisions is influenced by a person's 'sensemaking' framework, how is the process of organizational change in one organization likely to differ from that in another organization, and what are the implications for the management of change? How will different sensemaking frames of reference affect the outcomes of a change programme not only across a number of companies but within the same company? Sensemaking is able to frame and 'make sense' of all of these issues.

This led me to conclude that there is a need for an understanding of change that recognizes it as a problematized notion and accounts for people's understanding of given situations. Thus, the use of these conventional management practices partially explains the choice of these change programmes as solutions to organizational problems. The choices also demonstrate that while what went on in companies like Nova Scotia Power was not clearly 'successful', it was also not surprising. So while we can assume that Nova Scotia Power's decisions were driven by fads and fashions, the adequacy of the change material to explain the selection of these fads, and the gurus who promote them, lacks the depth of analysis required to explain individual decision-making and the impact of external factors.

Conclusion: a retrospective of my application of the sensemaking model

It is easy to look back and recognize how things could have been done differently. As part of the on-going nature of sensemaking, it is also easy to use retrospection to make decisions seem plausible. Yet, if I were able to start this research project with the knowledge I have since acquired, there are things I would have done differently.

First, I acknowledge that this study uses the single case of Nova Scotia Power to explain the process of change. I do not assume that all organizations are the same; rather, I recognize that while organizations have unique features, they are still bound by certain rules common to all organizations (i.e., meta rules of organizing, cf. DiMaggio and Powell, 1991) and they are still faced with similar challenges as they go through different stages of the organizational life-cycle (Greiner, 1972). 'Change' is one commonality in all organizations wishing to remain viable. It might be argued that organizations are idiosyncratic, but it is my opinion that organizations are bound by societal and ideological norms, resulting in relatively consistent behaviour and responses to environmental threats.

An understanding of how and why change is made sense of and interpreted, is relevant to all organizations. The issue is not what type of organization, or what type of change, but how the process of change is made sense of in a particular way. For example, organizational idiosyncrasies might affect how the change is made sense of within particular formative contexts, and how change is managed within different activity systems, using specific rules. I have stated that a strength of this study is the access I was afforded over a long period of time in one organization, but I do recognize the limitations of using only one in-depth study in the application of sensemaking to an analysis of change.

Second, while sensemaking provides a tool that can be used to check how individuals are making sense of events during a process of change, I did not choose this methodological approach (i.e., using sensemaking as a new way to explore the management of change) until after the data had been collected. Thus I was limited to the data that I did have.

Third, because I did start out with one methodological approach, I was limited to making retrospective sense of my data. This restricted, and in some ways biased, my analysis. But more importantly, it did not allow me to test any hypotheses.

I am sure that many people, in hindsight, would choose to do things differently. However, ultimately, I feel that this case study provides an impetus for future development of the sensemaking model by suggesting what might be possible by incorporating sensemaking with activity and rules theory.

Appendix A

North American-based companies involved in change programmes, 1980–97*

> **Key**
>
> C Canadian owned/based company
> ▼ Culture change
> ■ TQM
> ● BPR
>
> * Compiled from a review of seventy-eight North American business textbooks published between 1980 and 1998.

A&P ▼
AACSB ▼
Abbott Labs ■
Abitibi Price ▼
Acadia University C ▼
Adolph Coors ■
Advanced Filtration System ▼■
Aetna Life ▼■
AGI ▼
Air Canada C ▼
Air Florida ▼
Alberta Research Council C ■
Albertsons ■
Alcan ▼
Alcoa ▼
Allen-Bradley Co. ▼
Allied Ltd. ▼
Allied Signal ■
Almuth Public Library ▼
Aluminum Co. of America ■

Amanda Refrigeration ▼■
Amax ■
Amdahl ■
American Airlines ▼■
American Brands ■
American Cynamid ■
American Express ▼■
American Home Products ■
American Information Tech. ■
American International Group ■
American Motors ▼
American Standard ■
American Steel & W. ▼
American Stores ■
Ameritech ●
Amoco Chemicals ▼■
AMP of Canada Ltd. C ■
AMR ■
Anheuser-Busch ■
Apex Corp. ●

Apollo Computing ■
Apple ▼■
ARA Holdings ■
Arari ▼●
Archer Daniels Midland ■
ARCO ▼
Armco ■
Armstrong World Industries ■
Armtek ■
Arthur Anderson & Co. ▼■
Arvin Industries ■
Astra USA ▼
AT&T ▼■●
AT&T Credit Corp. ●
AT&T Universal Card Ind. ■
Avis ▼●
Avon ■
Bain & Co. ▼■●
Baker Hughes ■
Baker-Lovick ■
Ball ■
Banc One ▼■
Banca Di America e Di Italia ■
Bank of America ▼■
Bank of Montreal Ⓒ▼
Bankers Trust of America ■
BASF ■
Bassett Furniture Ind. ■
Bata Inc. Ⓒ▼■
Bausch & Lomb. ■
Baxter International ■
Baxter Travenol ■
Bayer USA ■
BCE Ⓒ▼
Beatrice Co. ■
Becton Dickinson ■
Beech-Nut ▼
Bell ▼■
Bell Atlantic ●
Bell South ■
Ben & Jerry's ■
Bethlehem Steel ▼■
Bethlehem Steel L.A. Plant ■
B. F. Goodrich ▼
Birkenstock Footwear ■

Black & Decker Canada Inc. Ⓒ■
Blockbuster Video ▼
Blue Bell ▼
Blue Diamond Drugs Ⓒ●
Body Shop, The ▼
Body Shop (Canada), The Ⓒ▼
Boeing ▼■
Boise Cascade Corp. ▼■
Bombardier Ⓒ▼
Borden ■
Borg-Warner Corp. ▼
Boston Globe ▼
BP America ■
Braniff ▼
Bridgestone's LA Vergne, Tenn. ■
Bristol Meyers ●■
British Petroleum ●
Brown-Forman ■
Brunswick ■
Burger King ▼■●
Burlington Holdings ■
Burlington Northern ■
Burroughs Corp. ▼
Burson Masteller ●
Cadbury Ⓒ■
Cadet Uniform Services Ltd. Ⓒ■
Cadillac ●
CAE Industries Ⓒ■
Calfed ●■
Camco Inc. Ⓒ■
Campbell Soup Co. ▼
Campbell Soup (Ont.). Ⓒ▼■
Canada Grocers Ltd. Ⓒ■
Canada Post Ⓒ▼
Canadian Airlines Ⓒ▼
Canadian Armed Forces Ⓒ■
Canadian Tire Ⓒ▼
Canon ■
Capital Cities Comm. ■
Carleton County Law Ass. ■
Carlisle ■
Caterpillar Tractor ▼■
CDC ▼
Champion International ■
Charles Machine ▼

Charles Schwab & Co ▼

Charlottetown Engineering Co. Ⓒ■

Chase Manhatten ■

Chemical Banking ■

Chesebrough-Ponds Inc. ■

Chevron ■

Chiat/Day Advertising ■

Chick-fil-A ■

Chrysler Corp. ▼■●

Chrysler (Windsor) Ⓒ▼

Chubb & Son ●

CIBC Ⓒ▼■

Cigna ■

Circi Craft Co. Ⓒ▼

Citibank ▼

Citicorp ▼■

City Govt. Tacoma W. ▼

Clorox ■

CNR Ⓒ▼

Coca Cola ▼■

Colgate-Palmolive ●

Columbia Pictures ■

Comerica ▼

Commonwealth Life ▼■

Compaq ▼■

Computerland ■

ConAgra ■

Connecticut General Life ■

Conrail ▼

Continental Airlines ●

Control Data ■

Cooper Tire & Rubber ■

Coors ●

Corning Glass ▼■●

Corning Telecommunications
   Prod. ■

Cray Research ▼■

Crocker Bank ▼■

Crown Cork & Seal ■

Crystal Brands ●

CSX ■

CTAL ▼

Culinar Inc. Ⓒ▼

Cummins Engine (NY) ▼■

Cypress Semiconductor ■

Cyprus Minerals ■

Dana Corp. ▼■●

Dayton-Hudson ■

De Mar ■

Dell Computers ▼■●

Delta Airlines ▼■

Denny's ■

Detroit Edison ■

Dialog ■

Diamond International ▼

Digital Equipment ▼■●

Dime Savings Bank ■

Disney ▼■

Dixie Yarns ■

Dofasco Ⓒ▼■

Dome Petroleum ▼

Donnelly Mirrors ■

Douglas Aircraft ■

Dow-Corning ▼

Dow Jones ●■

Dresser Industries ■

Du Maurier Ltd. Ⓒ■

Duke Power & Light ■

Dupont ▼■●

Dupont Canada ▼■

DWG ■

Eastern Airlines ▼■

Eastman Kodak ▼■●

Eaton's Ⓒ▼■

Echlin ■

Ecolab ■

EG&G ■

Electronic Data Systems ▼■

Eli Lilly ■

Emerson ▼■

Emery Air Freight ▼

Emhart ■

Engelhard Corp ▼

Envirodyne Industries ■

Equitable Life Assurance ■

Ernst & Young ▼■

Esprit ▼

Esprit Asia Holdings ▼

Exxon ▼■

Faber College ▼

Fabergé ■

Fairfax AFX ■

Fairfield High School ●

FBI ▼■

Federal Aviation Adm. ▼

Federal Department Stores ■

Federal Express ▼■

Federal National Mortgage ■

Fieldcrest Cannon ■

Financial Corp. of American ■

Firestone Rubber & Tire ▼

First Chicago Bank ▼■

First Interstate Bankcorp. ■

Fisher Scientific Group ■

Fleet Financial ■

Fleetwood Enterprises ■

Fleming Co. ■

Flexcom Co. ▼

Flight Time Corp. ■

Florida Power & Light ■

Fluor ■

Foley's Department Store ▼

Food Lion ■

Ford Kentucky Truck Plant ■

Ford Motor Co. ▼■●

Ford Motor Co (Windsor, Ont.) Ⓒ●

Ford Sharonville Plant ■

Ford Taurus ■

Fortune Corp. ■

Foster Creek Post Office ■

Four Seasons Hotel Ⓒ▼

Freeport-McMoRan ■

Frito Lay ▼■

Fruehauf ■

Fruit of the Loom ■

Gannett ■

Gateway 2000 ■

GE ▼■●

GE (Refrigeration Plant) ▼

GenCorp. ■

General Cinema ■

General Dynamics ■

General Foods (Dog Food) ▼

General Foods (Topeka) ▼■

General Mills ▼■

General Motors ▼■●

Genetech ■

Georgia-Pacific Chemicals ▼■

Gerber Products ▼

Gibraltar Financial Group ■

Gillette ■

Girl Scouts ▼■

Glacier Metals ▼

Glenfed ▼■

GM (Cadillac Division) ▼■

GM Brookhaven Miss. ■

GM Cadillac Division ■

GM Cadillac, Livonia, Mich. ■

GM NDH Bearings Plant ■

Goldman Sachs & Co. ▼

Goldome ■

Goodyear ■

Gould Inc. ■

Grand Rapids Spring & Wire Co. ●

Great American First Savings ■

Great Western Financial ■

Greenbay Packers ▼

Greenfield Recorder ▼

GTE ■●

Guilford Mills ■

Halliday Realtors ■

Hallmark ▼■

Hampton Inns ■

Hanson Industries NA ■

Hard Rock Cafe ■

Harley Davidson ■

Harsco ■

Hartmarx ■

Harvard University ▼■

Harwood Manufacturing ▼

Hees International Ⓒ▼

Heinz ▼■

Herman Miller Inc. ■

Hershey Foods ▼

Hertz-Penske ▼

Heublin ■

Hewlett-Packard ▼■

H. F. Anderson ■

Hoechst Celanese ■

Holiday Inn ▼

Home Depot ▼■
Home Federal Savings & Loan ■
Honda ■
Honda Canada Ⓒ▼
Honeywell ▼■●
Honeywell (Aerospace) ▼
Hospital Corp. of America ●
H-P (Canada) Ⓒ▼
Hudson Bay Co. Ⓒ▼
Hughes Aircraft ▼
Hydro Quebec Ⓒ▼
Hymac Ltée. Ⓒ●
Hyundai ▼●
IBM ▼■●
IBM Credit Corp. ▼
IBS ■
Illinois Tool Works ▼●
Imperial Oil Ⓒ▼
Inco Ltd. Ⓒ■▼
Indiana Bell ■
Ingersol-Rand ▼
Inland Steel Industries ▼
Inspiration Resources ▼
Intel ▼■
Interco ■
International Controls ■
International Flavors & Fragrances ■
International Harvester ●■
International Paper ■
IRS ▼
ITT ▼■
Jaguar ▼
James River Corp. of Virginia ■
J. C. Penney ▼■
Jim Walter ■
John Deere ■
John Hancock Mutual Life ■
Johnson & Johnson ▼■
J. P. Morgan ▼■
Kaiser Aluminum ▼
Kaiser Tech. ■
Kawasaki ▼
Keithley Instruments ■
Kellwood ■
Kimball International ■

Kimberly Clark ▼●
KL Spring & Stamping ▼
KMart ■
Knight-Ridder ●
Knoll International ▼
Knowledge Adventure ▼
Kodak ▼■
KPMG Peat Marwick ▼●
Kraft ▼
Kroger ▼
Kyocera ▼
L'Eggs ■
Lafarge ▼
Land's End ▼
Lantech ■
Leggett & Platt ▼
Leslie Fay ▼
Lever Brothers ▼
Levi Strauss & Co. ▼■
Lewiston Sun Journal ●
Liberty Mutual ▼■
The Limited ▼
Lincoln Electric ▼
Liz Claiborne ■
Lockheed Corp. ▼■●
Loewen Ondaatje McCutcheon Ⓒ■
London Life Ⓒ▼
Lord. Corp. ▼
Lotus Development ▼■
Louisiana Land & Exploration ▼
LTV ▼
Lufthansa Airlines ▼
M&M Mars ▼
Maax Ⓒ▼
Mack Trucks ▼
Magna International Ⓒ▼
Magnavox ▼
Manufacturers Hanover ▼
Manulife ▼
Manville ▼
March of Dimes ▼
Marlow Industries ▼
Marpac Ind. ■
Marriott Corp. ▼■
Martin Marietta ▼■

Mary Kay ▼■
Masco ▼
Massey-Ferguson Ⓒ▼
Matsushita Electric ▼
Maxus Energy ▼
May Department Stores ▼
Mayo Forest Products Ⓒ▼
Mazda ■
McCormick & Co. ▼■
McDonalds ▼■
McDonalds Canada Ⓒ▼
McDonnell Douglas ▼
McGraw-Hill ▼
McKesson ▼
McKim Advertising ▼
McKinsey & Co. ▼
MCI ▼
Mead ▼■
Medtronic ▼
Mercedez-Benz ■
Merck ▼■
Meritor Financial Group ▼
Merrill Lynch ▼
Mesa Petrolium ▼
Methodist Hospital ■
Metropolitan Hospital ▼
Metropolitan Life ▼
Milacron ▼
Miller Brewing Co. ■
Mills College ▼■
Millstone Plant ■
Minstar ■
Miscrosoft ▼■
MIT ▼■
Mitchell Energy ■
Mitsubushi Chemical ▼
MMM (3M) ▼■
Mobil ■
Mohasco ■
Moldcraft Plastics ■
Molson Breweries Ⓒ●
Montgomery Ward & Co. Inc. ■
Monsanto ▼■
Morgan Guaranty Trust ■
Morgan Stanley ■

Motorola ▼■
Motorola Cellular ▼
Mrs. Fields Cookies ▼
Mutual Life Insurance ▼
Nabisco ▼
Napco Ind. ■
NASA ▼
National Gypsum ▼
National Intergroup ▼
National Steel ▼●
Navistar International ▼
NBC ▼
NBD Bank ▼
NCR ▼
Nerco ▼
New Jersey Bell ▼
New Morgan Guaranty Bank ■
New York Life ▼
New York Times ▼
New York University ■
New York Yankees ▼■
Newport Daily News ▼
Nike ▼■
Nippon Kokon ■
Nissan ▼■
Nordstrom ▼■
North West Airlines ▼■
Northern Telecom ▼
Northrop ▼
Northwestern Mutual ▼
Northwestern National ▼
Norton ▼
Norwest Bank ■
Novacor Chemicals Ⓒ▼
Nucor ▼■
Nynex ▼
NYPD ■
Oakland Athletics ■
Occidental Petroleum ▼
Odetics ■
Ohio Matress ▼
Olivetti ■
Ontario Hydro Ⓒ▼
Owens-Corning Fib. ▼
Owens-Illinois ▼

Oxford Industries ▼
P&G (Lima, Ohio) ●
Paccar ■
Pacific Gas & Electric ■
Pacific Telesis Group ▼
Pancanadian Petro ⒞▼
Paratech ●
Parks Canada ⒞▼
Paul Revere Insurance Group ■
Peak Electronics ■
Penn Central ▼
People's Express ▼●
PepsiCo. ▼■●
Perkin-Elmer ▼
Perot Systems ●
Pfizer ▼
Phelps Dodge ▼
Philadelphia Flyers ●
Phillip Morris ▼
Phillips-Van Heusen ▼
Pilgrim Plant ▼
Pillsbury ▼■
Pitney Bowes ▼
Pizza Hut ■
Plant World ●
Polaroid ▼■●
Porsche ▼
PPG Industries ■
Pratt & Witney ⒞■
Premark International ■
Preston Trucking Co. ■
Price Club/Cosco ▼
Princess Margaret Hospital ⒞■
Principle Group ▼
Pro Fasteners ●
Proctor & Gamble ▼■●
Prospect Associates ▼
Prudential Insurance ▼
Prudential of America ▼
P. S. Ross & Associates ▼
Quadrucci ▼
Quantum ▼
Quasar ■
Ralston Purina ▼
Ramada Intnl. Hotels ▼

Raytheon ▼
RCA ▼■
Red Lobster ▼
Reimer Express ⒞▼
Relcon Ltd. ⒞■
Remington ▼
Republic Airlines ▼
Revlon ▼■
Reynolds Metals ■
Richardson-Greenshields ⒞▼
Ringer Hut ■
Ritz-Carlton Hotel Co. ▼■
RJR Nabisco ▼■
Rochester Products Plant ■
Rockwell International ▼■●
Rohm & Haas ■
Rolm ▼
Royal Bank ⒞●
Royal Trust ⒞●
R. R. Donnnelly & Sons ▼
Rubbermaid ▼■●
Rushton Coal Mine ■
Ryder System ▼■
Saab ■
Safeco Insurance Co. ▼
Safeway Stores ▼
Saloman ▼
San Diego Zoo ▼
Sante Fe Southern Pac. ▼
Sanyo ▼■
Sara Lee ▼■
SAS ▼
Satisfaction Guar. Eat. ▼
Saturn ▼■
Savage Pumps Inc. ▼
Savin Corp. ■
Schlumberger ▼
Schneider ⒞▼■
Scientech ▼
Scott Paper ▼
SDRC ▼
Seagrams & Sons ■
Sears Roebuck ▼■
Security Pacific ▼
Sequent Computer Systems ■

Sharp Inc. ▼■
Shaw Industries ▼
Shell Canada ⓒ▼
Shell Oil ▼
Shell UK ■
Siemens ▼
Siemens AG Germany ■
Simpson's ⓒ▼
Singer ▼■
SmithKline Beecham ▼
Solectron ●
Solectron Corp. ■
Sony ▼■●
Southern ▼
Southland Corp. ▼■
Southwest Airlines ▼
Southwest Industries ▼
Southwestern Bell ▼■
Spar Aerospace ⓒ▼
Speedy Muffler ⓒ■
Springs Industries ■
St. Joe Paper Co. ▼
St. Michael's Hospital ⓒ▼
St. Regis Paper Co. ▼
Standard Aero ⓒ■
Standard Products ■
Stanley Works ▼■●
Staples ▼
Starbucks ▼
State Employment Agency ■
Steelcase ▼
Sth. Ontario Utility ⓒ▼
Stone Container ●
Stroh's Beer ▼
Sun Banks ▼
Sun Microsystems ⓒ▼●
Super Valu Stores ●
Taco Bell ▼●
Tandem ▼●
Teachers Insurance & Annuity ●
Tektronix ▼
Tenneco ▼■
Tennessee Valley Authority ▼■
Texaco ▼
Texas Air ▼

Texas El Dorando ▼
Texas Instruments ▼■
Time Inc. ▼
Time Warner ▼
Times Mirror ▼
Timex ▼
Toronto Star ⓒ●
Toshiba ▼■
Toyota ▼■
Toyota (Cambridge) ⓒ▼
Toyota (Lexus) ▼
Toys 'R Us ▼
Transamerica ▼
Trans Australia Air. ▼
Travelers ▼■
Triad Systems Corp. ▼
Triangle Industries ▼
Triathlon Vehicles Lease ▼
Tribune ▼
Trinova ▼
TRW ▼■
Turner Broadcasting ▼
TWA ▼
Twentieth-Century Fox ▼
Tyco Labs ▼
U. of Virginia ▼■
Unilever ■
Union Carbide ▼
Union Pacific ▼■
Union Texas ▼
Unisys ▼■
United Airlines ▼■
United Merch, & Manuf. ▼
United Services Auto. Ass. ■
United States Navy ■
United Technologies ▼■
United Way ▼
Unitel ⓒ▼
Universal ▼
University of Alberta Hospital ⓒ■
University of Ottawa Students
    Union ⓒ▼
UPS ▼■
USAA ▼■
US Air Force ▼

US Army ■
US Federal Trade Commission ▼
USG ▼
US Interior Dept. ▼
US Marine Corp. ▼■
US Military ▼
US Postal Service ▼■
US Small Business Administration
■
US Steel ▼■
UST ▼
US West ▼
USX ■
Valasis Comm. ▼
Veristek ■
Versatech ▼
Vestron ■
VF ■
Via Rail ©▼■
Virgin Group ▼
Volvo ■
Volvo (Kalmar Plant) ▼
Vulcan Materials ■
Wainwright Industries ▼
Walgreens ■
Wallace Co. ▼■

Wal-Mart ▼■
Wal-Mart Canada ©▼
Wang Labs. ▼■
Warnaco Group ▼■
Warner Lambert ▼
Washington Post ▼
Wells Fargo Bank ▼
WestAmerica Bank ▼
West Point Pepperell ▼
Western ■
Western Union Telegraph ■
Westinghouse ▼■●
Westmoreland Coal ▼
Weston ▼
Weyerhaeuser ▼
Whirlpool Corp. ■
White Sands Missile Range ■
Winn-Dixie Stores ▼
W. L. Gore & Associates ■
Wood-Mizer ▼
Worthington Industries ▼
W. R. Grace ▼
Xerox ▼■●
Xerox Canada ©▼
Zenith ▼
Zytech ▼

Texts used

Arnold *et al.* (1992)
Baird *et al.* (1990)
Bateman & Zeithaml (1990)
Champoux (1996)
Cherrington (1989)
Cherrington (1994)
Coffey *et al.* (1987)
Coffey *et al.* (1994)
Cohen *et al.* (1988)
Daft (1986)
Daft and Steers (1986)
Das (1990)
Das (1998)
Davis and Newstrom (1985)
Dessler (1983)

Donnelly *et al.* (1987)
Feldman and Arnold (1983)
Field and House (1995)
Fombrun *et al.* (1984)
George and Jones (1996)
Gerloff (1985)
Gibson *et al.* (1985)
Gordon (1993)
Gram (1986)
Gray and Starke (1988)
Greenberg and Baron (1993)
Greenburg *et al.* (1996)
Griffen and Moorhead (1986)
Griffin *et al.* (1996)
Hellriegel *et al.* (1986)

Hellriegel *et al.* (1992)
Hellriegel *et al.* (1995)
Higgins (1986)
Higgins (1991)
Hitt *et al.* (1989)
Hodge and Anthony (1991)
Hodgetts (1990)
Hodgetts (1991)
Ivancevich (1987)
Jenks (1990)
Johns (1983)
Johns (1988)
Johns (1992)
Legge (1996)
Luthans (1985)
Luthans (1995)
Madura (1998)
McShane (1992)
Middlemist and Hitt (1988)
Moorhead (1988)
Moorhead (1998)
Moorhead and Griffin (1992)
Nelson and Quick (1996)
Nickels *et al.* (1997)
Northcraft and Neale (1990)

Pliniussen (1994)
Randolph and Blackburn (1989)
Robbins (1983)
Robbins (1988)
Robbins (1989)
Robbins (1996)
Robbins (1998)
Robbins and Stuart-Kotze (1986)
Robbins and Stuart-Kotze (1990)
Schermerhorn (1984)
Schermerhorn *et al.* (1982)
Schermerhorn *et al.* (1985)
Schermerhorn *et al.* (1988)
Schermerhorn *et al.* (1991)
Schermerhorn *et al.* (1992)
Schermerhorn *et al.* (1994)
Schermerhorn *et al.* (1995)
Schermerhorn *et al.* (1997)
Starke *et al.* (1990)
Steers and Porter (1987)
Stuart-Kotze (1980)
Tosi *et al.* (1990)
Van Fleet (1991)
Vecchio (1991)

Appendix B

Interview guidelines used in the initial, culture change
phases of the research

1 How long have you worked for NSPC and in what department?
2 After looking at the results of the 1986 attitude survey, do you feel that
  the culture change has made any difference in how senior management
  treats employees?
3 Do you think that present communication between management and
  employees is adequate?
4 In your opinion, is there enough recognition for doing your job?
5 Will your immediate supervisor let you take responsibility in decision-
  making for routine matters, and do you feel you have enough responsibility?
6 (Because of the 'open door' policy initiated with the culture change)
  would you feel comfortable in approaching your supervisor's boss if you
  were unhappy with how your supervisor had handled a situation?
7 Can you tell me why you think NSPC is undergoing this cultural change
  and what the objectives are?
8 Now that the values have been defined, what changes, if any, have you
  made in your daily routine?
9 How has the cultural change been implemented in your unit?
10 What are your feelings about this cultural change?
11 What do you see as the benefits of this cultural change for the employees
   and the organization?
12 Do you see any disadvantages with this change for the employees and
   the organization?
13 What do you believe to be the general opinion of this change?
14 Is progress being made with the organization, and do you see change
   happening in the workplace through the living of the values?
15 Is NSPC a better place to work? Are you satisfied with working for this
   company? If not, what would you suggest to improve the organization?
16 Do you see the colour of hard hats as an issue? If so, do you want all
   one colour or the situation to remain as is?

Notes

1 Introduction

1 An April 2002 Internet search indicates that in the last 5 years there have been at least 1,337 articles devoted to Six Sigma, 756 on TQM, 513 on BPR, and just under 300 on culture change. Recent popular books include, Breyfogle, Cupello, and Meadows (2001), Lawler, Mohrman and Benson (2001), and Champy (2002).
2 See Appendix A.

2 Identifying cues: a history of Nova Scotia Power

1 I have borrowed this wonderful metaphor from Pyrch (1998).
2 The notion of 'Tammany Hall politics' comes from political practices in the US, in particular New York, and refers to the various efforts of a political faction to get their candidate elected to high office with the promise of favours (political and financial) in return. See Steinberg (1972).
3 By now the Point Aconi plant had opened and the Glace Bay plant had been closed.
4 Handy (1983), for example, argues that culture is structure, while Mills and Murgatroyd (1991) contend that organizational culture in an outcome of a structured series of formal and informal rules.
5 The process was not unlike a politician holding meetings of potential voters throughout a constituency.
6 Although gendered (e.g., drafts*man*, fore*man*, line*man*) I have used the company's own terms to refer to selected respondents.
7 See Nova Scotia Power (1991b).
8 It is interesting that classic studies of leadership which, thirty years earlier, argued that effective leaders combine 'initiating structure' with 'consideration' for employees had little or no impact on this company (cf. Stogdill and Coons, 1957).
9 Nova Scotia Power (1990b).
10 The company 'Employee Handbook' for 1990, for example, begins with the following statement from Louis Comeau: 'The Employee Handbook 1990 provides you with information about Nova Scotia Power and our work policies. At Nova Scotia Power we value Our Employees, Our Customers, Our Environment and Our Province. I am particularly proud of the strong team of employees who are committed to serving our Customers, protecting our Environment and serving our Province. If you have any questions about this material, please contact your supervisor.' (All capitals are in the original.)
11 Hatfield was my previous name.
12 That was how the company described my activities at the time.

13 Nova Scotia Power, 1990b.
14 On the cover of James Champy's (1995) book, for example, we are informed that 'Re-engineering the Corporation began a business revolution'; that 'the principles of re-engineering necessarily require not only a sea-change in the ways people work, but also a radical new approach to management. After working with dozens of companies in the throes of re-engineering, Jim Champy is uniquely qualified to write the book that brings management fully into the re-engineering revolution'.
15 Later, they became involved in the re-engineering of nearby NBPower of New Brunswick.
16 Anonymous informant.
17 Of the three authors, Wayne J. Crawley was the director of corporate effectiveness and internal audit at Nova Scotia Power, Gary K. Oickle was the company's chief financial officer and Bryan J. Mekechuk was a principal in Ernst & Young Consultant's Toronto office.
18 This is a slogan that comes straight from the manual of re-engineering. Champy (1995: 163) makes this point throughout his book, citing, among others, a slogan from Federal Express, 'Be all that you can be': 'But "be all that you can be", the old army recruiting slogan, for many people means "to be a manager". . . . America's great achievement in the last fifty years or so – and re-engineering's achievement more recently – has been to open up managerial status, rewards, and responsibilities to everyone.'
19 These foci, and many others, are central to BPI and re-engineering. Harrington (1991:139–40), for example, argues that: '*Value* is defined from the point of view of the customer or the business process.' James Champy (1995: 163–4) writes: 'Re-engineering's role has been to insist on the bottom-line rationale of self-management and teamwork, and of circulating knowledge, and bearers of knowledge from the bottom up.' For Harrington (1991: 61): 'Many types of teams become involved in the BPI activities . . . [including:]

- Process improvement team (PIT)
- Subprocess improvement team (sub-PIT)
- Task team (TT)
- Department improvement team (DIT).'

Speaking on 'streamlining the process' Harrington (1991: 131) argues that, 'Streamlining suggests the trimming of waste and excess, attention to every minute detail that might lead to improved performance and quality. It suggests contouring to provide the smoothest flow, the least resistance to progress and performance with the minimum amount of effort. With streamlining, the process will operate with the least disturbance to its surroundings.'
20 David Mann, like Godsoe and Comeau, has strong political ties to the party in power. In this case a Liberal government. A former senior manager of Nova Scotia Power said at the time that he was 'shocked and surprised that they still hired someone with political connections' when they didn't have to. But the combination of big industry and politics is still closely related in this province and as such, politics shapes leadership and the culture of large companies in Nova Scotia.
21 Within a few months Forbes left Nova Scotia Power and joined the Aliant company as executive vice-president and chief financial officer.

3 Strategic sensemaking

1 The two planes involved were diverted to Tenerife from other airports.
2 English was a second language for the air traffic controllers and two of the pilots.

3 Lenin (1947), in an entirely different context, makes a similar point in regard to political leadership, arguing that leadership is about being 'one step forward, two steps
back'. In other words, the leader must take people forward with new ideas that somehow build on existing concerns and experiences. In a similar vein, Gramsci (1978)
argues for 'organic leadership' whereby the organizational leader draws strength by
referencing cultural values and understandings but doing so in a way that is new.

4 Contrast this with Mary Douglas's (1986: 69–70) comment on institutional theory.

5 I use the *Challenger* disaster as an integrative case in my teaching and have long been
struck by the different interpretations of causality that arise out of a search for the
antecedents of the explosion.

6 Focused on outcome rather than process, Weick's (1995: 58) own term for this is
'circumscribed accuracy'.

7 'Group think' (Janis, 1971) is an extreme example of this.

8 This is perhaps reminiscent of Weber's work on bureaucracy and rationality (1947)
and the protestant ethic and the spirit of capitalism (1967), i.e., that dominant modes
of thinking precede certain actions.

4   The story of organizational change

1 Although, more recently, Six Sigma and the Balanced Scorecard approaches have
gained popularity, neither had achieved the same status as the earlier change
programmes.

2 c.f. Zimmerman (1994); Blancett (1995); Griffith (1995); Stetler (1995); Kissler
(1996); Lenz and Sikka (1998). For some indication of the problems associated with
the introduction of TQM in the US health-care system see Hospitals (1992). For a
critique of the introduction of business change programmes to the Canadian health-
care system see Armstrong *et al.*, (1997).

3 See also Beer *et al.* (1990); Bak (1992); Hospitals (1992); Armstrong *et al.* (1997);
Stewart (1997); Westphal (1997); Schaffer and Thompson (1998); Wiele and Brown
(1998); Wiele (1998).

4 See also Buchanan (1997); Carter (1999); Geisler (1997); Grey and Mitev (1995);
Grint (1994); Grint and Case (1998).

5 Transformational and visionary leadership (cf. Bass, 1985, 1990) regained popularity
with the culture change movement.

6 What is interesting here is that Harrington (1991) and Davis (1984) both reference
supposed 'hard nosed' business attitudes to make their accounts plausible. In Davis'
(1984: 1) case this is done to make culture change acceptable to the business community: '[In 1983] Corporate America, long obsessed with the cold facts of the bottom
line, had begun to take a hard look at corporate culture, a subject many thought
was "soft".' Harrington (1991), on the other hand, refers to his 'no-nonsense' blueprint to create distance between his views and 'exotic' (or does he mean foreign?)
views on corporate culture.

7 If that proves a failure I can only guess that Champy's next book will be titled:
Re-engineering the Employee!

8 For a critique of the concept of 'globalization' within management thinking, see
Mills and Hatfield (1998).

9 The same is true in regard to the social construction of the 'ideal employee' (see
Townley, 1994).

10 I am using the term 'political' in the broad sense rather than the more narrow party
political reference.

11 That is not to suggest that Comeau had no alternative. There are clearly other ways
of handling organizational problems (cf. Rinehart, 1986). Indeed, as I will argue

later, when I look at the work of Blackler, the existence of several, often competing, scripts needs explanation.

12 One of the key 'findings' of the survey was that 'there was little recognition of good performance' (Nova Scotia Power, 1990b).

13 In Halifax, as in other North American cities, Rotary Clubs bring together members of the local business community and university business administrators. For example, the Vice-President (a former Dean of Commerce), and the Director of the Executive MBA of Saint Mary's University are active Rotarians.

14 The numerous cases enumerated in Appendix A are almost all drawn from textbook references.

15 See, for SAS, Campbell-Smith (1986), Carlzon (1987), Hampden-Turner (1990), Sampson (1984); BA, Bruce (1987), Hampden-Turner (1990), Poulet and Moult, 1987; and IBM, Dreyfuss (1989), Hamilton (1989), Mills and Murgatroyd (1991).

16 While I have attempted to suggest criteria for guru status it is likely that the term is used with greater abandon than I have suggested, often referring to someone who has/claims a track-record of consulting and writing.

17 Champy (1993) and Hammer (1996) argue that a 70 per cent failure rate attributed to re-engineering is not due to the programme itself but, rather, how the change is implemented and managed.

18 I would argue that this, in turn, had some link to the 'full-employment' practices at that time and a response to many of the challenges of the late-1960s, which had forced a rethink of the 'human element' at work.

19 See, for example, Davies (1984) – Davies' earlier work informed the 1980 edition of *Business Week* on organizational culture; Deal and Kennedy (1982); Frost *et al.*, (1985); Handy (1983); Morgan (1986); Ott (1989); Peters and Waterman (1982); Schein (1985); Smircich (1983); Van Maanen (1991); Wilkins and Ouchi (1983).

20 Cincinnati Gas and Electricity (CG&E) also influenced the company.

21 For example, British Airways' introduction of a culture change programme in the early 1980s was undertaken with a view to creating the appearance of a more efficient company in preparation for privatization (Campbell-Smith, 1986). Nova Scotia Power's introduction of a re-engineering programme in the early 1990s was undertaken with a similar purpose.

22 See, in particular Champy (1995) and Hammer and Champy (1993).

23 Re-engineering is a prime example of a theory that complements perceived knowledge. With its customer service focus and claims of 'revolutionary' ideas (Hammer, 1990: Hammer and Champy, 1993) re-engineering fits well into the context following the collapse of the Eastern bloc, whereby capitalism has the appearance of a revolutionary force, with the profit motive triumphing over bureaucratic welfarism.

5 Sensemaking and identity construction

1 This committee was composed of the President, four vice presidents and the consultant as facilitator. Its mandate was to make employees aware of the re-engineering project by focusing on enhancing customer service and identifying 'new stars who could be trained and rewarded by identifying good and poor performance' (Core Team Meeting Notes, 25 January 1994).

2 In Comeau's sense of the company his predecessor did not do such a good job. When he took over the company in 1983 it was 'not in very good shape. From the basic point of government relations and public and community relations, it was a disaster' (Comeau, quoted in Bruce, 1991).

3 This is not to say that there wasn't support for the culture change from some Cape Breton employees, but the greatest negativity and backlash to the programme came from this region.

4 This is not confined to industrial workers but is very much a way of life in the region. Evidence of this can be seen in the fact that in 1971 Sydney 'was the first city in Canada since Confederation to be affected by a police strike and, in 1984, was the first city to be subjected to a second police strike' (Ferguson, 1987: 172).

5 In January 2000, two incidents were reminders of Cape Breton's heritage. At one and the same time Cape Breton was faced with the closure of its largest steel company and all but one of its coal mines. In the former case the news was full of desperate attempts to find a new buyer. In the latter case, miners were staging an unofficial 'illegal' strike, a sit-in of the mine and a hunger strike to win concessions from the government. Interestingly, the miners' strike came close to closing down some of Nova Scotia Power's Cape Breton operations.

6 A new plant manager had recently been appointed to one of the plants to replace the previous manager, who had died suddenly. The new manager was selected based on his ability get along with people and motivate his workforce. Morale had become a serious problem in the plant owing to the previous manager's style of leadership.

7 The director of Employee and Organizational Development found himself out of work following the re-engineering programme, when it was decided to outsource all HR functions.

8 This would appear to complement Goffman's work on the presentation of self (1982) and asylums (1984). Indeed Weick (1995) draws on Goffman's (1974) work on 'framing'.

6 Application of the sensemaking model to the Nova Scotia Power case

1 Had I initially chosen to approach the case study using a sensemaking model, my data collection would have been influenced and grounded in that approach, which would have led me to seek out events to support particular issues. But my late arrival to sensemaking prevented me from asking questions that might have focused more on employees' understanding of change, and less on perceptions of success or failure and the mechanics of culture change. For example, my observations would have included more time spent on watching managers 'manage'.

2 Roethlisberger and Dickson (1939) were among the first management writers to identify this problem in the form of informal groups. More recent writers have substituted the notion of the 'weak' culture to argue for greater management control over corporate values and beliefs.

3 The problem, as a number of commentators have noted, is that routines can mitigate against future change and innovation (cf. Bate, 1994; Argyris, 1993).

4 When privatization was announced employees received assurances that there would be no lay-offs (Myrden, 1994). However, with the introduction of re-engineering the language of BPR and employees limited knowledge of its application elsewhere suggested that staff reductions were inevitable.

5 In 1991, the 'general corporate objective' of Nova Scotia Power was to improve 'effectiveness' by 'being the best and remaining competitive'. This was to be achieved by changing the culture of the organization through the modelling of values which were designed to help employees carry out the corporate mandate (Nova Scotia Power, 1991b).

6 For example, that 'mutual respect among employees is the foundation of excellence at Nova Scotia Power. . . . I believe in people, in the sense that you achieve your

goals through people, and people only produce those results when they feel good about their work' (Nova Scotia Power, 1991c).

7 Brian Mulroney, the Canadian Prime Minister during the era of Nova Scotia Power's privatization, has been described as a 'fixture on the world stage with two other conservative world leaders, former US, President Ronald Reagan and former British prime minister Margaret Thatcher' (cited in Cameron, 1994: 481).

7 Making sense of sensemaking: suggestions for sensible modifications of the sensemaking model

1 For discussion of the value of this approach see Tinker and Neimark (1987) and Benschop and Meihuizen (2002).

2 I use the word 'his' deliberately in this case to reflect the gendered character of engineering at Nova Scotia Power. In fact, it could be argued that 'masculinity' is an important aspect of the established notions that shape a person's sense of engineering (cf. Cockburn, 1985).

3 For example, in 1990, the year prior to Nova Scotia Power's privatization, $25 billion of state-owned enterprises were sold off world-wide (Goodman, 1991: 26).

Bibliography

Aaltio, I., & Mills, A. J. (eds). (2002) *Gender, Identity, and the Culture of Organizations*. London: Routledge.

Abrahamson, E. (1996) Management Fashion. *Academy of Management Review*, 21(1), 254–85.

Ackroyd, S., and Hughes, J. (1992) *Data Collection in Context* (second ed). London: Longman.

Adler, P. A., and Adler, P. (1994) Observational Techniques. In N. K. Denzin and Y. S. Lincoln (eds), *Handbook of Qualitative Research* (pp. 377–92). Thousand Oaks, CA: Sage.

Allaire, Y., and Firsirotu, M. (1984) Theories of Organizational Culture. *Organization Studies*, 5, 193–226.

Alvesson, M., and Berg, P. O. (1992) *Corporate Culture and Organizational Symbolism*. Berlin: de Gruyter.

Annison, M. H. and Medical Group Management Association (1993) *Managing the Whirlwind: Patterns and Opportunities in a Changing World*. Englewood, CO, Medical Group Management Association.

Armstrong, P., Armstrong, H., Choiniere, J., Mykhalovskiy, E., and White, J. (1997) *Medical Alert: New Work Organizations in Health Care*. Toronto: Garamond Press.

Arnold, H. J., Feldman, D. C., and Hunt, G. (1992) *Organizational Behaviour. A Canadian Perspective*. Toronto: McGraw-Hill Ryerson.

Atkinson, P., and Hammersley, M. (1994) Ethnography and Participant Observation. In N. K. Denzin and Y. S. Lincoln (eds), *Handbook of Qualitative Research* (pp. 248–61). Thousand Oaks, CA: Sage.

Baird, L. S., Post, J. E., and Mahon, J. F. (1990) *Management. Functions and Responsibilities*. New York: Harper & Row.

Bak, C. (1992) Lessons from the Veterans of TQM. *Canadian Business Review*, Winter, 17–19.

Baker, G. R., Barnsley, J., and Murray, M. (1993) The Development of Quality Improvement in Canadian Health Care Organizations. *Leadership in Health Services*, 2(5), 18–23.

Bass, B. M. (1985) *Leadership and Performance beyond Expectations*. New York: Free Press.

Bass, B. M. (1990) From Transactional to Transformational Leadership: Learning to Share the Vision. *Organizational Dynamics*, 18, 19–31.

Bate, P. (1994) *Strategies for Cultural Change*. Oxford: Butterworth Heinemann.

Bateman, T. S., and Zeithaml, C. P. (1990) *Management. Function and Strategy*. Homewood, Ill.: Irwin.

Becker, S. (1993) TQM Does Work. Ten Reasons Why Misguided Efforts Fail. *Management Review*, 82(5), 30–34.

Beer, M., Eisenstat, R. A., and Spector, B. (1990) Why Change Programs Don't Produce Change. *Harvard Business Review*, Nov–Dec, 158.

Benschop, Y. and Meihuizen, H. E. (2002) Reporting Gender: Representations of Gender in Annual Reports. In Aaltio, I. and Mills, A. J. (eds) *Gender, Identity, and the Culture of Organizations* (pp. 160–84). London: Routledge.

Bendix, R. (1974) *Work and Authority in Industry*. Berkeley, CA: University of California Press.

Berg, B. L. (1989) *Qualitative Research Methods*. Boston: Allyn and Bacon.

Berg, P. O. (1985) Organizational Change as a Symbolic Transformation Process. In P. Frost, L. Moore, M. R. Louis, C. Lundber, and J. Martin (eds), *Organizational Culture* London: Sage.

Best, J. W. (1981) *Research in Education*. Englewood Cliffs, NJ: Prentice-Hall.

Blackler, F. (1992a). Formative Contexts and Activity Systems: Postmodern Approaches to the Management of Change. In M. Reed and M. Hughes (eds), *Rethinking Organization* (pp. 273–94). London: Sage.

Blackler, F. (1992b). Knowledge and the Theory of Organisations: Organisations as Activity Systems and the Reframing of Management. Paper presented at the *Knowledge Workers in Contemporary Organisations Conference*, Lancaster, UK: Lancaster University.

Blackler, F. (1993) Knowledge and the Theory of Organisations: Organisations as Activity Systems and the Reframing of Management. *Journal of Management Studies*, 30(6), 863–84.

Blackler, F., and Brown, C. (1981) A New Philosophy for Management: Shell Revisited. *Personnel Review*, 10, 15–21.

Blackler, F., Crump, N., and McDonald, S. (1999) Managing Experts and Competing through Innovation: An Activity Theoretical Analysis. *Organization*, 6(1), 5–31.

Blackler, F., Reed, M., and Whitaker, A. (1993) Editorial Introduction: Knowledge Workers and Contemporary Organizations. *Journal of Management Studies*, 30(6), 1017–20.

Blancett, S. S., and Flarey, D. L. (1995) *Re-engineering Nursing and Health Care: The Handbook for Organizational Transformation*. Gaithersburg, MD: Aspen Publishers.

Boje, D. M., Gephart, Jr., R. P., and Thatchenkary, J. (eds) (1996) *Postmodern Management and Organization Theory*. Thousand Oaks, CA: Sage.

Brown, C. A. (1992) Organization Studies and Scientific Authority. In M. Reed and M. Hughes (eds), *Rethinking Organizations: New Directions in Organizational Analysis and Theory* (pp. 67–84). London: Sage.

Bruce, A. (1991) Louis Comeau's Private Role in Public Power. *Commercial News*, pp. 31–3.

Bruce, M. (1987) Managing People First – Bringing the Service Concept to British Airways. *ICT* (March/April), 21–6.

Bryman, A. (ed.) (1988) *Doing Research in Organizations*. London: Routledge.

Buchanan, D., Boddy, D., and McCalman, J. (1988) Getting in, Getting on, Getting out, and Getting back. In A. Bryman (ed.), *Doing Research in organizations* (pp. 53–67). London: Routledge.

Buchanan, D. A. (1997) The Limitations and Opportunities of Business Process Re-engineering in a Politicized Organizational Climate. *Human Relations*, 50(1), 51–72.

Burns, T., and Stalker, G. (1961) *The Management of Innovation*. London: Tavistock.

Burrell, G. (1987) No Accounting for Sexuality. *Accounting, Organizations, and Society*, 12, 89–101.

Burrell, G., and Morgan, G. (1979) *Sociological Paradigms and Organizational Analysis*. London: Heinemann.

Calás, M., Smircich, L. (1992), Re-writing Gender into Organizational Theorizing: Directions from Feminist Perspectives. In M. Reed and M. Hughes (eds), *Rethinking Organization* (pp. 227–53) London: Sage.

Campbell-Smith, D. (1986) *Struggle for Take-Off. The British Airways Story*. London: Coronet/Hodder and Stoughton.

Cameron, S. (1994) *On The Take*. Toronto: Macfarlane Walter and Ross.

Carlzon, J. (1987) *Moments of Truth*. Cambridge, MA: Ballinger Publishing Co.

Carr, E. H. (1990) *What is History?* Harmondsworth: Penguin.

Carter, T. (1999) *The Aftermath of Re-engineering: Downsizing and Corporate Performance*. New York: Haworth Press.

Case, P. (1994) Virtually the End of History: A Critique of Business Process Re-engineering. Paper presented at the *Modernity/Postmodernity Conference*, Oxford: Oxford Brookes University.

Champoux, J. (1996) *Organizational Behavior*. New York: West.

Champy, J. (1995) *Re-engineering Management: The Mandate for New Leadership*. New York: Harper Business.

Chang, R. Y. (1994) *Mastering Change Management: A Practical Guide for Turning Obstacles into Opportunities*. Irvine, CA: R. Chang Associates Publication Division.

Cherns, A. (1976) The Principles of Socio-Technical Design. *Human Relations*, 29, 783–92.

Cherns, A. B. (1987) Principles of Socio-Technical Design Revisted. *Human Relations*, 403, 153–62.

Cherrington, D. J. (1989) *Organizational Behavior. The Management of Individual and Organizational Performance*. Boston, MA: Allyn & Bacon.

Cherrington, D. J. (1994) *Organizational Behavior. The Management of Individual and Organizational Performance* (second edn). Boston, MA: Allyn & Bacon.

Chiaramonte, P., and Mills, A. J. (1998) Organizational Analysis Goes to the Movie: Inserting Humanities into the Management Curriculum. *Journal of Management Systems*, 10(3), 17–30.

Child, J. (1972) Organisation Structure, Environment and Performance – the Role of Strategic Choice. *Sociology*, 6(1), 1–22.

Choi, T. Y., and Behling, O. C. (1997) Top Managers and TQM Success: One More Look After All These Years. *Academy of Management Executive*, XI(1), 37–47.

Clark, J. (1995) *Managing Innovation and Change: People, Technology and Strategy*. London and Thousand Oaks, CA: Sage Publications.

Clark, T., and Salaman, G. (1996) The Management Guru as Organisational Witch Doctor. *Organization*, 3, 85–108.

Clark, T., and Salaman, G. (1998) Telling Tales: Management Gurus' Narratives and the Construction of Managerial Identity. *Journal of Management Studies*, 35(2), 137–61.

Clegg, S. (1981) Organization and Control. *Administrative Sciences Quarterly*, 26, 532–45.

Clegg, S. R. and Hardy, C. (1996) Introduction: Organizations, Organization and Organizing. In S. R. Clegg, C. Hardy, and W. R. Nord (eds), *Handbook of Organization Studies* (pp. 1–28). London: Sage.

Coch, L., and French, J. R. P. (1948) Overcoming Resistance to Change. *Human Relations*, 1, 512–32.

Cockburn, C. (1985) *Machinery of Dominance*. London: Pluto Press.

Coffey, R. E., Cook, C. W., and Hunsaker, P. L. (1987) *Management and Organizational Behavior*. Burr Ridge, Ill.: Irwin.

Coffey, R. E., Cook, C. W., and Hunsaker, P. L. (1994) *Management and Organizational Behavior*. Burr Ridge, Ill.: Irwin.

Cohen, A. R., Fink, S. L., Gadon, H., and Willits, R. D. (1988) *Effective Behavior in Organizations* (fourth ed.). Homewood, Ill.: Irwin.

Cohen, L., and Manion, L. (1980) *Research Methods in Education*. London: Croom Helm.

Cohen, M., March, J. and Olsen, J. (1972) A Garbage Can Model of Organizational Choice. *Administrative Science Quarterly* 17: 1–25.

Collinson, D. and Hearn, J. (1994) Naming Men as Men: Implications for Work, Organization and Management. *Gender, Work and Organization* 1(1): 2–22.

Colville, I. (1994) Review Article: Searching for Karl Weick and Reviewing for the Future. *Organization*, 1(1), 218–24.

Colville, I. D., Waterman, R. H., and Weick, K. E. (1999) Organizing and the Search for Excellence: Making Sense of the Times in Theory and Practice. *Organization*, 6(1), 129–48.

Comeau, L. (1994a) Re-engineering for a More Competitive Tomorrow. *Canadian Business Review*, pp. 51–2.

Comeau, L. R. (1994b). President's Address to the Shareholders. In Minutes of the 1994 Annual Meeting of Shareholders of Nova Scotia Power Incorporated.

Conrad, R. (30 June 1995) NSP Extinguishes 250 Jobs. *The Chronicle Herald*, pp. 1–2.

Cooke, B. (1999) Writing the Left out of Management Theory: The Historiography of the Management of Change. *Organization*, 6(1), 81–105.

Cox, T. H. J. (1990) Problems with Organizational Research on Race and Ethnicity Issues. *Journal of Applied Behavioral Sciences* 26: 5–23.

Crawley, W., Mekechuk, B., and Oickle, G. K. (June/July 1995) Powering up for Change. *CA Magazine*, pp. 33–8.

Cressey, D. R. (1974) Intensive Interviews. In W. B. Sanders (ed.), *The Sociologist as Detective. An Introduction to Research Methods* (pp. 188–98). New York: Praeger Publishers.

Crompton, R. (1987) Gender and Accountancy: A Response to Tinker and Neimark. *Accounting, Organizations and Society*, 12(1), 103–10.

Czarniawska-Joerges, B. (1992) *Exploring Complex Organizations: A Cultural Perspective*. Newbury Park, CA: Sage.

Daft, R. L. (1986) *Organization Theory and Design* (second ed.). St. Paul, MN: West.

Daft, R. L., and Steers, R. M. (1986) *Organizations. A Micro/Macro Approach*. Glenview, Ill.: Scott, Foresman and Co.

Daft, R. L., and Weick, K. E. (1984) Towards a Model of Organizations as Interpretation Systems. *Academy of Management Review*, 9(2), 284–95.

Das, H. (1990) *Organization Theory with Canadian Applications*. Toronto: Gage.

Das, H. (1998) *Strategic Organizational Design*. Scarborough, Ont: Prentice-Hall Canada.

Davies, S. (1984) *Managing Corporate Culture*. Cambridge, MA: Ballinger.

Davis, K., and Newstrom, J. W. (1985) *Human Behavior at Work: Organizational Behavior* (seventh ed.). New York: McGraw-Hill.

Davis, K., and Scott, W. G. (1964) *Readings in Human Relations* (second ed.). New York: McGraw-Hill.

Deal, T. E., and Kennedy, A. A. (1982) *Corporate Cultures*. Reading, MA: Addison-Wesley.

Delbridge, R. (1998) *Life on the Line in Contemporary Manufacturing*. Oxford: Oxford University Press.

Dellheim, C. (1986) Business in Time: The Historian and Corporate Culture. *The Public Historian*, 8(2), 9–22.

Deming, E. (1986) *Out of the Crisis*. Cambridge, MA: MIT-CAES.

Dessler, G. (1983) *Applied Human Relations*. Reston, VA: Prentice-Hall.

Dietrich, N., and Thomas, B. (1972) *Howard, The Amazing Mr. Hughes*. London: Coronet.

DiMaggio, P. J., and Powell, W. W. (1991) The Iron Cage Revisited: Institutional Isomorphism and Collective Rationality in Organizational Fields. In W. W. Powell and P. J. DiMaggio (eds), *The New Institutionalism in Organizational Analysis* (pp. 63–82). Chicago: University of Chicago Press.

Donnelly, J. H., Gibson, J. L., and Ivancevich, J. M. (1987) *Fundamentals of Management* (sixth ed.). Plano, TX: Business Publications, Inc.

Douglas, M. (1986) *How Organizations Think*. Syracuse, NY: Syracuse University Press.

Doyle, K. (1992) Who's Killing Total Quality? *Incentive*, *16*(8), 12–19.

Dreyfuss, J. (14 August 1989) Reinventing IBM. *Fortune*.

Duck, J. D. (1998) Managing Change: The Art of Balancing. In Harvard Business Review (ed.), *Harvard Business Review of Change* (pp. 55–82). Boston: Harvard Business School Press.

du Gay, P. (1994) Colossal Immodesties and Hopeful Monsters: Pluralism and Organizational Conduct. *Organization*, *1*(1): 125–48.

du Gay, P. (1996) *Consumption and Identity at Work*. London and Thousand Oaks, CA: Sage Publications.

Dunkerley, D. (1988) Historical Methods and Organizational Analysis. In A. Bryman (ed.), *Doing Research in Organizations* (pp. 82–95). London: Routledge.

Dusky, L. (July 1990) Bright Idea: Anatomy of a Corporate Revolution. *Working Women*, pp. 58–63.

Easterby-Smith, M., Thorpe, R., and Lowe, A. (1993) *Management Research: An Introduction*. London: Sage.

Eldridge, J. E. T., and Crombie, A. D. (1974) *The Sociology of Organisations*. London: George Allen & Unwin Ltd.

Engestrom, Y. (1987) *Learning by Expanding: An Activity Theoretical Approach to Developmental Research*. Helsinki: Orienta-Konsultit Oy.

Ernst & Young (1992a). *International Quality Study: Automotive Industry Report*. New York: American Quality Foundation.

Ernst & Young (1992b). *International Quality Study: Best Practices Report*. New York: Amsterdam Quality Foundation.

Etzioni, A. (1975) *A Comparative Analysis of Complex Organizations*. New York: The Free Press.

Feldman, D. C., and Arnold, H. J. (1983) *Managing Individual and Group Behavior in Organizations*. Toronto: McGraw-Hill.

Ferguson, K. (1987) The Sydney Police Strike. In C. Gilson (ed.), *Strikes. Industrial Relations in Nova Scotia, 1957–1987* Hantsport, Nova Scotia: Lancelot Press.

Ferguson, K. (1994) On Bringing More Theory, More Voices, and More Politics to the Study of Organization. *Organization*, *1*(1), 81–99.

Festinger, L. (1957) *A Theory of Cognitive Dissonance*. Stanford, CA: Stanford University Press.

Fetterman, D. (1989) *Ethnography: Step by Step* (first ed.). London: Sage.

Field, R. H. G., and House, R. J. (1995) *Human Behavior in Organizations. A Canadian Perspective*. Scarborough, Ont: Prentice Hall.

Filley, A. C., and House, R. J. (1969) *Managerial Process and Organizational Behavior*. Glenview, NJ: Scott, Foresman and Company.

Flax, J. (1990) *Thinking Fragments: Psychoanalysis, Feminism and Postmodernism in the Contemporary West*. Berkeley, CA: University of California Press.

Fombrun, C., Tichy, N. M., and Devanna, M. A. (1984) *Strategic Human Resource Management*. New York: Wiley.

Fondas, N. (1997) Feminization Unveiled: Management Qualities in Contemporary Writings. *The Academy of Management Review* 22(1): 257–82.

Fontana, A., and Frey, J. H. (1994) Interviewing: The Art of Science. In N. K. Denzin and Y. S. Lincoln (eds), *Handbook of Qualitative Research* (pp. 361–76). Thousand Oaks, CA: Sage.

Forster, N. (1995) The Analysis of Company Documentation. In C. Cassell and G. Symon (eds), *Qualitative Methods in Organizational Research* (pp. 147–229). Thousand Oaks, CA: Sage.

Fortune (3 May 1993). The Promise of Re-engineering. *Fortune*, pp. 94–7.

Foucault, M. (1979) *Discipline and Punish: The Birth of the Prison*. New York: Vintage Books.

Foucault, M. (1980) *Power/Knowledge*. New York: Pantheon.

Frank (13 April 1993). Jobs Threat at Nova Scotia Power. *Frank Magazine*, p. 6.

Frank (11 June 1996). Hands on Leslie's Nice Little Earner. *Frank Magazine*, pp. 14–15.

French, W. L., and Bell, C. (1972) *Organization Development: Behavioral Science Interventions for Organization Improvement*. Englewood Cliffs, NJ: Prentice-Hall.

Frost, P. J., Moore, L. F., Louis, M. R., Lundberg, C. C., and Martin, J. (eds) (1985) *Organizational Culture*. Newbury Park: Sage.

Galt, V. (19 December 1996). Universities Look for Corporate Support in Research. *The Globe and Mail*.

Garfinkel, H. (1967) *Studies in Ethnomethodology*. Englewood Cliffs, NJ: Prentice Hall.

Gartner, W. B., and Naughton, M. J. (1990) Summary of Out of the Crisis. In J. L. Pierce and J. W. Newstrom (eds), *The Manager's Bookshelf* (pp. 310–15). New York: Harper & Row.

George, J. M., and Jones, G. R. (1996) *Understanding and Managing Organizational Behavior*. Reading, MA: Addison-Wesley Publishing Co.

Gergen, K. (1992) Organization Theory in the Postmodern Era. In M. Reed and M. Hughes (eds), *Rethinking Organization*. London: Sage.

Gerloff, E. A. (1985) *Organizational Theory and Design. A Strategic Approach for Management*. New York: McGraw Hill.

Gherardi, S. (1995) When Will He Say: 'Today the Plates are Soft'? The Management of Ambiguity and Situated Decision-Making. *Studies in Culture, Organizations and Societies*, 1(1), 9–29.

Gibson, J. L., Ivancevich, J. M., and Donnelly, J. H. (1985) *Organizations. Behavior. Structure. Processes* (fifth ed.). Plano, TX: Business Publications, Inc.

Gibson, J. L., Ivancevich, J. M., and Donnelly, J. H. (1997) *Organizations. Behavior, Structure, Processes.* (ninth ed.). Chicago: Irwin.

Gilson, C. H. J. (ed.). (1987) *Strikes. Industrial Relations in Nova Scotia 1957–1987*. Hansport: Lancelot Press.

Glaser, B. G., and Strauss, A. L. (1967) *The Discovery of Grounded Theory: Strategies for Qualitative Research*. New York: Aldine.

Goffman, E. (1974) *Frame Analysis*. Cambridge, MA: Harvard University Press.

Goffman, E. (1984a). *Asylums*. Harmondsworth: Penguin.

Goffman, E. (1984b). *The Presentation of Self in Everyday Life*. Harmondsworth: Penguin.

Goodman, R., and Kruger, E. (1988) Data Dredging or Legitimate Research Method? Historiography and Its Potential for Management Research. *Academy of Management Review*, 13(2), 315–25.

Gordon, J. R. (1993) *A Diagnostic Approach To Organizational Behavior* (fourth ed.). Boston: Allyn & Bacon.

Gram, H. A. (1986) *The Canadian Manager. An Introduction to Management*. Toronto: Holt, Rinehart and Winston of Canada.

Gramsci, A. (1978) *The Modern Prince and Other Writings*. New York: International Publishers.

Gray, J. L., and Starke, F. A. (1988) *Organizational Behavior. Concepts and Applications.* (fourth ed.). Columbus, OH: Merrill Publishing Co.

Greenberg, J., and Baron, R. A. (1993) *Behavior in Organizations* (fourth ed.). Boston, MA: Allyn & Bacon.

Greenberg, J., Baron, R. A., Sales, C. A., and Owen, F. A. (1996) *Behavior in Organizations. Canadian Edition*. Scarborough, On.: Prentice Hall.

Greiner, L. (1972) Evolution and Revolution as Organizations Grow. *Harvard Business Review*, 50 (July–August), 37–47.

Grey, C., and Mitev, N. (1995) Re-engineering Organizations. A Critical Appraisal. *Personnel Review*, 24(1), 73–90.

Griffin, R. W., and Moorhead, G. (1986) *Organizational Behavior*. Boston, MA: Houghton Mifflin.

Griffin, R. W., Ebert, R. J., and Starke, F. A. (1996) *Business. Second Canadian Edition*. Scarborough, On.: Prentice Hall.

Griffith, J. R., Sahney, V. K., and Mohr R. A. (1995) *Re-engineering Health Care: Building on CQI*. Ann Arbor, Mich: Health Administration Press.

Grint, K. (1994) Re-engineering History: Social Resonances and Business Process Re-engineering. *Organization*, 1(1), 179–201.

Grint, K., and Case, P. (1998) The Violent Rhetoric of Re-engineering: Consultancy on the Offensive. *Journal of Management Studies*, 35(5), 557–79.

Guba, E. G., and Lincoln, Y. S. (1994) Competing Paradigms in Qualitative Research. In N. K. Denzin and Y. S. Lincoln (eds), *Handbook of Qualitative Research* (pp. 105–17). Thousand Oaks, CA: Sage.

Gummesson, E. (1991) *Qualitative Methods in Management Research*. London: Sage.

Hackman, J. R., and Oldham, G. (1980) *Work Redesign*. Reading, MA: Addison-Wesley.

Hall, G., Rosenthal, J., and Wade, J. (1993) How to Make Re-engineering Really Work. *Harvard Business Review* (November–December), 119–31.

Hamilton, S. (September, 1989). Culture Shock Hits Big Blue. *Business (UK)*.

Hammer, M. (1990) Re-engineering Work: Don't automate, obliterate. *Harvard Business Review*, 68(4), 104–12.

Hammer, M. (1995) *The Re-engineering Revolution*. New York: HarperCollins.

Hammer, M. (1996) *Beyond Re-engineering*. New York: HarperCollins.

Hammer, M., and Champy, J. (1993) *Re-engineering the Corporation*. New York: HarperCollins.

Hammersley, M. (1990) What's Wrong With Ethnography? The Myth Of Theoretical Description. *Sociology*, 24(4), 597–615.

Hampden-Turner, C. (1990) *Corporate Culture. From Vicious to Virtuous Circles*. London: Hutchinson.

Handy, C. (1983) *Understanding Organizations*. Harmondsworth: Penguin.

Harrington, H. J. (1991) *Business Process Improvement*. New York: McGraw-Hill.

Hartley, J. F. (1995) Case Studies in Organizational Research. In C. Cassell and G. Symon (eds), *Qualitative Methods in Organizational Research* (pp. 208–29). Thousands Oaks, CA: Sage.

Harvey, T. R. and Wehmeyer, L. B. (1995) *Checklist for Change: A Pragmatic Approach to Creating and Controlling Change*. Lancaster, PA, Technomic Pub. Co.

Heifetz, R. A. and Laurie, D. L. (1998) Adaptive Strategy. *Executive Excellence*, December issue.

Hellriegel, D., Slocum, J. W., and Woodman, R. W. (1986) *Organizational Behavior* (fourth ed.). St. Paul, MN: West.

Hellriegel, D., Slocum, J. W., and Woodman, R. W. (1992) *Organizational Behavior*. St. Paul, MN: West.

Hellriegel, D., Slocum, J. W., and Woodman, R. W. (1995) *Organizational Behavior*. St. Paul, MN: West.

Hatfield, J. (1994) Implementation and Results of a Planned Culture Change in a Public Utility. In proceedings of *The Annual Conference of the Administrative Sciences of Canada*, 15 (pp. 102–11). Halifax, Nova Scotia.

Hatfield, J. (1995) Volte Farce: Power Failure and Change in a Canadian Electrical Company. Paper presented at the *Standing Conference on Organizational Symbolism (SCOS)*, Turku, Finland.

Hatfield, J. (1996) A Case Study of Organisational Change in a Canadian Electrical Company. In proceedings of the *Administrative Sciences Association of Canada (ASAC)*, 1 (pp. 1–20). Montreal, Quebec.

Hatfield, J. (1997) Framing the Space: Making Sense of Organisational Change Programmes. Paper presented at the *15th International Colloquium of the Standing Conference on Organisational Symbolism (SCOS)*. Warsaw, Poland.

Hatfield, J. (1998a). Competition as a Sensemaking Device in the Management of Meaning: A Case Study. *Paper presented at the 16th International Colloquium of the Standing Conference on Organizational Symbolism (SCOS)*. Brazil, 3–7 July.

Hatfield, J. (1998b). No Sense Changing: Sensemaking and the Management of Change. *Paper presented at Critical Approaches to Organizations session of the annual meeting of the Canadian Sociology and Anthropology Association (CSAA)*. Ottawa, 31 May–3 June.

Hatfield, J., and Mills, A. J. (1997) Guiding Lights and Power Sources: Consultants Plug into the Management of Meaning in an Electrical Company. *Paper presented at the 13th Colloquium of the European Group for Organisational Studies conference*. Budapest, Hungary.

Hatfield, J. and Mills, A. J. (1998) A Shock to the System: Re-engineering the Employee – A Case Study of BPR in Canadian Utility Company. *Paper presented at the 14th Colloquium of the European Group for Organization Studies conference*. Maastricht, the Netherlands, 9–12 July.

Helms Mills, J. and Mills, A. J. (2000) Rules, Sensemaking, Formative Contexts and Discourse in the Gendering of Organizational Culture. In N. Ashkanasy, C. P. M. Wilderom, and M. F. Peterson (eds), *Handbook of Organizational Culture and Climate* (pp. 55–70). Thousand Oaks, CA: Sage.

Hendry, C. (1996) Understanding and Creating Whole Organizational Change through Learning Theory. *Human Relations*, 49(5).

Henwood, K., and Nicolson, P. (1995) Grounded Theory and Qualitative Research. *The Psychologist*, 8(115–19).

Herbert, T. E. (1976) *Dimensions of Organizational Behavior*. New York: Macmillan Publishing Inc.

Herbert, T. T. (1981) *Dimensions of Organizational Behavior*. New York: Macmillan Publishing Co.

Higgins, J. M. (1991) *The Management Challenge*. New York: Macmillan.

Hill, M. R. (1993) *Archival Strategies and Techniques*. Newbury Park, CA: Sage.

Hill, P. (1971) *Towards a New Philosophy of Management*. London: Gower.

Hitt, M. A., Middlemist, R. D., and Mathis, R. L. (1989) *Management. Concepts and Effective Practice* (third ed.). St. Paul, MN: West Publishing Co.

Hobsbawm, E. (1994) *Age of Extremes*. London: Michael Joseph.

Hochschild, A. R. (1983) *The Managed Heart*. Berkeley, CA: University of California Press.

Hodge, B. J., and Anthony, W. P. (1991) *Organization Theory. A Strategic Approach* (fourth ed.). Boston, MA: Allyn & Bacon.

Hodgetts, R. M. (1990) *Modern Human Relations at Work* (fourth ed.). Chicago: The Dryden Press.

Hodgetts, R. M. (1991) *Organizational Behavior. Theory and Practice*. New York: Macmillan.

Holpp, L. (1989) Ten Reasons why Total Quality Is Less than Total. *Training*, *26*(10), 93–103.

Hospitals (5 June 1992). TQM Backlash Prompts Questions. *Hospitals*, p. 30.

Howes, C. (23 January 1994). Employees 'Reeling' from New Fads. *Sunday Daily News.*

Huczynski, A. (1993) *Management Gurus: Who Makes Them and How to Become One*. London: Routledge.

Hunt, J. (1979) *Managing People at Work*. London: Pan Books.

Hurtig, M. (1992) *The Betrayal of Canada* (second ed.). Toronto: Stoddart.

Huse, E. F., and Bowditch, J. L. (1973) *Behavior in Organizations*. Reading, MA: Addison-Wesley.

Itzin, C. and Newman, J. (1995) *Gender, Culture and Organizational Change: Putting Theory into Practice*. London and New York: Routledge.

Ivancevich, J. M., and Matteson, M. T. (1987) *Organizational Behavior and Management*. Homewood, Ill: Irwin.

Ivancevich, J. M., and Matteson, M. T. (1990) *Organizational Behavior and Management*. (second ed.). Homewood, Ill: Irwin.

Jackson, B. (1995) Re-engineering the Sense of Self: The Manager and the Management Guru. Paper presented at the 13th International Colloquium of the *Standing Conference on Organizational Symbolism*. Turku, Finland.

Jackson, B. (1996) The Goose that Laid the Golden Egg?: A Rhetorical Critique of Stephen Covey and the Effectiveness Movement. Paper presented at the *Open University Conference on Management Consulting*. London.

Jackson, W. (1988) *Research Methods. Rules for Survey Design and Analysis*. Scarborough, Ont: Prentice-Hall Canada Inc.

Jacques, R. (1996) *Manufacturing the Employee: Management Knowledge from the 19th to 21st Centuries*. London: Sage.

Janesick, V. J. (1994) The Dance of Qualitative Research Design: Metaphor, Methodolatry, and Meaning. In N. K. Denzin and Y. S. Lincoln (eds), *Handbook of Qualitative Research* (pp. 199–208). Thousand Oaks, CA: Sage.

Janis, I. L. (1971) Groupthink: The Desperate Drive for Consensus at Any Cost. *Psychology Today*, *12*, 43–76.

Jenkins, K. (1994) *Re-thinking History*. London: Routledge.

Jenks, V. O. (1990) *Human Relations in Organizations*. New York: Harper & Row.

Jick, T. (1993) *Managing Change. Cases and Concepts*. Boston: Irwin McGraw-Hill.

Jobb, D. (1994) *Calculated Risk. Greed, Politics, and the Westray Tragedy*. Halifax, NS: Nimbus Publishing.

Johns, G. (1983) *Organizational Behavior. Understanding Life at Work*. Glenview, Ill: Scott, Foresman and Co.

Johns, G. (1988) *Organizational Behavior. Understanding Life at Work* (second ed.). Glenview, Ill: Scott, Foresman and Co.

Johns, G. (1992) *Organizational Behavior. Understanding Life at Work* (third ed.). New York: HarperCollins.

Johns, G. (1996) *Organizational Behavior. Understanding Life at Work* (fourth ed.). New York: HarperCollins.

Jones, P. (1985) *Theory and Method in Sociology*. Slough: University Tutorial Press.

Juran, J. (1988) *Juran on Planning for Quality*. New York: Free Press.

Kanter, R. (1983) *The Change Masters*. New York: Simon and Schuster.

Kanter, R. M. (1989) *When Giants Learn To Dance*. London: Simon & Schuster.

Katz, D., and Kahn, R. L. (1966) *The Social Psychology of Organizations*. New York: John Wiley and Sons.

Kay, E. (November 1996). Trauma in Real Life. *The Globe and Mail Report on Business Magazine*, pp. 82–92.

Keidel, R. (1994) Rethinking Organizational Design. *Academy of Management Executive*, 8(4), 12–27.

Keleman, M. (1999) Total Quality Management in the UK Service Sector: A Social Constructivist Study. In S. R. Clegg, E. Ibarra-Colado, and L. Bueno-Rodriquez (eds), *Global Management*. London: Sage.

Kelly, J. E. (1982) *Scientific Management, Job Redesign and Work Performance*. London: Academic Press.

Kets de Vries, M. F. R. (1989) The Leader as Mirror: Clinical Reflections. *Human Relations*, 42(7), 607–23.

Kets de Vries, M. F. R. (1980) *Organizational Paradoxes. Clinical Approaches to Management*. New York: Tavistock

Kets de Vries, M. F. R. (1989) Alexithymia in Organizational Life: The Organization Man Revisited. *Human Relations*, 42(12), 1079–93.

Kets de Vries, M. F. R. (1990) Leaders on the Couch: The Case of Roberto Calvi. Paper presented at the *Clinical Approaches to the Study of Managerial and Organizational Dynamics Symposium*, Ecole des Hautes Commerciales de Montreal.

Kets de Vries, M. F. R., and Miller, D. (1984) *The Neurotic Organization*. San Francisco, CA: Jossey-Bass.

Kets de Vries, M. F. R., and Miller, D. (1986) Personality, Culture and Organization. *Academy of Management Review*, 11(2), 266–79.

Kieser, A. (1989) Organizational, Institutional, and Societal Evolution: Medieval Craft Guilds and the Genesis of Formal Organizations. *Administrative Science Quarterly*, 34, 540–64.

Kieser, A. (1994) Why Organization Theory Needs Historical Analyses – And How This Should Be Performed. *Organization Science*, 5(4).

Kieser, A. (1997) Rhetoric and Myth in Management Fashion. *Organization*, 4(1), 49–74.

King, N. (1995) The Qualitative Research Interview. In C. Cassell and G. Symon (eds), *Qualitative Methods in Organizational Research* (pp. 14–36). Thousands Oaks, CA: Sage.

Kissler, G. D. (1996) *Leading the Health Care Revolution: A Re-engineering Mandate*. Chicago: Health Administration Press.

Klein, S. M., and Ritti, R. R. (1980) *Understanding Organizational Behavior*. Boston, MA: Kent Publishing.

Köhler, W. (1961) *Gestalt Psychology*. New York: Mentor Books.

Kotter, J. P. (1990) What Leaders Really Do. *Harvard Business Review* (May–June), 103–111.

LeBlanc, A. (1994) Power Play. *The Globe and Mail*. Toronto, Ontario: B24.

Legge, K. (1996) On Knowledge, Business Consultants and the Selling of TQM. Paper presented at the Organizational Learning Symposium, Lancaster University, Sept. 1–3.

Lenin, V. I. (1947) *Selected Works*. (Vol. 1). London: Lawrence and Wishart.

Lenz, P. R., and Sikka, A. (1998) *Re-engineering Health Care: A Practical Guide*. Tampa, Fla: American College of Physician Executives.

Levy, N. (2002) *Sartre*. Oxford: Oneworld Publications.

Lewin, K. (1951) *Field Theory in Social Science*. New York: Harper & Row.

Lippitt, G. L., Langseth, P., and Mossop, J. (1985) *Implementing Organizational Change*. San Francisco, CA: Jossey-Bass.

Luthans, F. (1985) *Organizational Behavior*. (fourth ed.). New York: McGraw-Hill.

Luthans, F. (1995) *Organizational Behavior* (seventh ed.). New York: McGraw-Hill.

MacLeod, F. (1994) *An Analysis of Continuous Improvement Process Teams and their Impact on Knowledge and Acceptance of TQM Concepts at a Manufacturing Service Organization*. MBA, Saint Mary's University.

Madura, J. (1998) *Introduction to Business*. Cincinnati, OH.: South-Western College Publishing.

Maier, M. (1993) 'Am I the Only One Who Wants to Launch?' Corporate Masculinity and the Space Shuttle Challenger Disaster. *Masculinities* 1(2): 34–45.

Maier, M. and Messerschmidt, J. W. (1998) Commonalities, Conflicts and Contradictions in Organizational Masculinities: Exploring the Gendered Genesis of the Challenger Disaster. *The Canadian Review of Sociology and Anthropology* 35(pp. 325–44).

Mangham, I. L. (1987) *Organization Analysis and Development: A Social Construction of Organizational Behaviour*. Chichester (West Sussex) and New York: Wiley.

Martin, J. (1992) *Cultures in Organizations: Three Perspectives*. Oxford: Oxford University Press.

Martin, J., and Frost, P. (1996) The Organizational Culture War Games: A Struggle for Intellectual Dominance. In S. R. Clegg, C. Hardy, and W. R. Nord (eds), *Handbook of Organization Studies* (pp. 599–621). London: Sage.

Martin, J., and Seihl, C. (1983) Organization Culture and Counter Culture: An Uneasy Symbiosis. *Organizational Dynamics, Autumn*, 52–64.

McConnell, M. (1987) *Challenger: A Major Malfunction*. Garden City, NY: Doubleday.

McLennan, R. (1989) *Managing Organizational Change*. Englewood Cliffs, NJ: Prentice-Hall.

McNeill, P. (1985) *Research Methods*. London: Tavistock Publications.

McShane, S. L. (1992) *Canadian Organizational Behavior*. Homewood, Ill: Irwin.

McShane, S. L. (1998) *Canadian Organizational Behaviour*. (third ed.) Toronto: Irwin.

Mead, G. H. (1962) *Mind, Self and Society*. Chicago: Chicago University Press.

MediaWatch (1982) *Sex Role Stereotyping: A Content Analysis of Radio and Television Programmes and Advertisements*. Vancouver: MediaWatch.

Messerschmidt, J. (1995) Managing to Kill: Masculinities and the Space Shuttle Challenger explosion. *Masculinities* 3(4): 1–22.

Meyer, J. W., and Rowan, B. (1983) The Structure of Educational Organizations. In J. W. Meyer and W. R. Scott (eds), *Organizational Environments. Ritual and Rationality* (pp. 71–97). Beverly Hills, CA: Sage.

Middlemist, R. D., and Hitt, M. A. (1988) *Organizational Behavior. Managerial Strategies for Performance*. St. Paul, MN: West Publishing.

Miller, D. (1990) *The Icarus Paradox*. New York: HarperBusiness.

Mills, A. J. (1988a). Organization, Gender and Culture. *Organization Studies*, 9(3), 351–69.

Mills, A. J. (1988b). Organizational Acculturation and Gender Discrimination. In P. K. Kresl (ed.), *Canadian Issues, X1– Women and the Workplace* (pp. 1–22). Montreal: Association of Canadian Studies/International Council for Canadian Studies.

Mills, A. J. (1995) Man/aging Subjectivity, Silencing Diversity: Organizational Imagery in the Airline Industry – The Case of British Airways. *Organization*, 2(2), 243–69.

Mills, A. J. (1999) Gendering Organizational Analysis – A Retrospective. Paper presented at the Colloquium on Feminism(s) Challenge the Traditional Disciplines. Montreal: McGill University, 23 October.

Mills, A. J., and Hatfield, J. C. H. (1998) Air Canada vs. Canadi>n: Competition and Merger in the Framing of Airline Culture. *Studies in Cultures, Organizations and Societies*, 4(1), 1–32.

Mills, A. J., and Hatfield, J. C. H. (1999) From Imperialism to Globalization: Internationalization and the Management Text. In S. R. Clegg, E. Ibarra, and L. Bueno (eds), *Theories of the Management Process: Making Sense Through Difference*. Thousand Oaks, CA: Sage.

Mills, A. J., and Murgatroyd, S. J. (1991) *Organizational Rules: A Framework for Understanding Organizations*. Milton Keynes: Open University Press.

Mills, A. J., and Simmons, T. (1995) *Reading Organization Theory: Critical Approaches to the Study of Behaviour and Structure in Organizations*. Toronto: Garamond Press.

Mills, A. J., and Simmons, T. (1998) *Reading Organization Theory: Critical Approaches to the Study of Behaviour and Structure in Organizations.* (second ed.). Toronto: Garamond Press.

Mintzberg, H. (1973) *The Nature of Managerial Work.* New York: Harper & Row.

Mintzberg, H., Brunet, J. P., and Waters, J. A. (1986) Does Planning Impede Strategic Thinking? Tracking the Strategies of Air Canada From 1937 to 1976. In R. Lamb and P. Shrivastava (eds), *Advances in Strategic Management* (pp. 3–41). Greenwich, CT: JAI Press.

Moorhead, G., and Griffin, R. W. (1988) *Organizational Behavior. Managing People and Organizations.* Boston: Houghton Mifflin.

Moorhead, G., and Griffin, R. W. (1992) *Organizational Behavior. Managing People and Organizations.* (third ed.). Boston: Houghton Mifflin.

Moorhead, G., and Griffin, R. W. (1998) *Organizational Behavior. Managing People and Organizations.* Boston: Houghton Mifflin.

Morgan, G. (1986) *Images of Organization.* Beverly Hills, CA: Sage.

Morse, J. M. (1994) Designing Funded Qualitative Research. In N. K. Denzin and Y. S. Lincoln (eds), *Handbook of Qualitative Research* (pp. 220–35). Thousand Oaks, CA: Sage.

Mumby, D. K. (ed.) (1993) *Narrative and Social Control: Critical Perspectives.* Newbury Park, CA: Sage.

Murgatroyd, S., and Morgan, C. (1993) *Total Quality Management and the School.* Milton Keynes: Open University Press.

Myrden, J. (20 April 1993) Holding Reins of Power. *The Chronicle Herald,* p. B1.

Myrden, J. (25 January 1994) Nova Scotia Power Privatization. *The Mail Star,* p. D12.

Nelson, D. L., and Quick, J. C. (1996) *Organizational Behavior. The Essentials.* Minneapolis, MN: West.

New York Times (1996) *The Downsizing of America.* New York: Times Books Random House.

Nickels, W. G., McHugh, J. M., McHugh, S. M., and Berman, P. D. (1997) *Understanding Canadian Business* (second ed.). Toronto: Irwin.

Nord, W., and Fox, S. (1996) The Individual in Organizational Studies: The Great Disappearing Act? In S. Clegg and C. Hardy (eds), *Handbook of Organizational Studies* (pp. 148–75). Thousand Oaks, CA: Sage.

Northcraft, G. B., and Neale, M. A. (1990) *Organizational Behavior. A Management Challenge.* Chicago: The Dryden Press.

Nova Scotia Power (1990a) *Nova Scotia Power 1989/90 Annual Report* (No. 70). Nova Scotia Power Corp.

Nova Scotia Power (1990b) *Culture Change at Nova Scotia Power. Employee Bulletin,* Nova Scotia Power Corp.

Nova Scotia Power (1991a) 'Check-Up' on Culture Change. *Powergram,* No. 185 (Employee Newsletter). Nova Scotia Power Corp.

Nova Scotia Power (1991b) *Meeting Customer Expectations into the 21st Century: Vision 2001.* Nova Scotia Power Corporate Plan.

Nova Scotia Power (1991c). *Annual Report, 1990/91* (No. 71). Nova Scotia Power Corporation.

Nova Scotia Power (1991d) *President's Bulletin.*

Nova Scotia Power (1992) *Employee Development. Training Booklet.* Nova Scotia Power Corp.

Nova Scotia Power (1993a). *Employee Attitude Survey. Task Force.* Nova Scotia Power.

Nova Scotia Power (4 March 1993b). Effectiveness Update. *Employee Bulletin No. 1,* pp. 1–2. Nova Scotia Power.

Nova Scotia Power (31 March 1993c) Effectiveness Update. *Employee Bulletin No. 2,* pp. 1–2. Nova Scotia Power.

Nova Scotia Power (14 May 1993d) Effectiveness Update. *Employee Bulletin No. 3*, pp. 1–2. Nova Scotia Power.

Nova Scotia Power (31 May 1993e) Effectiveness Update. *Employee Bulletin No. 4*, pp. 1–2. Nova Scotia Power.

Nova Scotia Power (1993f) *1992 Annual Report*. Nova Scotia Power Corp.

Nova Scotia Power (1993g) *Organization Charts*. Nova Scotia Power Inc.

Nova Scotia Power (1994a) *1993 Annual Report*. Nova Scotia Power Inc.

Nova Scotia Power (1994b) *To Be The Best*. Business Plan. Nova Scotia Power Inc.

Nova Scotia Power (1994c) *Minutes of the 1994 Annual Meeting of Shareholders*. Nova Scotia Power Inc.

Nova Scotia Power (1995a) *1994 Annual Report*. Nova Scotia Power Inc.

Nova Scotia Power (1995b) *Minutes of the 1995 Annual Meeting of Common Shareholders*. Nova Scotia Power Inc.

Nova Scotia Power (1996a) *1995 Annual Report*. Nova Scotia Power Inc.

Nova Scotia Power (1996b) *Organization Charts*. Nova Scotia Power Inc.

Nova Scotia Power (1996c) *Notice of 3 April 1996 Annual Meeting of Common Shareholders*. Nova Scotia Power Inc.

Nova Scotia Power (1996d) *Minutes of the 1996 Annual Meeting of Common Shareholders*. Nova Scotia Power Inc.

Nova Scotia Power (1997a) *1996 Annual Report*. Nova Scotia Power.

Nova Scotia Power (1997b) *Notice of 24 April 1997 Annual Meeting of Common Shareholders*. Nova Scotia Power Inc.

Nova Scotia Power (1998a) *1997 Annual Report*. Nova Scotia Power Inc.

Nova Scotia Power (1998b) *Notice of 23 April 1998 Annual Meeting of Common Shareholders*. Nova Scotia Power Inc.

Nova Scotia Power (1998c) *Minutes of 1988 Meetings of Common Shareholders of Nova Scotia Power Inc. 23 April 1998 and 2 December 1998*. Nova Scotia Power Inc.

Nova Scotia Power (1998d) *Notice of Special Meeting of Common Shareholders to be Held Wednesday, 2 December 1998*. Nova Scotia Power Inc.

Nova Scotia Power (1999a) *1998 Annual Report*. Nova Scotia Power Inc.

Nova Scotia Power (1999b) *Notice of 7 May 1999 Annual Common Shareholders*. NS Power Holdings Inc.

Oliver, T. (1986) *The Real Coke, The Real Thing*. New York: Random House.

O'Mahoney, J., and Newell, S. (1998) BPR: An Indistinguishable Concept in Practice. *Paper presented at the 14th Colloquium of the European Group for Organisation Studies*. Maastricht, Netherlands, 9–11 July.

Ott, S. J. (1989) *The Organizational Culture Perspective*. Pacific Groves, CA: Brooks/Cole Publishing Co.

Ouchi, W. (1981) *Theory Z*. Reading, MA: Addison-Wesley.

Pascale, R. T., and Athos, A. G. (1981) *The Art of Japanese Management: Applications for American Executives*. New York: Simon & Schuster.

Peters, T., and Waterman, R. (1982) *In Search of Excellence – Lessons from America's Best Run Companies*. New York: Warner Communications.

Pettigrew, A. (1979) On Studying Organizational Cultures. *Administrative Science Quarterly*, *24*, 570–81.

Pfeffer, J., and Salanik, G. (1978) *The External Control of Organizations*. New York: Harper & Row.

Pierce, J. L. and Newstrom, J. W. (eds) (1990) The Manager's Bookshelf. (second ed.). New York: Harper & Row.

Pliniussen, J. (ed.) (1994) *Introduction to Canadian Business and Management*. Toronto: McGraw-Hill Ryerson.

Poulet, R., and Moult, G. (1987) Putting Values Into Evaluation. *Training and Development Journal* (July), 62–6.

Prasad, A. (1997) The Colonizing Consciousness and Representations of the Other: A Postcolonial Critique of the Discourse of Oil. In P. Prasad, A. J. Mills, M. Elmes and A. Prasad (eds) *Managing the Organizational Melting Pot: Dilemmas of Workplace Diversity* (pp. 285–311). Thousand Oaks, CA: Sage.

Punch, M. (1986) *The Politics and Ethics of Fieldwork.* Beverly Hills, CA: Sage.

Pyrch, T. (1998) Mapmakers on Mapmaking. *Systematic Practice and Action Research*, *11*(6), 651–68.

Randolph, W. A. and R. S. Blackburn (1989) *Managing Organizational Behavior.* Boston, MA: Irwin.

Reed, M. (1992) *The Sociology of Organizations: Themes, Perspectives and Prospects.* London: Harvester Wheatsheaf.

Reichers, A. E., Wanous, J. P., and Austin, J. T. (1997) Understanding and Managing Cynicism About Organizational Change. *Academy of Management Executive*, *XI*(1), 48–59.

Rinehart, J. (1986) Improving the Quality of Working Life through Job Redesign: Work Humanization or Work Rationalization. *The Canadian Review of Sociology and Anthropology*, *23*(4), 507–30.

Robbins, S. P. (1983) *Organization Theory. The Structure and Design of Organizations.* Englewood Cliffs, NJ: Prentice-Hall.

Robbins, S. P. (1988) *Essentials of Organizational Behavior* (second ed.). Englewood Cliffs, NJ: Prentice-Hall.

Robbins, S. P. (1989) *Organizational Behavior. Concepts, Controversies, and Applications* (fourth ed.). Englewood Cliffs, NJ: Prentice-Hall.

Robbins, S. P. (1996) *Organizational Behavior. Concepts, Controversies, and Applications* (seventh ed.). Englewood Cliffs, NJ: Prentice-Hall.

Robbins, S. P. (1998) *Organizational Behavior. Concepts. Controversies. Applications.* Englewood Cliffs, NJ: Prentice-Hall.

Robbins, S. P., and Stuart-Kotze, R. (1986) *Management. Concepts and Practices. Canadian Edition.* Scarborough, Ont: Prentice-Hall.

Robbins, S. P., and Stuart-Kotze, R. (1990) *Management.* (second ed.). Scarborough, Ont: Prentice-Hall.

Root, J. (1984) *Pictures of Women.* London: Pandora Press.

Rose, M. (1978) *Industrial Behaviour.* Harmondsworth: Penguin.

Rüling, C.-C. (1998) Exploring Management Fashion: Refining A Sociological Approach. *Paper presented at the 14th Colloquium of the European Group for Organisation Studies (EGOS).* Maastricht, Netherlands, 9–11 July.

Rummel, R. W. (1991) *Howard Hughes and TWA.* Washington, DC.: Smithsonian.

Said, E. W. (1993) *Culture and Imperialism.* New York: Vintage.

Sampson, A. (1984) *Empires of the Sky. The Politics, Contests and Cartels of World Airlines.* New York: Random House.

Schaffer, R. H. and H. A. Thomson (1998) Successful Change Programs Begin with Results. *Harvard Business Review on Change.* Harvard Business Review. Boston, MA: Harvard Business School Publishing: 189–213.

Schein, E. (1987) *The Clinical Perspective of Fieldwork.* Newbury Park, CA: Sage.

Schein, E. H. (1985) *Organizational Culture and Leadership.* San Francisco, CA: Jossey-Bass.

Schermerhorn, J. R. (1984) *Management for Productivity.* New York: John Wiley & Sons.

Schermerhorn, J. R., Hunt, J. G., and Osborn, R. N. (1982) *Managing Organizational Behavior.* New York: Wiley.

Schermerhorn, J. R., Hunt, J. G., and Osborn, R. N. (1985) *Managing Organizational Behaviour* (second ed.). New York: John Wiley.

Schermerhorn, J. R., Hunt, J. G., and Osborn, R. N. (1988) *Managing Organizational Behavior.* (third ed.). New York: Wiley.

Schermerhorn, J. R., Hunt, J. G., and Osborn, R. N. (1991) *Managing Organizational Behavior.* (fourth ed.). New York: Wiley.

Schermerhorn, J. R., Hunt, J. G., and Osborn, R. N. (1994) *Managing Organizational Behavior.* (fifth ed.). New York: Wiley.

Schermerhorn, J. R., Hunt, J. C., and Osborn, R. N. (1995) *Basic Organizational Behavior.* New York: Wiley.

Schermerhorn, J. R., Hunt, J. C., and Osborn, R. N. (1997) *Organizational Behavior.* New York: Wiley.

Schermerhorn, J. R., Templer, A. J., Cattaneo, R. J., Hunt, J. G., and Osborn, R. N. (1992) *Managing Organizational Behavior* (first Canadian ed.). Toronto: Wiley.

Schultz, M. (1995) *On Studying Organizational Cultures. Diagnosis and Understanding.* Berlin: de Gruyter.

Schwartz, H. (1987) On the Psychodynamics of Organizational Disaster: The Case of the Space Shuttle Challenger, *Columbia Journal of World Business* 22(1): 59–67.

Serling, R. (1983) *Howard Hughes' Airline. An Informal History of TWA.* New York: St. Martin's/Marek.

Shalla, V. (1997) Technology and the Deskilling of Work: The Case of Passenger Agents at Air Canada. In A. Duffy, D. Glenday, and N. Pupo (eds), *Good Jobs, Bad Jobs, No Jobs* (pp. 76–96). Toronto: Harcourt Brace.

Siehl, C. (1985) After the Founder: An Opportunity to Manage Culture. In P. J. Frost, L. F. Moore, M. R. Louis, C. C. Lundberg and J. Martin (eds) *Organizational Culture* (pp. 125–40). London: Sage.

Silverman, D. (1970) *The Theory of Organizations.* New York: Basic Books.

Smircich, L. (1983) Concepts of Culture and Organizational Analysis. *Administrative Science Quarterly* (28), 339–58.

Smircich, L., and Morgan, G. (1982) Leadership: The Management of Meaning. *Journal of Applied Behavioral Science, 18,* 257–73.

Spradley, J. P. (1979) *The Ethnographic Interview.* New York: Holt, Rinehart & Winston.

Stake, R. E. (1994) Case Studies. In N. K. Denzin and Y. S. Lincoln (eds), *Handbook of Qualitative Research* (pp. 236–47). Thousand Oaks, CA: Sage.

Stanley, L. (1990) Doing Ethnography, Writing Ethnography: A Comment on Hammersley. *Sociology, 24*(4), 617–27.

Starke, F. A., Owen, B. E., Reinecke, J. A., Dessler, G., and Schoell, W. F. (1990) *Introduction to Canadian Business.* Scarborough, Ont: Allyn & Bacon.

Steers, R. M. (1981) *Introduction to Organizational Behavior.* Santa Monica, CA: Goodyear Publishing Inc.

Steers, R. M., and Porter, L. W. (1987) *Motivation and Work Behavior* (Fourth ed.). New York: McGraw-Hill.

Steinberg, A. (1972) *The Bosses.* London: Macmillan.

Stewart, T. A. (23 August 1993). Re-engineering: The Hot New Management Tool. *Fortune,* pp. 40–3, 46, 48.

Stewart, T. A. (3 March 1997). When Change Is Total, Exciting – and Scary. *Fortune,* pp. 169–70.

Stetler, C. B. and M. P. Charns (1995) *Collaboration in Health Care: Hartford Hospital's Experience in Changing Management and Practice.* Chicago: American Hospital Pubs.

Stogdill, R., and Coons, A. E. (eds) (1957) *Leader Behavior: Its Description and Measurement.* Columbus, OH: Bureau of Business Research, Ohio State University.

Strauss, A., and Corbin, J. (1994) Grounded Theory Methodology: An Overview. In N. K. Denzin and Y. S. Lincoln (eds), *Handbook of Qualitative Research* (pp. 273–85). Thousand Oaks, CA: Sage.

Strauss, A., Schatzman, L., Ehrlich, D., Bucher, R., and Sabshin, M. (1963) The Hospital and its Negotiated Order. In E. Friedson (ed.), *The Hospital in Modern Society*. New York: Macmillan.

Stuart-Kotze, S. (1980) *Introduction to Organizational Behavior. A Situational Approach*. Reston, VA: Prentice-Hall.

Strebel, P. (1998) Why Do Employees Resist Change?. *Harvard Business Review on Change* (pp. 139–58). Boston: Harvard Business School Press.

Tajfel, H. (ed.) (1979) *Differentiation Between Social Groups: Studies in the Social Psychology of Intergroup Relations*. London: Academic Press.

Tajfel, H., and Turner, J. (1979) An Integrated Theory of Intergroup Conflict. In W. G. Austin and S. Worched (eds), *The Social Psychology of Intergroup Relations*. Monterey, CA: Brooks/Cole.

Taylor, J. R., and Lerner, L. (1996) Making Sense of Sensemaking: How Managers Construct Their Organization Through Their Talk. *Studies in Cultures, Organizations and Societies*, 2(2), 257–86.

Tinker, T., and Neimark, M. (1987) The Role of Annual Reports in Gender and Class Contradictions at General Motors: 1917–76. *Accounting, Organizations and Society*, 12(1), 71–88.

Tosi, H. L., Rizzo, J. R., and Carroll, S. J. (1990) *Managing Organizational Behavior* (second ed.). New York: Harper & Row.

Townley, B. (1994) *Reframing Human Resource Management: Power, Ethics and the Subject at Work*. London: Sage.

Trento, J. J. (1987) *Prescription for Disaster: From the Glory Days of Apollo to the Betrayal of the Shuttle*. New York: Crown.

Trist, E. L., and Bamforth, K. (1951) Some Social and Psychological Consequences of the Longwall Method of Coal Getting. *Human Relations*, 4, 3–38.

Tuchman, G. (1994) Historical Social Science: Methodologies, Methods and Meanings. In N. K. Denzin and Y. S. Lincoln (eds), *Handbook of Qualitative Research* (pp. 306–23). Thousand Oaks, CA: Sage.

Turner, B. (1983) The Use of Grounded Theory for the Qualitative Analysis of Organisational Behaviour. *Journal of Management Studies*, 20(3), 333–48.

Turner, B. (1988) Connoisseurship in the Study of Organizational Cultures. In A. Bryman (ed.), *Doing Research in Organizations* (pp. 108–23). London: Routledge.

Turner, B. A. (1990) *Organizational Symbolism*. Berlin: de Gruyter.

Unger, R. M. (1987a) *Plasticity into Power*. Cambridge: Cambridge University Press.

Unger, R. M. (1987b) *Social Theory: Its Situation and Its Task*. Cambridge: Cambridge University Press.

Uzumeri, M. V. (1997) ISO 9000 and Other Metastandards: Principles for Management Practice? *The Academy of Management Executive*, XI(1), 21–36.

Van Fleet, D. D. (1991) *Behavior in Organizations*. Boston, MA: Houghton Mifflin.

Van Maanen, J. (1979) The Self, the Situation, and the Rules of Interpersonal Relations. In B. Staw and L. Cummings (eds), *Research in Organizational Behavior* Greenwich, Conn: JAI.

Van Maanen, J. (1988) *Tales of the Field*. Chicago: The University of Chicago Press.

Van Maanen, J. (1991) Disney Worlds: Culture on the Move. *Hallinnon Tutkinus*, 3, 227–38.

Van Maanen, J., Dabbs, J., and Faulken, R. (eds) (1982) *Varieties of Qualitative Research*. London: Sage.

236 *Bibliography*

Vaughan, D. (1996) *The Challenger Launch Decision*. Chicago: University of Chicago Press.

Vecchio, R. P. (1991) *Organizational Behavior* (second ed.). Chicago: Dryden Press.

Vidich, A. J., and Lyman, S. M. (1994) Qualitative Methods: Their History in Sociology and Anthropology. In N. K. Denzin and Y. S. Lincoln (eds), *Handbook of Qualitative Research* (pp. 23–59). Thousand Oaks, CA: Sage.

Vygotsky, L. S. (1978) *Mind in Society*. Cambridge, MA: Harvard University Press.

Walkerdine, V. (1990) *School Girl Fictions*. London: Virago.

Walston, S. L., and Burns, L. R. (1998) Does Re-engineering Really Make a Difference? An Examination of the Context and Competitive Outcomes of Hospital Re-engineering Programmes. *Paper presented at the 14th Colloquium of the European Group for Organization Studies*, Maastricht, the Netherlands, 9–11 July.

Walton, M. (1990) *Deming Management at Work*. New York: G.P. Putnam's Sons.

Walton, R. E. (1975) The Diffusion of New Work Structures: Explaining Why Success Didn't Take. *Organizational Dynamics* (Winter), 3–22.

Webb, E. J., Campbell, D. T., Schwartz, R. D., and Sechrest, L. (1984) The Use of Archival Sources in Social Research. In M. Bulmer (ed.), *Sociological Research Methods* (pp. 113–30). London: Macmillan.

Weber, M. (1947) *The Theory of Social and Economic Organization* (Henderson, A. R. and Parsons, T., trans.). London: Free Press.

Weber, M. (1967) *The Protestant Ethic and the Spirit of Capitalism* (Parsons, T., trans.). London: Allen & Unwin.

Weick, K (1969) *The Social Psychology of Organizing* , Reading, MA: Addison-Wesley.

Weick, K (1976) Educational Organizations as Loosely-Coupled Systems, *Administrative Sciences Quarterly* , 2 (1–19).

Weick, K. (1979) *The Social Psychology of Organizing* (second ed.). Reading, MA: Addison-Wesley.

Weick, K. (1985a). Sources of Order in Underorganized Systems: Themes in Recent Organizational Theory. In Y. S. Lincoln (ed.), *Organizational theory and inquiry* (pp. 106–36). Beverly Hills, CA: Sage.

Weick, K. (1985b). The Significance of Corporate Culture. In P. Frost, L. Moore, M. Louis, C. Lundberg, and J. Martin (eds), *Organizational Culture* (pp. 381–89). London: Sage.

Weick, K. (1989) Sources of Order in Underorganized Systems: Themes in Recent Organizational Theory. In Y. S. Lincoln (ed.) *Organizational Theory and Inquiry* pp. 106–36. Beverley Hills, CA: Sage.

Weick, K. (1990a) Technology as Equivoque: Sensemaking in New Technologies. In P. S. Goodman, L. S. Sproull and Associates. (eds), *Technology and Organizations* (pp. 1–44). San Francisco, CA: Jossey-Bass.

Weick, K. (1990b) The Vulnerable System: An Analysis of the Tenerife Air Disaster. *Journal of Management*, 16(3), 571–93.

Weick, K. (1993a) The Collapse of Sensemaking in Organizations: The Mann Gulch Disaster. *Administrative Science Quarterley*, 38, 628–52.

Weick, K. (1993b). Sensemaking in Organizations: Small Structures with Large Consequences. In J. K. Murningham (ed.), *Social Psychology in Organizations: Advances in Theory and Research* (pp. 10–37). Englewood Cliffs, NJ: Prentice-Hall.

Weick, K. (1995) *Sensemaking in Organizations*. London: Sage.

Weick, K. (1996) Drop Your Tools: An Allegory for Organizational Study. *Administrative Science Quarterly*, 41, 301–13.

Weick, K. (1997) Book Review Symposium. *Administrative Sciences Quarterly*, 42, 395–401.

Westphal, J. D., Gulati, R., and Shortell, S. M. (1997) Customization or Conformity? An Institutional Network Perspective on the Content and Consequences of TQM Adoption. *Administrative Sciences Quarterly*, *42*, 366–94.

Wilkins, A. L., and Ouchi, W. G. (1983) Efficient Cultures: Exploring the Relationship between Culture and Organizational Performance. *Administrative Science Quarterly*, *28*, 468–81.

Willmott, H. (1994) Bringing Agency Back (Again) into Organizational Analysis: Responding to the Crisis of Postmodernity. In J. Hassard and M.Parker (eds) *Towards a New Theory of Organizations* (pp. 87–130). London: Routledge.

Zimmerman, D. H. and J. J. Skalko (1994) *Re-engineering Health Care: A Vision for the Future*. Franklin, Wis: Eagle Press.

Index

Note: Page numbers followed by '*t*' indicate a table; and those followed by '*f*' indicate a figure.